Microfinance to Combat Global Recession and Social Exclusion

Ramesh Chandra Das
Editor

Microfinance to Combat Global Recession and Social Exclusion

An Empirical Investigation

Editor
Ramesh Chandra Das
Department of Economics
Vidyasagar University
Midnapore, West Bengal, India

ISBN 978-981-19-1128-6   ISBN 978-981-16-4329-3 (eBook)
https://doi.org/10.1007/978-981-16-4329-3

© The Editor(s) (if applicable) and The Author(s), under exclusive license to Springer Nature Singapore Pte Ltd. 2022

This work is subject to copyright. All rights are solely and exclusively licensed by the Publisher, whether the whole or part of the material is concerned, specifically the rights of translation, reprinting, reuse of illustrations, recitation, broadcasting, reproduction on microfilms or in any other physical way, and transmission or information storage and retrieval, electronic adaptation, computer software, or by similar or dissimilar methodology now known or hereafter developed.

The use of general descriptive names, registered names, trademarks, service marks, etc. in this publication does not imply, even in the absence of a specific statement, that such names are exempt from the relevant protective laws and regulations and therefore free for general use.

The publisher, the authors and the editors are safe to assume that the advice and information in this book are believed to be true and accurate at the date of publication. Neither the publisher nor the authors or the editors give a warranty, expressed or implied, with respect to the material contained herein or for any errors or omissions that may have been made. The publisher remains neutral with regard to jurisdictional claims in published maps and institutional affiliations.

This Palgrave Macmillan imprint is published by the registered company Springer Nature Singapore Pte Ltd.
The registered company address is: 152 Beach Road, #21-01/04 Gateway East, Singapore 189721, Singapore

This book is for my wife, Amrita, and daughter, Anureema

Foreword

The global economy has been suffering from a long-term recession which makes the economies moving backward in terms of loss of income and well beings. Besides, there has been increasing magnitudes of social exclusion in certain economies due to the recessionary effects. During the times of the crises, poor and the vulnerable class of the society suffer the most as they lose incomes and creditworthiness. The role of the formal financial institutions here is crucial since they too are impacted by the recession-induced loan losses that impair their businesses. Often, microfinance is considered an alternative to the mainstream financial institutions. In fact, there has been an increasing trend of the growth of the microfinance institutions across the globe, specifically to the African and Asian regions. And, the question is, can Microfinancing Institutions (MFIs) be immune to the happenings around or, will they survive from the crisis and recession?

As we know, MFIs emerged on the stage in response to the need for financial inclusion of the poor and excluded. Over the last three decades, there have been several measures to connect most of the poor and backward classes with the formal sector credit system to ensure the financial inclusion and inducing the overall growth and development of a country. Several innovations happened in this sphere. What is the level of efficacy of these different models? How far they are successful in connecting the poor to formal system? Major goal of microfinance is to empower women, economically and socially. Did the empowerment happen, as desired? What about needs other than finance, say, micro-insurance, microremittances, and so on?

The present edited book by Dr. Ramesh Chandra Das of Vidyasagar University, India, has been a good effort to answer the above and many more questions through the research papers from India and a few other countries and groups. The book has compiled the two subthemes of the book in two different parts for better understanding of the readers. The studies have the potential to motivate the policy makers of the concerned countries and groups covered in the book in particular and the policy makers at the global level in general. The studies covered will definitely interest the readers and rake up their brains to think further on the issues concerned. I congratulate the editor, authors and the publisher for their efforts.

Dr. K. J. S. Satyasai
Chief General Manager
Department of Economic Analysis
and Research (DEAR)
NABARD
Mumbai, India

Dr. K. J. S. Satyasai, Ph.D. is presently the Chief General Manager, Department of Economic Analysis and Research (DEAR), the National Bank for Agriculture and Rural Development (NABARD), India, and is an agricultural economist. He did his Ph.D. from Indian Agricultural Research Institute, New Delhi. He served as Foreign Professor at Konkuk University, South Korea, and as a faculty member at the Banker's Institute of Rural Development, India. He has recently steered a large sample survey, NABARD All India Rural Financial Inclusion Survey (NAFIS) conducted by NABARD. He has over 70 publications to his credit during his 35 years of career in applied economic research. He guided quite a few students as well. He recently coauthored a book on *Agricultural Development in Andhra Pradesh*.

Acknowledgements

Putting long-term efforts to see the birth of the proposed edited book, titled *Microfinance to Combat Global Recession and Social Exclusion: An Empirical Investigation*, it is now an unimaginable pleasure to me as the editor to share the holy news with the academic fraternity. But, the ultimate achievement to such a huge volume could not be made if the contributions of the cluster of academicians all around the world would not be combined. Thus, it would be blameworthy if I do not acknowledge the contributions of the concerned academicians and the other members of the society who are directly or indirectly involved with the academic venture.

First, I must acknowledge the cooperation of the Palgrave Macmillan Team for approving the proposal and continuously guiding me at all stages of developments of the book. Second, I am indebted to my research guides Professor Soumyen Sikdar of Indian Institute of Management, Calcutta, India, and former Professor Sarmila Banerjee of Calcutta University, India, for persistently inspiring me to undertake such types of academic projects. Third, I must express gratitude to Dr. Partha Gangopadhyay of School of Business, Western Sydney University, NSW, Australia, and Professor and former Vice Chancellor Asis Kumar Banerjee, Calcutta University, Dr. N. R. Bhanumurthy, Professor at National Institute of Public Finance and Policy, New Delhi, and Dr. K. J. S. Satyasai, Chief General Manager, Department of Economic Analysis and Research, NABARD, Mumbai, India, for their pristine efforts in supporting me throughout the entire project. Fourth, I am highly grateful to all the contributing authors for their valuable chapter contributions and showing their patience for such a long-standing academic venture. I do hereby acknowledge the values they have added to the existing literature through this volume.

Last but not the least, I am indebted to my parents, wife and daughter, brothers and other members of the family for their interminable encouragement, support and sacrifice in carrying out the project. Of course, no one other than me, as the editor, discloses to remain entirely responsible for any errors that still stay behind the book.

Ramesh Chandra Das

Contents

Part I Role of Microfinance in Mitigating Economic Recession of World's Economies

1 Introduction — Ramesh Chandra Das ... 3

2 Global Recession and Microfinance Institutions: Challenges and Opportunities — Avijit Brahmachary ... 11

3 Role of Microfinance as Counter-Recessionary Tool: A Macro-theoretic Analysis with Special Reference to Indian Economy — Mainak Bhattacharjee, Debashis Mazumdar, Sanghita Ghosh, and Dipti Ghosh ... 29

4 Performance of Microfinance Institutions Under Economic Growth and Fluctuations: Evidence from South Asian Countries — Ujjal Protim Dutta and Lipika Kankaria ... 51

5 Microfinance as a Strategy to Curb the Global Recession — Suman Chakraborty, Arpita Chaudhury, and Riddhima Panda ... 63

6	Developing Strategies to Improve Microfinance System in Turkey with Fuzzy Logic Hasan Dinçer, Serhat Yüksel, Çağatay Çağlayan, and Gözde Gülseven Ubay	81
7	Efficiency of Microfinance Institutions and Financial Inclusion in West Bengal: A DEA Approach Tarak Nath Sahu, CMA Sudarshan Maity, and Srimoyee Datta	97
8	Effects of Financial Widening Activities on Self-Employment Opportunities in Nigeria: Implications on Global Recession and Social Exclusion Ezebuilo Romanus Ukwueze and Henry Thomas Asogwa	113
9	Role of Microfinance to Promote the Growth of Unorganized Manufacturing Enterprises in India: An Analysis Akash Dandapat and Pinaki Das	131
10	Assessing Microfinance Potentiality in India with Special Reference to Odisha: Combating Global Recession Through Local Intervention Navin Kumar Rajpal and Sharmila Tamang	147

Part II Role of Microfinance in Reducing Social Exclusion of the Countries and Regions

11	Financial Inclusion Through Microfinance: Is It Possible? Arti Yadav, Vani Kanojia, and Megha Jain	161
12	Political Economy of Microfinance from the Gender and Politics Point of View: Enhancing Social Inclusion of Women to the Workforce Egemen Sertyesilisik	177
13	Assessing the Impact of Microfinance on Inequality: A Study of Major SAARC Nations Using Panel Causality Analysis Amit Chatterjee and Kshitij Patil	195

14	Sustainability of Indian Microfinance Institutions: Assessing the Impact of Andhra Crisis Amar Nath Das and Arindam Laha	209
15	Role of Microfinance Institutions in Social inclusion: A Study with Reference to India Bappaditya Biswas and Rohan Prasad Gupta	229
16	Role of Microfinance in the Reduction of Rural Poverty in West Bengal Kishor Naskar and Sourav Kumar Das	249
17	Microfinance and Women Empowerment: An Assessment of Disparity in Rural Women Access to Micro Credit in Nigeria Richardson Kojo Edeme, Henry Thomas Asogwa, and Yakub Yusuf	263
18	Predicting the Likelihood of Loan Default Among Marginalised Population: A Case Study on Rural Bengal Amit Kumar Bhandari	277

Index 295

Notes on Contributors

Henry Thomas Asogwa has M.Sc. in Economics from University of Nigeria and is currently a Ph.D. Student at Nnamdi Azikiwe University, Awka, in Anambra State, Nigeria, and also an Assistant Research Fellow at the Institute of Development Studies, University of Nigeria, Nsukka. He has published widely in recognized journals.

Amit Kumar Bhandari, Ph.D. is an Assistant Professor in the Department of Economics, Rishi Bankim Chandra Evening College, India. He is a Research Fellow at IZA Institute of Labour Economics, Bonn, Germany. He received his Ph.D. in Economics from the University of Kalyani, India. Formerly, he was a Lecturer in economics and finance at the Indian Institute of Social Welfare and Business Management, Kolkata. He has a broad interdisciplinary research interest in behavioural, development and financial economics. His research work has been funded by Indian Council of Social Science Research (ICSSR) and University Grants Commission (UGC), India.

Mainak Bhattacharjee is presently an Assistant Professor in Economics at Loreto College, Kolkata, India, and formerly, in the Heritage College, Kolkata, India. He has obtained M.Phil. and M.A. degrees in Economics from the Jadavpur University, Kolkata. He has been working in the areas of Macroeconomics and International Trade. He has contributed many research articles in reputed journals and chapters in edited volumes with international publications, along with having a number of undergraduate level text books to his credit.

Bappaditya Biswas, Ph.D. is presently working as an Assistant Professor in the Department of Commerce, University of Calcutta, India. He has over twelve years of teaching experience in undergraduate as well as postgraduate courses. He has published several articles in different journals and edited volumes of repute. He has successfully completed one UGC Minor Research Project and presently is Co-Investigator in two Major Research Projects under UGC-UPE Program. He has co-authored 4 books from McGraw Hill, India, for undergraduate students of commerce.

Avijit Brahmachary, Ph.D. is currently working as an Assistant Professor in Economics at Barrackpore Rastraguru Surendranath College, Barrackpore, Kolkata, West Bengal, India. His field of research interest is behavioural economics, rural economics and microfinance. He has contributed many articles in different journals and books at the national and international levels.

Çağatay Çağlayan is a 2nd grade Economics and Finance student in Istanbul Medipol University. He is also student of Health Management Department in Istanbul Medipol University. His research interests are sustainable energy economics, renewable energy and nuclear energy. He has some articles and international book chapters related to these topics.

Suman Chakraborty, Ph.D. is working as an Assistant Professor and Head of the Department of Economics of Raja N. L. Khan Women's College (Autonomous), West Bengal, India. His research and teaching experience is more than 14 years. His main area of interest of research is the study of socio-economic issues and also the issues of financial economics. He has published more than 12 papers in different reputed journal and book chapters.

Amit Chatterjee is currently serving as Assistant Professor at School of Economics, MIT-WPU, Pune, Maharashtra, India, since March 2018 with more than four years of teaching and research experience majorly in development and monetary economics. He has also served as Assistant Professor in NMIMS-Mumbai and has been associated with IGNOU. He is also a research scholar of Department of Economics at the University of Burdwan, West Bengal, and has published research papers at national and international journals of repute. He has also worked as Editor in McGraw Hill in more than 68 books related to various courses of economics at UG and PG levels for different universities in India and abroad.

Arpita Chaudhury is pursuing Ph.D. in Geography at Raja N. L. Khan. Women's College (Autonomous), Vidyasagar University, Paschim Midnapore (West Bengal), India. She is working as an Assistant Professor in the Department of General Studies, University of Engineering and Management, Kolkata, India. Her main area of interest of research is the study of socio-economic issues. She has published more than 10 papers in different reputed journal and book chapters.

Akash Dandapat is pursuing Ph.D. at Vidyasagar University, West Bengal, India. He has deep research interest into the unorganized sector and informal labour market. He completed B.Sc. (University Gold Medallist), M.Sc. (University Gold Medallist) and M.Phil. from Vidyasagar University.

Pinaki Das, Ph.D. is a Professor in the Department of Economics, Vidyasagar University, India. He has guided a number of research scholars and published four books and forty research papers. He has research interests on labour economics, social protection, food security, multidimensional poverty and women empowerment.

Ramesh Chandra Das, Ph.D. is currently Professor of Economics at Vidyasagar University, West Bengal, India, with more than twenty years of teaching and research experience in different fields of the subject. He has obtained Masters, M.Phil. and Ph.D. Degree in Economics from the University of Calcutta. He has contributed several research papers to national and international journals with reputes along with completions of three minor research projects sponsored by UGC, India. He has written text books on microeconomics and macroeconomics for different fields of students and academicians in economics and a number of edited books with international publishers such as IGI Global, Emerald, Springer, Routledge and Sage.

Sourav Kumar Das, Ph.D. is currently teaching Economics at Lalbaba College, Howrah, India. He obtained his Ph.D. degree in tribal livelihood from Vidyasagar University, India. His area of interest includes rural development, tribal livelihood, consumption pattern and terrorism. He also edited books on refugee crisis, tribal development and issues on globalization. He has contributed to numerous reputable national and international journals and has also edited a number of handbooks in the areas of tribal affairs, globalization and economic development.

Amar Nath Das, Ph.D. has been teaching Commerce in the Department of Commerce, Nabagram Hiralal Paul College, since the last 5 years. His areas of research interest include financial inclusion and microfinance. He has published a number of research articles in Scopus listed national and internationally reputed journals of social science.

Srimoyee Datta, Ph.D. is an Assistant Professor in the Department of Management Science, Bengal Institute of Science & Technology, Purulia, West Bengal, India. She has over ten years of teaching experience and keen interest in academic and research activities. She has published a number of research articles in reputed national and international journals.

Hasan Dinçer, Ph.D. is a Professor of Finance at Istanbul Medipol University, Istanbul, Turkey. He has more than 100 scientific articles and some of them are indexed in SSCI. He is also editor of many different books published by Springer and IGI Global.

Ujjal Protim Dutta, Ph.D. is presently working as an Assistant Professor in Economics at Rangia College in Assam, India. He previously worked as a Post-Doctoral Fellow in the Department of Humanities and Social Sciences at the India Institute of Technology Guwahati, India. He obtained his Ph.D. degree in Economics from National Institute of Technology Durgapur and holds a Masters' degree in Development Studies from Indian Institute of Technology Guwahati. He has published papers in journals like *Technology in Society*, *Child Indicators Research*, *South Asia Economic Journal*, *Journal of Health Management*, etc.

Richardson Kojo Edeme, Ph.D. is currently working in the Department of Economics, University of Nigeria, and also a Research Fellow, Institute of Business Research, University of Economics, Ho Chi Minh City, Vietnam. He holds Ph.D. in Economics from University of Nigeria, specializing in Public Finance and Policy. He has contributed to various book chapters and published widely in reputable journals in the area of public expenditure, trade analysis, infrastructure environmental sustainability, poverty and human development.

Dipti Ghosh is currently working as Junior Research Fellow in Economics at Jadavpur University, Kolkata, India. She has been associated with Bijoy Krishna Girls' College, Howrah, India, as a College Contractual Temporary Teacher of Economics. Her research interests lie in macroeconomics and Indian economy.

Sanghita Ghosh is presently associated with Jadavpur University, India, as Junior Research Fellow in Economics. She obtained M.Phil. and M.A. degrees in Economics from the same institution. Her research interest lies in the area of development economics and econometrics. Previously, she served at IMI, Kolkata, in the capacity of Research Associate. She has published articles in reputed journals.

Rohan Prasad Gupta is currently perusing M.Phil. in Commerce in the Department of Commerce, University of Calcutta, as a Junior Research Fellow. He has published more than ten research papers and articles in national and international journals and edited volumes.

Megha Jain is currently teaching as an Assistant Professor at Daulat Ram College, University of Delhi, and is under pursual of her research in Management (Economics) from Faculty of Management Studies (FMS), University of Delhi. She has many national and international publications with papers presented at IIMs, IITs. She is a joint columnist in Financial Express, Firstpost, Pioneer, Hindu Business line, etc. She is felicitated with Best Paper Awards at IIT Bombay Doctoral Consortium, IIT Madras Athenaeum Ph.D. Scholar Conference and Delhi Technical Campus, Noida, for different research papers on contemporary and structural developmental issues.

Lipika Kankaria is a Senior Research Scholar in the Department of Humanities and Social Sciences, National Institute of Technology Durgapur, India. She has obtained her Masters' degree from Calcutta University. Her research interest is primarily gender studies and exploring various aspects of gender issues in interdisciplinary research. She has presented several papers in international conferences in India and abroad as well as contributed book chapters in edited volumes.

Vani Kanojia is an aspiring Research Scholar at the University of Delhi. She has completed graduation from Hindu B.COM. (Hons.), University of Delhi, in 2013 and post-graduation from Delhi School of Economics in 2015. She has recently published a short opinion article at the Pioneer on "Practical Implications of Electric Vehicle in India" and another on "Adopt a Sustainable Lifestyle for Earth's Sake" which is highly appreciated by the academicians.

Arindam Laha, Ph.D. is currently a Professor of Economics in the Department of Commerce, the University of Burdwan, India. His areas of research interest include agrarian institutions, financial inclusion, financial literacy, human evelopment, and social and solidarity economy. He has written one book and has published a number of research articles in Web of Science and Scopus listed reputed journals and edited books. He has been awarded ILO's South–South Triangular Cooperation scholarship.

Debashis Mazumdar, Ph.D. has done his Masters in Economics from Jadavpur University, Kolkata; M.Phil. in Economics from Calcutta University; and Ph.D. in Economics from Rabindra Bharati University, Kolkata, India. At present, he is working as Professor of Economics at the Heritage College, Kolkata. He has written a good number of text books on managerial economics and contributed articles in many national and international journals.

Kishor Naskar, Ph.D. is an Assistant Professor of Economics in Budge Budge College, West Bengal. He obtained his M.Sc. degree in Agricultural Economics from University of Calcutta, Kolkata, West Bengal, in 2006 and Ph.D. degree in rural development from Vidyasagar University, India. He has published five book chapters along with three popular articles.

Riddhima Panda completed M.Sc in Economics from Calcutta University. She is working as an Assistant Professor (Guest) in the Department of Economics & Commerce, Syamaprasad College, Kolkata, India. Her main area of interest of research is the study of socio-economic issues and also the issues of financial economics. She has published more than 5 papers in different reputed journal and book chapters.

Kshitij Patil is an Economics Scholar at MIT World Peace University, Pune, Maharashtra, India. With a blend of an analytical mind and curiosity for Economics and Finance, he has been consistently performing well in his graduation and also earning valuable certifications in the field of finance. Currently pursuing the CFA charter, he is also passionate about social causes and has earned a UNESCO certification and carried out a primary research named "Socio-Economic Conditions of Maharashtrian farmers in Vidarbha Region".

Navin Kumar Rajpal, Ph.D. is an Assistant Professor in Economics at Sidho Kanho Birsha University, Purulia, West Bengal, India. He has about five years of teaching experience in several reputed institutes like NIT Tiruchirappalli, MNIT Jaipur and Lovely Professional University Punjab. His research papers have been published in reputed journals at national and international levels. His research interests are in the area of microfinance, financial inclusion, women entrepreneurship and empowerment.

Tarak Nath Sahu, Ph.D. is presently an Assistant Professor in the Department of Commerce and Department of Business Administration, Vidyasagar University, Midnapore, West Bengal, India. He has over 13 years of postgraduate teaching and research experience. He, a gold medalist at both graduate and postgraduate levels, has authored four books, edited five books and published more than seventy research articles.

Egemen Sertyesilisik, Ph.D. has received his B.A. degree on Political Science and Public Administration from the Bilkent University, Turkey, in 2007. He has received his M.A. degree on the Politics and the Mass Media from the University of Liverpool, UK. Furthermore, he has received an M.B.A. degree from the Yildiz Technical University in 2010. He has received his Ph.D. degree from the Marmara University.

CMA Sudarshan Maity, Ph.D. is presently Deputy Director, the Institute of Cost Accountants of India. He has over 18 years of administrative experience in various industries. He is an all-India rank holder in the Final Examination of the Institute of Cost Accountants of India. He has published more than thirty research articles in different reputed national and international journals.

Sharmila Tamang is an Independent Scholar and completed Ph.D. from Department of Economics, Mizoram (Central) University Aizawl Mizoram, India. Her research papers have been published in several reputed UGC enlisted, Emerging Source of Citation Index (Thomson Reuters) and ICI indexed journals. Her areas of research are entrepreneurship development, mid-day meal and microfinance.

Gözde Gülseven Ubay is a graduate student of Business Administration in İstanbul Medipol University. She was graduated from Economics and Finance Department in Istanbul Medipol University in 2020. Her research interests are energy economics, wind energy, hydrogen energy and renewable energy projects. She has some articles and international book chapters regarding these topics. Some of these studies are indexed in SSCI, SCI and Scopus.

Ezebuilo Romanus Ukwueze has Ph.D. in Economics (with area of specialization in Development Economics) and also Senior Lecturer in the Department of Economics, University of Nigeria, Nsukka, and Senior Research Fellow, Resource and Environmental Policy Research Centre (REPRC), the EFD unit for Nigeria. He has published widely in both local and internationally recognized journals.

Arti Yadav, Ph.D. is presently a Post-Doctoral Research Fellow at Indian Council of Social Science Research, India. She has also worked as Assistant Professor in the Department of Commerce, Daulat Ram College, University of Delhi. She earned her Ph.D. in Commerce from Department of Commerce, Aligarh Muslim University, and holds her master's degree from Delhi School of Economics, University of Delhi. She has also qualified UGC-NET/JRF. She has attended various seminars, conferences and faculty development programmes and published research papers in national and international journals.

Serhat Yüksel, Ph.D. is an Associate Professor of Finance at Istanbul Medipol University, Istanbul, Turkey. He has more than 80 scientific articles and some of them are indexed in SSCI. He is also editor of many different books published by Springer and IGI Global.

Yakub Yusuf is currently a Lecturer in the Department of Economics, Kogi State University, Anyigba. He holds M.Sc. Economics Degree in Economics from University of Nigeria. His area of research interest includes development and energy economics.

Abbreviations

ALPB	Average Loan Balance Per Borrower
AMI	Association of Microfinance Institution
ANOVA	Analysis of Variance
BancoSol	Banco Solidario Group
BDS	Business Development Services
BDT	Bangladeshi Taka
BFIL	Bharat Financial Inclusion
BJKS	Belgharia Jana Kalyan Samity
BPL	Below Poverty Line
BRI	Bank Rakyat Indonesia
BSM	Borrower Per Staff Member
BUDFOW	Business Development Fund for Women
BWDA	Bullock-Cart Workers Development Association
CAGR	Compounded Annual Growth Rate
CAR	Capital-Asset Ratio
CBN	Central Bank of Nigeria
CCM	Constant Coefficient Model
CCR	Charnes, Cooper and Rhodes
CDF	Cumulative Distribution Function
CECs	Children Education Centres
CGAP	Consultative Group to Assist the Poor
CHFs	Community Health Facilitators
CRR	Cash Reserve Ratio
CRS	Constant Returns to Scale
DE	Debt to Equity
DEA	Data Envelopment Analysis

DEMATEL	Decision Making Trial and Evaluation Laboratory
DMU	Decision Making Unit
DRS	Decreasing Returns to Scale
EGLS	Estimated Generalized Least Square
FDI	Foreign Direct Investment
FE	Fixed Effects
FEM	Fixed Effect Model
FFIs	Formal Financial Institutions
FI	Financial Institution
FY	Financial Year
GDP	Gross Domestic Product
GEEP	Government Enterprises Entrepreneurship Programme
GHS	General Household Survey
GINI	Gini Coefficient
GMF	Gramalaya Microfin Foundation
GMM	Generalized Methods of Moments
GREAT	Gramalaya Entrepreneurs Associates Tamil Nadu
GVA	Gross Value Added
HDI	Human Development Index
HHC	Household Belongs to Which Caste
HHS	Household Size
IFC	International Finance Corporation
IIMPS	India Invest Micro Pension Services
IMF	International Monetary Fund
IPO	Initial Public Offering
ITIs	Industrial Training Institutes
LICI	Life Insurance Corporation of India
MCDM	Multiple Criteria Decision-Making
MDGs	Millennium Development Goals
MFD	Deposit of the Microfinance Institution
MFI	Micro Finance Institution
MFIN	Microfinance Institutions Network
MFIs	Micro Finance Institutions
MFL	Loan from Microfinance Institution
MHCs	Mini Health Clinics
MIX	Microfinance Information Exchange
MOORA	Multi-Objective Optimization on the Basis of Ratio Analysis
MPCE	Monthly Per Capita consumption Expenditure
MRA	Microcredit Regulatory Authority
MSME	Micro Small and Medium Enterprises
MSMEDF	Medium and Small Micro Enterprise Development Fund
MSMEs	Micro, Small and Medium Enterprises
NAB	Number of Active Borrowers

NABARD	National Bank for Agriculture and Rural Development
NBFC	Non-Banking Financial Corporations
NBS	National Bureau of Statistics
NCEUS	National Commission for Enterprises in the Unorganised Sector
NFISIWG	National Financial Inclusion Special Interventions Working Group
NGO	Non-Governmental Organization
NIC	National Industrial Classification
NOCPL	New Opportunity Consultancy Pvt. Ltd.
NPA	Non-Performing Asset
NPS	New Pension Scheme
NSSO	National Sample Survey Organisation
OECD	Organisation for Economic Co-operation and Development
OLS	Ordinary Least Square
OSS	Operational Self-Sufficiency Ratio
OTE	Overall Technical Efficiency
PAR	Profit at Risks
PCCE	Per Capita Consumption Expenditure
PCI	Per Capita Income
PCL	Per Capital and Holding
PLE	Per Head Level of Education of a Household
PR	Portfolio at Risk
RBI	Reserve Bank of India
RBTF	Retirement Benefit Pension Fund
RE	Random Effects
REM	Random Effects Model
ROA	Return on Assets
ROE	Return on Equity
RoR	Rate of Return
RRB	Regional Rural Banks
RSETIs	Rural Self Employment Training Institutes
RTS	Returns to Scale
SAARC	South Asian Association of Regional Cooperation
SC	Scheduled Castes
SDG	Sustainable Development Goal
SERP	Society for Elimination of Rural Poverty
SFA	Stochastic Frontier Analysis
SGDP	Gross State Domestic Product
SHG	Self-Help Group
SHGs	Self-Help Groups
SIDBI	Small Industries Development Bank of India
SME	Small and Medium Enterprise
SPH	Status of Poverty of a Household
SPS	Social Protection Scheme

ST	Scheduled Tribes
SUR	Seemingly Unrelated Regression
TOPSIS	Technique for Order of Preference by Similarity to Ideal Solution
TSPI	Tulay Sa Pag-unlad, Inc.
UMEs	Unorganized Manufacturing Enterprises
UN	United Nation
UNECA	United Nations Economic Commission for Africa
VECM	Vector Error Correction Mechanism
VIKOR	VlseKriterijumska Optimizacija I Kompromisno Resenje
WAEMU	West African Economic and Monetary Union
WB	World Bank
WDI	World Development Indicators
WOFEE	Women Fund for Economic Empowerment
WSHG	Women Self Help Group
YGP	Yield on Gross Portfolio

List of Figures

Fig. 3.1	Equilibrium analysis (*Source* Drawn by the authors)	37
Fig. 3.2	Equilibrium analysis with parametric shifts (*Source* Drawn by the authors)	42
Fig. 3.3	Output dynamics with stability implications (*Source* Drawn by the authors)	46
Fig. 11.1	Advantages of microfinance (*Source* Sketched by the authors)	164
Fig. 12.1	Relationship among political economy of microcredit and microfinance, empowerment of women and sustainable development (*Source* Sketched by the author)	187
Fig. 14.1	Trend in sustainability scores of sample MFIs (*Source* Author's own presentation)	224

List of Tables

Table 2.1	F-value (PAR)	21
Table 2.2	F-value (ROA)	22
Table 2.3	F-value (CAR)	23
Table 4.1	Static models results	58
Table 4.2	Dynamic models results	60
Table 5.1	Regression equation between per capita consumption expenditure of households (PCCE) (proxy of poverty) as dependent variable and loan disbursement (MFL), deposits in microfinance bank and institutions (MFD) as explanatory variables for the selected country India (2008–2017)	74
Table 5.2	Regression equation between per capita consumption expenditure of households (PCCE) (proxy of poverty) as dependent variable and loan disbursement (MFL), deposits in microfinance bank and institutions (MFD) as explanatory variables for the selected country Bangladesh (2008–2015)	75
Table 5.3	Regression equation between per capita consumption expenditure of households (PCCE) (proxy of poverty) as dependent variable and loan disbursement (MFL), deposits in microfinance bank and institutions (MFD) as explanatory variables for the selected country Nigeria	76
Table 6.1	The Details of the criteria	90
Table 6.2	Weights of the criteria	91

LIST OF TABLES

Table 7.1	Descriptive statistics and correlation matrix among the variables (2016–17 to 2018–19)	104
Table 7.2	MFI-wise efficiency scores with their classification and ranking (2016–17 to 2018–19)	105
Table 7.3	Detailed results of Friedman test and Wilcoxon signed-rank tests	107
Table 8.1	Estimated results of effect of financial widening activities on self-employed Nigerians	123
Table 9.1	Amount and sources of loan and performance of UMEs in relation to microfinance in India, 2010–11 and 2015–16	139
Table 9.2	Multinomial logistic regression of status of growth of UMEs	142
Table 9.3	Heckman selection model—two-step estimates	143
Table 10.1	Socioeconomic and employment details	153
Table 10.2	Activity-wise employment details	154
Table 10.3	Saving and expenditure composition (INR)	156
Table 11.1	World's financial inclusion of adults (% 15+)	168
Table 11.2	Regional participation scenario of financial institutions	169
Table 13.1	Review of literature	199
Table 13.2	EGLS regression with cross-section SUR weights and standard errors	203
Table 13.3	ADF Fischer Unit Root Test and Granger Causality Analysis	205
Table 14.1	The results of the determinants of sustainability of MFIs (Dependent variable: Sustainability Score)	218
Table 14.2	The results of the Chow Test (F-statistics)	221
Table 15.1	Category wise composition of borrowers	235
Table 15.2	MFIs involved in Micro Insurance—Life Insurance	237
Table 15.3	MFIs involved in Micro Insurance—Health	238
Table 16.1	Percentage distribution of sample households (HH) with principal status activity (Panel a) and percentage distribution of population by age group (Panel b)	253
Table 16.2	Percentage distribution of households by income group (Panel a) and landholding (Panel b)	255
Table 16.3	Percentage distribution of consumption of commodities and services	256
Table 16.4	Fractiles of the distributions of sample households participating in SHGs according to MPCE	257
Table 16.5	Notation, Mean, and SD of the Variables used in Probit Regression Model to estimate the effect SHGs	259

Table 16.6	Probit estimation of SHGs over sample households on poverty	259
Table 17.1	Descriptive statistics showing differences among rural women group	269
Table 17.2	Disparity in rural women access to micro credit	269
Table 18.1	Socio-economic characteristics of respondents	285
Table 18.2	Results of logistic regression on the risk of loan default	287

PART I

Role of Microfinance in Mitigating Economic Recession of World's Economies

CHAPTER 1

Introduction

Ramesh Chandra Das

INTRODUCTION

Prolonged recession in the global economic fronts faced by the so-called developed economies and its magnitude fuelled by the emerging economies has perplexed the global leaders in finding permanent solution to combat it. The magnitude of recession has further been aggravated by the recent tariff war between China and US, and US and other nations such as India and Mexico. The outcomes of the economic crises are revealed through the declining income growth of the economies as well as increasing the magnitudes of poverty and social exclusion. As the big industrial houses at the global level are not so interested in investing their funds due to low marketability and hence low profitability, it has now become a distant solution for arresting such global recession. But the potential progress is probably latent within the potentialities of the small and medium-scale industries. Major part of the workforce is associated with the small and medium enterprises (SMEs) in most of the

R. C. Das (✉)
Department of Economics, Vidyasagar University, Midnapore, India
e-mail: ramesh051073@gmail.com

© The Author(s), under exclusive license to Springer Nature Singapore Pte Ltd. 2022
R. C. Das (ed.), *Microfinance to Combat Global Recession and Social Exclusion*, https://doi.org/10.1007/978-981-16-4329-3_1

countries of the world and, as most of the SMEs are informal or subcontracting units, their workers are with high consumption potentialities which usually demand augmenting. Strengthening the SMEs may thus lead to increase in the volume of demand, reducing excess supply or unemployment problem and thus combat recession. But where from the additional sources of funds will come? The answer lies within the microfinancial system which is present and performing well in almost all the countries in the today's world.

The history of microfinance can be traced back to the mid-nineteenth century, when the theorist Lysander Spooner wrote about the benefits of microfinance for entrepreneurs and farmers, and lifted people out of poverty. Friedrich Wilhelm Raiffeisen, independent of Spooner, founded the first cooperative banks to support farmers in rural Germany. The creation and shaping of the modern microfinance industry, which now provides support to more than 7 million poor women in Bangladesh, have inspired the world, but this success has proved difficult to replicate. In sparsely populated countries, it has proven to be much more difficult to pay for the cost of operating a retail store by providing services to nearby customers. This particular model (used by many microfinance institutions) has financial significance because it reduces transaction costs. Microfinance programmes must also be based on local resources. The poor borrow from informal money lenders and save from informal payees. They get loans and grants from charities. You buy insurance from a state-owned company. You will receive the remittance through a formal or informal wire transfer network. In 2004, the Consultative Group on Poverty Alleviation (CGAP) summarized some principles of development practice for a century and a half, and put them forward at the G8 summit on May 10. The principle is: The poor need not only credit, but also savings, insurance and remittance services; microfinance must be useful to poor households: it should help them increase income, accumulate wealth and/or cushion external shocks. Donor and government subsidies are scarce and uncertain. In order to benefit a large number of poor people, microfinance must be self-sufficient; microfinance means establishing permanent local institutions; microfinance also means integrating the financial needs of the poor into a country's mainstream financial system.

In the past thirty years, this field has made tremendous development, trying to connect most of the poor and underdeveloped classes to the credit network of the formal sector to ensure the scale and overall growth of the mission of inclusive finance, and promote the development of a country. This special development process is called microfinance or microfinance, which is operated by non-governmental organizations that act as self-help groups to establish connections between ordinary people and formal financial institutions. One of the main goals of microfinance activities is to empower women through financial support and the opportunity to obtain independent income, make economic contributions to the family and open self-employed businesses. This economic independence aims to improve the overall development of the country.

Traditionally, as a country's inclusive financial tool, microfinance has been regarded as a well-designed institutional innovation to ensure that a large amount of credit flows to poor families without or less strict collateral. However, it is generally believed that microfinance projects are not a panacea for grassroots poverty alleviation; on the contrary, they are only regarded as a means to solve problems, especially for emerging economies and underdeveloped groups. Microfinance intervention can increase access to resources, increase opportunities for self-employment and thereby reduce poverty. The premise is that the government takes appropriate measures to promote social mobilization, capital formation, capacity building and appropriate planning. Without effective intervention in the eligible macro-political environment, such micro-political intervention will not be able to successfully alleviate poverty.

Redirecting the flow of funds of the microfinance system to the SMEs will push up the capital base of the SMEs, increase the per head capital, increase the productivity of labour and finally the income and expenditure of the worker class in high magnitude and of the business class as relatively low magnitude. The combination of these two-income augmenting results will lead to increase in the volume of aggregate demand and solve the recessionary situation of the global economy. Besides, aggravation of microfinance activities will lead to inclusive growth, reduce the magnitudes of social exclusion and hence upgrade the overall development. The global policy-makers should focus on the redirection of microfinance funds upon SMEs and thus inspire global development.

Based upon the above background, the proposed book aims to examine whether microfinance activity can lead to combating global recession and ensuring social inclusion. After a thorough scrutiny and review of the edited book project by the publisher, *Palgrave Macmillan*, a final title is selected which is *Microfinance to Combat Global Recession and Social Exclusion—An Empirical Investigation*.

The edited book has eighteen chapters including this introductory chapter. The total eighteen chapters are further divided into two parts, Part I and Part II, to separate the issues related to the role of microfinance in combating economic recessions and that of ensuring social inclusion. In Part I, there are nine studies related to the linkages between microfinance and global recession, and in Part II, there are also nine studies which discuss the importance of microfinance in combating social exclusion across the countries and regions of the world. A brief outline of the chapters covered in Part I and Part II is supplied below to have a glimpse of ideas in each of the chapters.

Part I: Role of Microfinance in Mitigating Economic Recession of world's Economies

Chapter 2 tries to examine the performance of a few selected microfinance institutions to assess the impact of global financial crisis on these institutions. The secondary data analysis elicits that those institutions that offer multiple services such as savings, insurance and training simultaneously are less affected and struggled hard to keep the organizational spine straight at the outset of crisis.

Chapter 3 is intended to develop a macro-theoretic model based on Keynesian paradigm by incorporating an altered construct of financial sector comprised of banking sector to address the case of credit rationing faced by MSMEs in a closed economy setting with flexible interest rate. The pivotal result is that in the presence of credit rationing, the declining credit flow towards apparently non-quality sectors in the face of rising default risk due to the advent of economic downturn led by investment pessimism on part of the quality borrowers can be potentially destabilizing by having to accentuate the recession and henceforth, will be a self-defeating response for the banks by causing a further worsening of asset quality, inducing a more pronounced credit tightening or austerity in credit dissemination. The study thus recommends for enforcing credit flow towards this rationed sector which may be a plausible way to tackle the recession underway by effective enforcement of priority sector lending norms, etc.

Chapter 4 explores the role of growth and fluctuations of different macroeconomic variables affecting the performances of microfinance institutions (MFIs) in South Asian Countries. The findings of the study suggest that GDP is one of the significant variables that effect the performance of microfinance institutions as the GDP per capita of country goes up, the performance of microfinance institutions comes down and vice versa. Since the performance of the MFIs are inversely related to the economic growth, it can be inferred that economic shocks or recession have lesser effect on the performance of the MFIs in South Asian nations.

Chapter 5 tries to analyse the impacts of microfinance activities upon poverty alleviation, poverty being the outcome of recession, in three countries, India, Bangladesh and Nigeria. Taking loans from microfinance institutions and deposits in the microfinance institutions as the explanatory variables of the model, it is derived that there are positive and significant impacts of financial activities of microfinance institutions on poverty alleviation for the selected nations except Nigeria.

Chapter 6 examines how to improve the effectiveness of microfinance system in Turkey through different factors. Applying the fuzzy DEMATEL method in order to determine which of these factors is more important, the study identifies that legal infrastructure and credit unions have the most importance in this process.

Chapter 7 attempts to measure the efficiency of the MFIs operating in West Bengal, India, for the years 2016–2017 to 2018–2019 through input-oriented CCR model under Data Envelopment Analysis. The result of the study reveals the fact that all the nine inefficient MFIs have the scope of producing 1.17 times to 4.32 times of output with the same level of input. To overcome the present recessionary situation, there may be a requirement in an increase of investment and aggregate demand of consumer spending by escalating efficiency of MFIs.

Chapter 8 investigates the effect of financial widening activities on self-employment opportunities in Nigeria using World Bank Financial Inclusion Survey 2014 and examines the effect of financial widening activities such as mobile money, banking services, e-payment options, savings, access to financial institutions outlets among others on self-employment opportunities created by the agricultural sector. Using logit estimation model, the study demonstrates how mobile money, banking services, e-payment options, savings, access to financial institutions outlets and services among others have significantly strengthened agricultural transactions and enhanced self-employment opportunity and poverty reduction.

Chapter 9 attempts to analyse the access of microfinance and its role to promote the growth of unorganized manufacturing enterprises (UMEs) in India and points out the determinants that influence financial access with the help of NSSO Unit Level data of 67th (2010–2011) and 73rd (2015–2016) rounds. It reveals that less than 10% of UMEs has financial access. But the performance is higher among the UMEs which received loans than those didn't receive loans. Microfinance has played an important role in the growth of employment, gross value added and fixed assets of UMEs. Establishment and registered enterprises, enterprises which maintain accounts, have partnership and have larger size of the firm, are more likely to access loans and they are more likely to be expanding in nature.

Chapter 10 tries to link the impact of rural economic transaction through microfinance programme and its contribution in generating rural production and consumption linkages through incorporating 240 WSHG rural members from two major districts, Balasore and Mayurbhanj, of Odisha in India. The study finds significant impact of the programme in generating production/services at local level and assesses its replications in various economic indicators such as expenditure, saving and further investments.

Part II: Role of Microfinance in Reducing Social Exclusion of the Countries and Regions

Chapter 11 aims primarily to contemplate the role of microfinance towards financial inclusion, and hence, it examines the behaviour of microfinance towards curbing financial inequality. The study further highlights the problems and prospects associated with the role of microfinance in financial inclusion in different regions in the world. Adopting descriptive methodology using various secondary data sources, the present study arrives at the conclusion that a major part of the regions has reached the financial inclusion mission with some lacunae. The study thus suggests the use of digitalization and innovation aspects in the present digitalized world to the fullest in order to achieve the sustainability of the qualitative results.

Chapter 12 tries to establish whether microfinance performance has co-movements with financial inclusion and income inequality that consolidates the interconnection among demand, income and recession reduction. The empirical model serves to explain income inequality using panel cointegration to ascertain the reduction basis through VECM and deploying alternate regression models such as GMM-OLS with panel data for past six years across ten states in India. The empirical results demonstrate the microfinance institutions' offerings building strong risk management practices undertaking the short-run and long-run impacts.

Chapter 12 investigates theoretically the political economy of microfinance from the gender and politics point of view under the specific focus of its role upon social inclusion of women to the workforce and empowerment of women. The study establishes that the microfinance activity makes the women section more empowered leading to more social inclusion. Through its analysis, it supports the claim of the Maslow hierarchy pyramid, 'once people obtain their basic needs they proceed to the next step and reach to the self-actualization step'.

Chapter 13 studies the impact of microfinance on inequality for five SAARC countries, for the period 2000–2018 using the Panel Estimated Generalized Least Squares (EGLS) model, and tests the causal links using the Granger Causality test, the magnitude and direction of relationship of various macroeconomic variables and Gini Index. It is found that the number of borrowers significantly reduces inequality, while on the other hand the value of loans is found to be having a positive relationship with inequality. It further draws that higher value of loans might actually lead the poor into debt-traps, and thus, focussing on increasing the number of borrowers is vital.

Chapter 14 examines the impact of the Andhra crisis on the sustainability of MFIs using the Microfinance Information Exchange Database in a pooled dataset format of the Indian MFIs. In addition to the crisis, the study examines the implications of other financial and operating performance in explaining sustainability of MFIs in the changing scenario. Results reveal a positive and significant influence of crisis, return on assets, return on equity, yield on gross portfolio and a negative and significant impact of financial expenses to assets and operating expenses to assets in explaining variation of sustainability score of selected MFIs.

Chapter 15 primarily focuses on the case-based analysis of different MFIs to study the role of microfinance institutions in social inclusion with reference to India. The findings depict that significant inclusion has been seen in the recent years in Indian context, but there is need for more such policy integrations which would aid the MFIs in providing sustainable inclusion in India.

Chapter 16 examines empirically the influence of activities under SHGs on poverty with the help of probit model based on mainly primary data survey on the basis of Stratified Random Sampling in West Bengal. The study reveals that SHGs have a significant impact on poverty reduction.

Chapter 17 aims to assess the disparity in rural women access to microcredit in Nigeria using the cross-sectional data extracted from the 2016 Nigeria General Household Survey. Findings suggest that there is huge disparity among rural women access to microcredit. The study thus recommends that there is desirous need for effective implementation of financial inclusiveness so as to bridge the gap in access to microcredit among women in rural Nigeria.

The final chapter, Chapter 18, tries to identify the key factors of microloans that contribute to the risk of default using the data from a cross-section survey conducted among 500 rural borrowers living from the rural areas of West Bengal applying a multivariate statistical technique. The determinants include various borrower-specific and loan-related characteristics. It reveals that the risk of default increases for female borrowers than male, aged borrowers, lower household income and number of dependent family members if loans taken from non-formal borrowers. On the other side, the risk of default decreases with the education level of the borrowers, assets holdings other than agricultural land and an increase in business experiences of the borrowers.

The essence of the studies covered in the book is manifolds. There have been the studies which reveal that microfinance activities may be a tool for combating economic recessions, and on the other hand, some studies reveal that recession has impacted the performance of the microfinance institutions. With respect to the role of microfinance upon social inclusion, the studies in general opine that microfinance activities have been proved to be the panacea of social exclusion. For further development of the institutional aspects of the microfinance, certain studies are there which recommend the digitalization of the sector through the information and telecommunication services to be fit for the modern business arena.

The proposed book is thus highly impactful so far as recession management and social inclusion are concerned. It would provide thought provoking solutions to the existing problems of the global economic and social fronts, and there would be the incidence of accentuating literature base in this area. There may be immense academic value of the outcomes of the proposed book which may then be percolated to the other section of the economy and society. The book is thus recommended satisfactorily to the potential readers for its contents and thoughts.

CHAPTER 2

Global Recession and Microfinance Institutions: Challenges and Opportunities

Avijit Brahmachary

INTRODUCTION

The global financial crisis was first observed in 2008 in the developed nations and gradually accelerated throughout the world around 2010. The crisis hit both the real and financial sector simultaneously. Though the epicentre of the crisis was mainly observed in developed countries due to sub-prime lending crisis, the rampancy has speeded quickly to the developing countries through investment, trade and monetary channels (Sahoo & Mahapatra, 2013; World Bank, 2008). The financial breakdown unexpectedly hit the capital flows to developing nations and led destabilization in their financial system and averts the high economic growth objective of the emerging nations. Though initially the economic drag concentrated within the property market, it has stretched quickly on all other sectors bringing an economic collapse in the system.

A. Brahmachary (✉)
Department of Economics, Barrackpore Rastraguru Surendranath College, Kolkata, India
e-mail: avijiteco@rediffmail.com

© The Author(s), under exclusive license to Springer Nature Singapore Pte Ltd. 2022
R. C. Das (ed.), *Microfinance to Combat Global Recession and Social Exclusion*, https://doi.org/10.1007/978-981-16-4329-3_2

The crisis was very serious in the developing nations since they usually suffer from multiple problems such as reduced access to external liquidity sources, unorganized asset market, extensive withdrawals of deposits and obviously decreased volume of balance of payment position (Brahmachary, 2019).

Now, it is well known that Microfinance Institutions (MFIs) offer integrated monetary services to low income unbanked economically active borrowers who need small or micro volume of finance for their business or some other purposes (CGAP, 2010). Such borrowers have no credit history recorded to the MFIs and usually suffer from zero collateral. The formal financial institutions are not interested always to deal with these people due to moral hazard and adverse selection problem associated with credit disbursement and therefore, these people remain unbanked. With the advent of microfinance movement throughout the world, MFIs bring these people under their financial umbrella and witnessed a successful achievement in this operation. The wave accelerated from 2005, the year which United Nations Organizations placed microfinance as a tool to attain the Millennium Development Goals (MDGs) and declared the year 2005 as the 'Year of Microcredit'.

The global financial meltdown in 2008–2010 hit the regular operation of MFIs and put an impediment to serve financial services among the poor people. However, study reveals that such blow was not very severe as like formal financial institutions (FFIs) and most of the MFIs recovered their deterioration very quickly and found further avenues for business expansion mainly in informal sectors due to the incapability of FFIs for their recession wound.

Microfinance and Global Crisis

Microfinance has evidently been considered as one of the prime poverty alleviation programme around the world mainly in developing and underdeveloped economies. It is fact that supply led formal financial programme has several leakages and therefore, requires different reconstruction in the ongoing projects. These programmes usually suffer from the problem of moral hazard and adverse selection. To minimize these problems in the credit market, different initiatives were initiated from the formal agencies but unfortunately none of them were very productive and successful.

The lesson from different parts of the globe such as Bangladesh, India, Indonesia, Bolivia, Thailand gave a direction that moral hazard problem in the credit market can be handled successfully with microfinance programme. It is fact that there was a great need for a constructive mechanism to provide a variety of financial services to the poor people. But due to lack of adequate collateral they remained unbanked and microfinance programme in different forms has addressed the issue throughout the globe successfully. Here peer pressure within the group has worked well as collateral and has been instrumental in getting a loan. As compared to formal financial institutions here bank offers loan to the group, not to the individual member. And the borrower is borrowing from the group without getting direct individual loan from formal agencies.

The global recession was initiated with the advent of sub-prime crisis in United States in 2007–2008 and accelerated from mid-2008 throughout the world when U.S treasury refused to rescue the global financial giant Lehman Brothers. Just after the announcement of Lehman Brother's bankruptcy news, the financial crisis climbs on very rapidly over the world leading a currency market distortion, credit crunch, employment lay off and lower production resulting economic downturn. Economist was analyzed that the incidence of global financial meltdown was inevitable due to excessive greed, mispricing of assets and distorted speculation in the mortgage market suddenly burst the bubble resulting a financial meltdown throughout the globe. Though initially it was the problem of investment banks and therefore, the effect was primarily observed in United States and other developed nations only. But due to integrated global financial market, immediately the shock had speeded over in other parts of the globe (Brahmachary, 2019). Fortunately, MFIs in developing and underdeveloped countries were less affected due to such crisis.

IMPACT OF GLOBAL ECONOMIC CRISIS ON MFIS

The aftermath of crisis in developing and emerging nations like Thailand, Indonesia, Brazil, India etc. was witnessed by negative GDP growth, high inflation, currency depreciation and increased BOP deficit. World Bank summarized the immediate impacts of the crisis on financial markets as follows (Sahoo & Mahapatra, 2013):

a. The malfunction of some monetary institutions in the credit market due to huge greed and inefficient management a credit crunch triggered and consequently a liquidity shortage throughout the world widened.

b. The severe liquidity shortage forced different financial organisations to sell their own holding to protect their own corpus and thereby a panic sell-off in the market. This action of foreign institutions triggered a destabilization in the banking and equity market of the home country.
c. Cost of financing has increased due to liquidity crunch, currency depreciation and financial instability in the globe.
d. Due to shortage of fund and increased price of capital in the international market ability to finance in the development programme such as poverty reduction schemes, supply led subsidized pro poor programme, financial inclusion of the poor people etc. backpedal significantly.

However, the impact of the crisis can be analyzed into two separate dimensions (Sahoo & Mahapatra, 2013)—(i) Impact on Microfinance Institutions and (ii) Impact on MFI clients. It is assumed that during financial crisis MFIs tried to provide maximum liquidity and working capital to the micro-enterprises, small borrowers and other lending to informal sectors. The demand for credit from MFIs was very high since economic clot reduced volume of macro-output and hence a huge unemployment which generated in the economy in this time was compelled individuals to engage in different informal sectors for their bread and butter. It was found that the crisis was observed more severely in those financial sectors which are more integrated in the global financial markets. The impact of the crisis emerged as the secondary impact on MFI sector and the setback was less severe than formal financial institutions. However, the areas where remarkable stress was observed are as follows:

a. Mild stress was observed on the loan portfolio since 2008 and expansion of microcredit in the globe dropped up to 2011. Portfolio quality decayed significantly in large MFIs and portfolio at risks has increased representing weak financial health of the institutions. Consequently, the credit risks have grown substantially.
b. The immediate effect of the crisis on MFIs was observed in respect of volume of funds. Due to financial turmoil funding from formal national and international institutes dropped significantly and they have to rely on the funding of domestic savings deposits only. As

a result, the new lending was curtailed and further business expansion became stagnant. In this time the basic fight of the institutions was to survive and therefore, they primarily concentrated on the existing clients. Some MFIs reported that during this period the loan default has increased since the borrower hypothesized that there is little chance to survive the institute and if survive, very little hope to receive further loan.

c. Currency depreciation eroded the funding and refinance scheme of the MFIs and thereby a deterioration of the fund volume and asset quality.

These were the impacts of crisis on microfinance institutions. However, the impacts of the recession on MFI clients are also significant. The intense inflation with accelerated food and industrial output prices dropped the real income of the individuals and hence a collapse of loan repayment—from 98 in 2007 to 70% in 2010. Due to sluggish growth of the overall economy during global meltdown, new employment generation remained stationary or dropped in many parts of the world. Consequently, poverty loomed extremely among the deserved section of the society and though the demand for microfinance was very high but due to pressure on profit margin ultimately the financial sustainability bruised significantly.

Duflos and Gaehwiler (2008) observed that the pre-existing food inflation hit the MFIs more severe than the global financial crisis. They found that due to exorbitant food price in 2008–2009, clients have withdrawn their savings, restrain from further loan for productive activities, curtailed non-food consumption and suffer from liquidity or cash crisis. Many MFIs reported that the purchasing power of the clients dropped significantly and demand for cash has increased resulting higher default ratio in time of repayment.

Fortunately, in this gloomy situation also the demand for subsistence consumption goods remains unaltered. Micro enterprises which are usually financed by MFIs mainly concentrated their production in these consumption goods where demand shock was not observed significantly due to global crisis. Initially, just aftermath of global financial meltdown though some blow was observed in the micro financial sector but within a very short time span they have managed the seer attack due to emphasize on those businesses which are engaged in consumer goods production where demand is stationary.

Objectives and Methodology of the Study

Against this backdrop, the basic objective of the present study is to analyze the impact of global financial crisis on the microfinance institutions and to find out the opportunities to MFIs aftermath of the crisis. Historical experience will help us to understand how the microfinance sector has been affected by the global financial crisis in 2008–2010 and what kind of organizational reconstruction is needed to redefine the sector as a tool to combat the economic crisis particularly in informal sector. For this purpose, three popular microfinance institutions have been chosen from three different countries namely, Bolivia, Bangladesh and India to analyze that whether there is any significant difference in mean of some financial parameters of these three MFIs from pre to post global crisis or not.

Secondary data has been collected from Microfinance Information Exchange (MIX) Market dataset which is available via the World Bank open data catalogue. The MIX Market dataset provides diversified data to analyze the performance of microfinance institutions (MFIs) throughout the world. To fulfil our objective comprehensively here we have tried to analyze the performance of said MFIs in terms of some financial indicators namely, Profit at Risk (PAR), Return on Assets (ROA) and Capital-Asset Ratio (CAR) between pre and post recession period. Required data on these financial indicators has been collected from MIX Market, World Bank and arranged it as per the requirement of the study. Here, we have used the statistical tool ANOVA (analysis of variance) to analyze the differences of group means in terms of above financial indicators for the three respective MFIs. For our study year 2010 has been considered as the threshold year. The phase of operation of MFIs before 2010 has been identified as pre-recessionary period and after 2010 onwards the period has considered as post recessionary phase. The data range for the study is 2003–2017. The computation of mean variance between two phases (before and after recession) helps to analyze the impact of crisis on MFIs in the global scenario and can be decisive for future policy design in the country to combat economic recession.

Brief Outlook on MFIs

Before explaining the result of the study let us give a brief outlook on the three MFIs which have considered here for our study.

Banco Solidario of Bolivia

Bolivia is one of the countries in the world that successfully leads the microfinance programme in 1980s. The platform needed to successful implement of microfinance programme was perfect in Bolivia. People of Bolivia lost their confidence on banking system due to persistent economic and financial turmoil in the country and were leaning towards the private lender. The situation was more severe in case of unbanked people. The country was gradually moving to the recession stage. Many traders started to trade with neighbour giant Brazil and the production, employment of own country dropped drastically.

The microfinance sector took a positive role in this regard. Here microfinance played an important role in bringing all the economies out of recession. The success of the Grameen Bank of Bangladesh and its expansion was played as a catalyst for the popularization and expansion of microfinance programme in Bolivia. Banco Solidario (BancoSol) is one of the important MFI not only in the country but also in the world too. It started working in Bolivia as an NGO in 1987 and actively participates in monetary transactions like saving, lending etc. From 1992 it began to function fully as a bank. Currently, above 50% of Bolivian borrowers borrow from this bank. BancoSol offers loan to the group as well as the individual member separately. These members are known as Solidarity Group.

Reviewing the nature of Bolivian microfinance shows that it works on two different levels. One is in urban areas where poor people live. Some of them may receive formal financial services and others do not due to lack of adequate income and wealth. A large portion of those people who do not get the opportunity to receive financial services come from rural to urban for employment. These people have been brought into the service network of BancoSol for two purposes—(a) Capable people do not go anywhere else, and (b) those who do not have the ability to take financial services through group activities (Solidarity group). The other level is the rural population, most of who suffer from poverty and lack of resources. Due to poverty and lack of mortgages, they can't borrow from the formal institutions (Marconi & Mosley, 2005).

Since in case of BancoSol there was no specific liability or social goals, therefore, for business expansion they designed microfinance model from business perspective. Group based microfinance has worked very successful here for not having any specific social responsibility issues.

It is proved that most of the MFIs that have previously sought to advance certain social goals have failed in either direction. Either their target vision has been corrupted, or else the existence of the target has been endangered. BancoSol succeeded because they performed microfinance activities on their own methodology and the social responsibility to bring the poor people under the financial umbrella has been fulfilled automatically while doing their businesses (Lal & Lobb, 2016).

Grameen Bank

Grameen bank of Bangladesh is one of the oldest community development banks and provides microfinance to a large number of individuals. It is the brainchild of Muhammad Yunus, a Nobel laureate professor of University of Chitagong, Bangladesh. The famine of 1974 in Bangladesh leads to a new thinking in the mind of Professor Yunus about easy access to financial services for the poor people whose credit demand during this period was very high. During famine collateral-fewer poor people are compelled to take loans from professional moneylenders at usurious rate of interest. A pilot research project initiated by professor Yunus with U.S funding covered 42 families in Jobra and neighbour villages to study the effectiveness of financial access of these families on their business and household consumption. The positive observations of the project inspired Muhammad Yunus to initiate a new organization for providing micro financial services among the poor under the belief that if such micro loans are offered to a large number of populations, it will act as a stimulant for business and may be instrumental for poverty reduction in Bangladesh. Observing the success of the pilot project it extended to other districts with the financial support of Bangladesh Bank in 1979.

In 1983, the project was converted to an independent bank by the ordinance of Bangladesh government and thus Grameen Bank was established to offer microcredit among the poor household in Bangladesh. Ford foundation and other notable donor agencies started to offer their financial integration scheme with Grammen Bank to extend the outreach of the Bangladesh microfinance (Yunus, 2003).

The loan portfolio of Grameen Bank during global recession in 2008–2010 was deteriorated and struggled initially a lot. Funding from donor agencies decreased significantly and the refinance scheme from the central bank of Bangladesh shortened in an unguarded state. However, the initial outbreak of the crisis softens the capital-asset ratio of the bank but quickly recovered from its distress situation in 2012–2013. Professor Yunus, the 'Banker of the Poor' opined that though big banks floundered and suffered considerably due to financial meltdown in 2008–2010, the blow to Grameen Bank of Bangladesh was very mild and negligible. He concluded that in 2010–2011, the total loan disbursement by the Grameen Bank was over 100 million U.S Dollar and repayment rate was around 99%. Many researchers advocated that Grameen Bank model of microfinance can go all over the world including developed countries. As on 2010 the net income of the bank was 9 million U.S dollar and total asset was 1.5 billion U.S dollar (Hossain, 2013; Mustafa et al., 2018).

Bandhan Microfinance in India

India is one of the breeding countries of microfinance in the world and officially considered by the government as a pivot programme for financial inclusion in 1990s. The official involvement of microfinance activities in India was started in 1992 under the aegis of National bank for Agriculture and Rural Development through a pilot project and thereafter, RBI and government of India came forward with a bunch of policies to promote the group-based microfinance programme in the country more comprehensively (NABARD, 2018).

Bandhan Microfinance limited started its operation in 2001 as a nonprofit organization providing microloans to left out in the cold people in the society. Initially Bandhan started its microfinance operations from Bagnan, a village of West Bengal. The basic objective of the organizations was twofold—(i) financial inclusion of the poor and (ii) women empowerment through livelihood security. In 2006, Bandhan was recognized as non bank financial company and in 2010 Bandhan established themselves as the largest MFI in the country. Now it has active presence in the 34 states and union territories with special focus on eastern and north-eastern states of the country.

In August 2015, Bandhan Bank got licence from the central bank of India (RBI) to function as a fully fledged bank in the country and later listed in the stock exchanges (namely, National Stock Exchange and Bombay Stock Exchange) for daily trading. As on 2019, the total number of banking outlets of Bandhan was 4288 and total number of employees is 37331. The total number of clients of the bank in this time is around 1.9 crore. The net income of the bank as on 2017 was 160 million U.S dollar and total assets of the bank were 4.2 billion dollar. Out of total

4288 outlets, 1009 were direct bank branches, 3084 are doorstep service centers (DSCs) and 195 are GRUH centre (GRUH Finance is a housing loan providing institutes formerly was a subsidiary of HDFC Bank limited and now is a part of the Bandhan Bank).

Prior to 2010, Bandhan microfinance was growing at a rapid pace but global financial meltdown made soften the operations of the Badhan when it was not recognized as bank as today. The unfortunate global crisis along with the ordinance of Andhra Pradesh government in India in 2010 reduced the volume of fund support in microfinance sectors and some well known MFIs including Bandhan. Almost 2 years after global recession Bandhan struggled seriously to survive in the microfinance industry and gradually recognized as the extended arms of formal banking system to reach among unbanked deserved people in the country. Unlike profitable MFIs, Bandhan microfinance pays considerable attention to balance their financial and social objectives simultaneously. Banks and other agencies gained confidence about recession insulation characteristics of microfinance industry and started funding MFIs again from 2012–2013 with enough support of Reserve Bank of India. However, Bandhan tried to reconstruct their balance sheet from this time and accelerated their microfinance operation after the recognition of formal bank by RBI in 2015 (Bandyopadhyay, 2016).

Results and Discussions

As stated above, in this study we have considered three famous MFIs namely BancoSol, Grameen Bank and Bandhan microfinance limited from Bolivia, Bangladesh and India. Here, the basic objective is to analyze the performance of these MFIs in terms of some financial indicators namely, Profit at Risk (PAR), Return on Assets (ROA) and Capital-Asset Ratio (CAR) in pre and post recession period. For analysis here we have used the statistical tool ANOVA (Analysis of Variance) single factor to identify that whether there is any significant variance of group mean of the above financial indicators is exists or not from pre to post recession phase.

The Profit at Risk (PAR) of a financial organization indicates the relationship between risk and profit of that organization. According to professor Hawley, profit is a reward for risk taken in business. It is mainly used in financial service sector to measure the downside risk to profitability of a portfolio of both physical and financial assets. It is analyzed for a specific time period. In case of financial sector, it is believed that high volatility in the financial market during global recession will put significant difference of group means of PAR from pre to post recessionary period. But the study reveals that microfinance sector suffered less from recessionary shock and therefore, here our assumption is that there is no significant difference of mean in respect of PAR for the concerned three MFIs under our study from pre to post recession phase.

Hence the hypotheses of the study are—

Null Hypothesis H_0: There is no significant difference of group mean from pre to post recession period in respect of PAR

Alternative Hypothesis H_1: There is a significant difference of group mean in respect of PAR.

In Table 2.1 we have summarized the F-value of PAR for the three MFIs under our study.

The result shows that (Table 2.1) in case of three MFIs under our consideration the calculated F-value is less than the critical or table value of F at respective degrees of freedom. Hence, we can accept the null hypothesis that there is no significant variance of mean in respect of PAR value between pre and post recessionary period. The result authenticates our hypothesis that recession has limited or mild impact on MFIs and therefore, it can be concluded that microfinance industry to some extent recession insulated.

However, if we look at the value of F on three MFIs, it indicates that the impact in terms of PAR on Grameen Bank and Bandhan Bank is very negligible whereas mild impact has observed in case of BancoSol of Bolivia. Since the comparative analysis between different MFIs is beyond the scope of present study and depends on some political, demographic and country specific factors which require different dimension of dataset is, therefore, left from present study for the time being. But

Table 2.1 F-value (PAR)

MFIs	F-value calculated	F-value critical	Degrees of freedom	Probability
BancoSol	3.895	9.330	1,12	0.01
Grameen Bank	0.024	9.074	1,13	0.01
Bandhan Bank	0.951	9.074	1,13	0.01

Source Author's Calculation

from Table 2.1, however, we can unanimously conclude that in terms of PAR recession has very little impact on the three MFIs under our consideration.

The other financial parameter which we have included here is return on assets (ROA). The return on assets of an organization indicates that how profitable a company's assets are in generating revenue. ROA shows that the potential of MFIs to earn profit with its existing assets. Our assumption is that there is no significant difference of group means in respect of ROA from pre to post recessionary phase. Hence, here our hypotheses are—

H_0: There is no significant difference of mean of ROA between pre and post recession for MFIs

H_1: There is a significant difference of mean of ROA between these two phases.

The F-value of ROA for three MFIs has summarized in Table 2.2.

Table 2.2 shows that for all the three MFIs, F-value is significant at 1% level of significance at respective degrees of freedom. It confirms the acceptance of null hypothesis that there is no significant difference of group means in respect of ROA for these three well known MFIs before and after global recession and thereby ascertain that microfinance sector is recession proof and can be put in pivotal position for financing informal sector in the country.

Lastly, here we have considered the capital-asset ratio of the MFIs to understand that whether there is any deterioration of the asset quality of MFIs after the financial meltdown in 2008–2010 or not. The capital-asset ratio helps to measure that whether an organization has sufficient capital to support its asset. Capital of a MFI refers to the net worth of the organization and asset includes all the things they own. Capital to Asset Ratio

Table 2.2 F-value (ROA)

MFIs	F-value calculated	F-value critical	Degrees of freedom	Probability
BancoSol	4.649	8.862	1,14	0.01
Grameen Bank	2.015	9.074	1,13	0.01
Bandhan Bank	0.031	9.074	1,13	0.01

Source Author's Calculation

Table 2.3 F-value (CAR)

MFIs	F-value calculated	F-value critical	Degrees of freedom	Probability
BancoSol	61.507	8.861	1,14	0.01
Grameen Bank	11.207	9.074	1,13	0.01
Bandhan Bank	35.639	9.074	1,13	0.01

Source Author's Calculation

(CAR) helps to determine that whether the MFIs have enough capital to support its total assets. Study reveals that due to global meltdown in 2008, the quality and volume of capital of MFIs have deteriorated initially and thereby put a challenge to the MFI industry in the long run. The ANOVA result based on the secondary data on CAR has summarized in Table 2.3. Again, here the hypotheses are—

H$_0$: There is no significant difference of mean of CAR between pre and post recession for MFIs

H$_1$: There is a significant difference of mean of CAR between these two phases.

Unlike ROA and PAR here the null hypothesis is rejected since calculated F-value is greater than the critical F-value at respective degrees of freedom. Thus, the alternative hypothesis is accepted here which indicates that there is a significant difference of capital to asset ratio of MFIs between pre and post recessionary phase. Though, the result shows a negative impression on the performance of MFIs after financial meltdown, but it somehow in line with our expectations. Literature and study throughout the world found that due to global meltdown and resulting liquidity crunch lead a decreased volume of asset and capital of the MFIs initially. It retards further opening of new loan accounts. Simultaneously, funds from different donor agencies and refinance schemes have stopped totally thereby a deterioration of capital-asset ratio of most of the MFIs. Our result (Table 2.3) proves the proposition successfully. However, study reveals that MFIs were managed in this gloomy environment over the time and performed as a potential business avenue to finance informal sector in the economy.

Though it is true that only F-test is not sufficient and robust statistical tool to establish a strong conclusion that microfinance institutions are recession free but definitely it provides a crude statistical indication about the trend and our findings clearly supports that microfinance institutions can manage the recessionary phase more efficiently than the formal financial sectors. Thus, from the overall analysis of this paper, we can strongly conclude that the impact of financial meltdown has less injury in case of MFIs as compared to other financial institutions. Sahoo and Mahapatra (2013) opined that since the clients of MFIs are usually local unbanked poor and mainly focus on their basic needs only their loan demand and use of such loan cannot be compared with formal financial institutions. These transactions have no integration with global banking and currency markets and therefore, less affected due to any global financial shocks. Some large MFIs in the emerging nations including India though faced some blow just after the global financial meltdown in 2008–2010 but survived very quickly within 2012 due to their less cohesion with the global market. Evidences from different parts of the world show that the currency turmoil, credit crunch, falling demand etc. were managed by MFIs in an alternative anecdotal way and survived in the market significantly. Since they dealt with large customers whose volume of loan was small and mainly channelized loan for either direct consumption or some productive purposes which is also in turn consumption oriented and therefore, the global recession does not affect the demand side of the system. Only problem came from supply side due to credit crunch from large formal institutions.

However, in this time most of the MFIs dependent on their own client savings and less on other formal sources. Due to such supply shock and fear of loan default, some large MFIs restrain themselves for further loan during this period which induced a negative impact on their balance sheet. Small MFIs who have hardly been able to manage other financial support and walked on their own client base have zero effect of such recession. Within very short time span all these were MFIs able to manage their business portfolio profitably, at least no serious harmful impact were not seen there. Rather, it was observed that for own sustainability large global financial institutions started to finance MFIs again aftermath of the crisis and considered these MFIs as the extended arms of their own business. They rightly assessed that microfinance institutions have a potential market base in the informal sector and evidently they have managed their own market prudentially even in the recessionary phase also.

Conclusion

The above analysis reveals that MFIs in developing and underdeveloped countries were less affected due to global economic crisis in 2008–2010. Though the study of CGAP in 2009 on 400 MFIs across the world revealed that the clients of these institutions have been affected severely due to food and financial crisis but our results assert that the crisis is less severe for MFIs as compared to other formal sector in developing and underdeveloped economies. It is because MFIs are usually dealing with those clients who have no toxic assets and derivatives as like large formal institutions and use 'peer pressure' as the proxy of so-called collateral in time of financial transactions. As a result, no significant distortion was found in the MFI market even when the globe was struggling with financial turmoil and speculative bubble. It was found that though MFIs faced a shortage of supply of funds due to global crisis from formal institutions, their demand for credit remains unchanged and investment portfolio within an inch same. The portfolio quality of microfinance was not distorted and reduced in the recessionary period due to the reason that most of the clients are from informal sector and global recession affected the informal sector less than the formal sector (Visconti, 2012). Historically it is true that when recession or such negative phenomenon in the market emerge overreaction and panic selling softening the financial market and a tremendous blow to the formal sector. Fortunately, MFIs mostly deal with informal sector and thereby less affected due to shock. Economists opined that microfinance cannot be recession proof, but definitely recession resistant due to their special kind of stakeholders—the informal sector who have limited or zero access to formal credit market due to inappropriate collateral.

The data analysis clearly suggests that as compared to other financial institutions MFIs were affected less due to global financial recession in 2008–2010 and proved their potential about shock resistance. Observing such achievement of MFIs World Bank opined that microfinance has a potential to tackle global recession at micro scale and should be supplemented in rural and semi urban areas as an alternative of formal financial institution with close monitoring. They also pointed out that though every financial institution including MFIs is elastic with business cycles but the impact of unprecedented economic turmoil in 2008–2010 was not very critical for MFIs. Most of the MFIs in the world were able to cope with the crisis and gradually proved themselves as a strong financial organization in the country. The inquietude of global financial market gives a robust chance to the MFIs for further growth and to prove the power to combat economic slowdown in rural and semi urban areas.

Though it is true that the governance of MFIs is very crucial for their active functioning and recession insulated activities in the present world, still it is true that MFIs are less affected during the global financial crisis. Operational transparency, fair practice, client's treatment, inclusiveness etc. are very crucial for MFIs governance and future sustainability. Recession sometimes brings deglobalization and protectionism which obviously harmful for developing and underdeveloped countries. In this juncture, MFIs can play a crucial role in the economy and better governance of MFIs will help to become self-sufficient and less dependence on external donor agencies which are extremely volatile and fragile.

References

Bandyopadhyay, T. (2016). *Bandhan: The making of a bank*. Random House. ISBN: 978-8-1840-0498-4

Brahmachary, A. (2019). *Impact of monetary policy on Indian economic growth and price stability in 21st century: An exploratory study*. Paper published in the book entitled by 'The impacts of monetary policy in the 21st century: Perspectives from emerging economies' (Das, R. S. Ed., 2019, pp. 351–360). Emerald Publishing. ISBN: 978-1-78973-320-4.

CGAP. (2010). *Andhra Pradesh 2010: Global implications of the crisis in Indian microfinance*.

Duflos, E., & Gaehwiler, B. (2008). *Impact and implications of the food crisis on microfinance*. https://www.cgap.org

Hossain, M. D. (2013). Social capital and microfinance: The case of Grameen Bank, Bangladesh. *Middle East Journal of Business, 8*(4). https://doi.org/10.5742/MEJB.2013.84311. https://www.researchgate.net/publication/271299707

Lal, R., & Lobb, A. (2016, February). *BancoSol and microfinance in Bolivia* (Harvard Business School Case 516-005). https://www.hbs.edu/faculty/pages/item.aspx?num=50707

Marconi, R., & Mosley, P. (2005). *Bolivia during the global crisis 1998–2004: Towards a 'macroeconomics of microfinance'* (Sheffield Economic Research Paper Series. SERP Number: 2005007).

MIX Market. (2020). *Mixmarket data set*. https://www.themixorg/mixmarket/dataset. Access on 22 February 2020.

Mustafa, F., Khursheed, A., & Fatima, M. (2018). Impact of global financial crunch on financially innovative microfinance institutions in South Asia.

Financial Innovation 4, *13* (open access). https://doi.org/10.1186/s40854-018-0099-8.

NABARD. (2018). *NABARD and microfinance.* National Bank for Agricultural and Rural Development.

Sahoo, S., & Mahapatra, D. (2013). Global economic Turmoil—Redefining Microfinance Institutions (MFIs). *Elk Asia Pacific Journal of Finance and Risk Management, 4*(2). ISSN: 0976-7185 (print).

Visconti, M. R. (2012). *Global recession and microfinance in developing countries: Threats and opportunities.* https://www.reserchgate.net/publication/228119606

World Bank Report. (2008). http://documetns.worldbank.org/

Yunus, M. (2003). Banker to the poor: Micro-lending and the battle against world poverty. *Public Affairs.* ISBN: 978-1-58648-198-8.

CHAPTER 3

Role of Microfinance as Counter-Recessionary Tool: A Macro-theoretic Analysis with Special Reference to Indian Economy

Mainak Bhattacharjee, Debashis Mazumdar, Sanghita Ghosh, and Dipti Ghosh

Introduction

The fundamental idea behind the role of microfinance in containing recession in developing countries lies in the recognition of the importance

---

M. Bhattacharjee (✉)
Department of Economics, Loreto College, Kolkata, India
e-mail: mainkbh4@gmail.com

D. Mazumdar
The Heritage College, Kolkata, India
e-mail: debashis.mazumdar@thc.edu.in

S. Ghosh · D. Ghosh
Jadavpur University, Kolkata, India

© The Author(s), under exclusive license to Springer Nature Singapore Pte Ltd. 2022
R. C. Das (ed.), *Microfinance to Combat Global Recession and Social Exclusion*, https://doi.org/10.1007/978-981-16-4329-3_3

of micro-medium-small sector (comprising small business) in employment generation and thereof, injection of demand into the system at the time when demand is at crisis. In this connection, it is beyond any dispute that this petty sector is characterized by the borrowers at large with low net worth, which is why the commercial banking institutions are perhaps apathetic in extension of credit. Now a plausible implication of this lending apathy is that the borrowers in this small sector are subject to credit rationing which is the case when the demand of credit exceeds its supply led by the lenders' non-willingness to extend credit. One clear ramification of the above dispensation is that at the time of economic downturn triggered by the lack effective demand in the system, this particular case of credit rationing would cause to aggravate the privation of demand, thereof amplifying the recession both in scale and spell, in as much such a credit constraint acts to suppress the demand. This is what essentially buttresses the argument underlying the role of microfinance in taming economic downturn and reining in the recession. In India, micro-small-medium sector assumes a predominate space in overall economic activities and livelihood generation in terms of employment, in what is corroborated by the findings of 73rd survey of National Sample Survey (NSS) indicating an employment share of 11 crore in 2015–2016 and the estimate of annual report on MSME (Annual Report, Ministry of MSME, 2018–2019), indicating a nominal GDP share of 30% in 2016–2017 and much larger share of 45% in aggregate manufacturing output during the same period (Report of Expert Committee Micro Small and Medium Enterprises, June 2019). Nevertheless, such a significant presence of this particular gamut is paradoxically overshadowed by a poignantly bleak outlook in what can be elicited from the case of the expanse of this particular sector being predominantly confined to the small entities at large, with the 97% of total employment in MSME comes from micro firms in 2017–2018. Now this scenario of preponderance of micro entities has implication on the structural bottlenecks in the vertical development of this sector, which is that the micro firms have not able to development into small and medium entities and this is in turn explains why the firms in MSME sector at large are deprived of economies of scale, technological economies and innovation. To this end, the inhibiting factors are primarily at work are, namely, absence of formalization, infrastructural lacuna, lack of branding, inadequate access to formal credit and risk and delayed payments. The problem of insufficient credit flow mainly emanates from the lack of formalization, whereby traditional banking system finds it difficult to assess the creditworthiness of MSME firm at large due to lack of information on financial performance of their businesses and high operating cost owing to the absence of collateral. Besides, small scale of operations poses a stringent constraint for the firms at large in accessing risk capital.

It in this backdrop, the theoretical model forthcoming, developed in line with the standard Keynesian paradigm along with necessary alliterations of the notion of 'financial accelerator' (Bernanke et al., 1994), seeks to elucidate how this credit-constraint along with snags in raising risk capital facing MSMEs at large can potentially militate against macroeconomic stability by acting destabilizing force at the time of some economic downturn, in the light of the Keynesian paradigm with reference to the inter-linkage between real sector (consisting of goods market) and financial sector (consisting of formal banking system).

Review of Literature

Micro Finance Institutions are considered as an important instrument to alleviate poverty. There is a whole spectrum of researches that relates microfinance to poverty alleviation. Among those, some studies by Khandker (2003), Khanam et al. (2018), and Mecha (2017) reveal that the micro-loans have a positive impact on the poverty alleviation. Banerjee and Jackson (2016) in their article found microfinance led to increasing levels of indebtedness among already impoverished communities and exacerbated economic, social and environmental vulnerabilities.

Berthelemy and Varoudakis (1996) in their study have shown that growth and financial development occur in a two-way manner. The real sector growth expands financial markets which in turn, with the development of the banking sector and its increased net yield on savings, raise capital accumulation and thus growth. Their theoretical model exhibits multiple stable equilibria the existence of which has been therefore tested econometrically.

Visconti (2011) in his paper acknowledges that Microfinance institutions (MFIs) in developing countries that are not fully integrated with international markets are likely to be less affected by the worldwide turmoil, due to their segmentation and resilience to external shocks. Similar result is also documented by the researchers Loncar et al. (2009). They find that compared to Eastern Europe the MFIs in India, Northern Africa and Latin America have largely protected overall from the global financial crisis. On the other hand, Visconti (2012) reports that MFIs cannot be considered immune from these economic problems caused by such economic events and although they can provide, to some extent, a social safety net, they are sooner or later expected to suffer from the general unrest, given the nature of events, if most of its customers are simultaneously affected, the MFIs might themselves be in need of assistance to withstand even this crisis. The study by Visconti (2011) has also showcased the impact of different types of microfinance risks on the MFI and its stakeholders during the recession period, with an allusion to how the intrinsic characteristics of microfinance, such as closeness to the borrowers, limited risk and exposure and little if any correlation with international markets has an anti-cyclical effect.

Rodriguez (2002) finds that in Bolivia institutions serving primarily or exclusively low-income women showed a higher level of sustainability in times of crisis. Women, who are large percentage of microfinance clients, tend to have above average debt service reliability. Therefore, such evidence suggests that MFIs which continue to focus on the poor and keep strong ties with their customers may be able to maintain their resistance to the current global financial crisis.

A study by Bella (2011) reports that MFIs in Central America and the Caribbean (including Mexico), Eastern Europe, and the Middle East and Central Asia appear most sensitive to changes in the domestic and international economic environment, while from an institutional perspective, banks and nonbank financial institutions show the closest links.

In a study conducted by Patten et al. (2001) recognized The Bank Rakyat Indonesia (BRI) unit system as one of the largest and most successful microfinance institutions in the world. According to this study, microfinance appears to have played a notably counter-cyclical role in Indonesia that has been more drastically affected by the East Asian monetary crisis in the late 1990s. Therefore, it suggests essential features in the future design of sustainable microfinance institutions, products and delivery systems.

In contrary to Patten, Marconi and Mosley (2006) show that macroeconomic role of microfinance appears to have varied enormously between country cases. Specifically, the study has figured out that the Micro Finance Institutes (MFIs) to intensify rather than restrain the crisis in Bolivia. The explanation for this lies in the behaviour of government towards microfinance and in the structure of demand along with the institutional design.

Nowadays it is observed that international commercial banks and donors have become more interested to finance in MFIs that are offering innovative services to their customers. The first example of MFI with commercial capitalization is Profound, an investment fund that raised 23 million dollars to finance MFIs operating in Latin America (CGAP, 2007). Silva and Chavez (2015) said that microfinance is not only focused to provide loans but it is also dedicated to update its services in terms of latest technology.

Researchers like Ahlin and Lin (2006) analyzing 112 MFIs selected from 48 countries indicated that macroeconomic shocks are major factors to affect MFI operations and these questions the potential of investment in MFIs during period of crunch and also highlighted that MFI key performance indicators also play a significant part in MFI success. A study by Krauss and Walter (2009) assessed correlation of MFIs with domestic and international market performance indicators revealed that MFIs are not vulnerable to domestic and international market shocks.

Galema et al. (2011), using mean variance spanning tests found that investors can avoid risk of investment by investing in a MFI offering financially innovative services with well dispersed credit portfolio.

Mazumdar et al. (2018) analyze the performance of such SHGs in some of the economically backward districts of West Bengal based on primary data collected from some sample drought-prone and non-drought-prone blocks of Paschim Medinipur and Bankura districts of West Bengal. An intra-regional difference in performance of sampled SHGs in terms of per-capita deposit, per-capita credit, credit-deposit ratio and repayment-credit ratio has been observed in SHGs functioning in drought-prone and non-drought-prone blocks within the backward districts. Further, the Probit model estimates suggest that the SHG can climb easily upon the performance ladder with younger and educated members, greater percentage of members above the poverty level, better utilization of credit received. Studies like Gilberto M. Llanto and Ryu Fukui (2003); Mustafa et al. (2018) reported that the noticeable progress of MFIs towards commercialization is enhanced with the adoption of more technologically advanced innovative services.

The Model

The model comes in Keynesian lines with closed economy setting and having two sector structure involving goods market and credit market (with commercial banks as the financial intermediary. In the goods market, we have aggregate demand for consumption goods from private determined by disposable income, aggregate investment demand comprising of investment by large firms representing the quality borrower (I_q) and that made by MSME firms representing the non-quality borrowers (I_{nq}) and government expenditure with subject to fiscal restraint. Moreover, it is necessary to clarify that the aggregate investment is financed by the credit lent by commercial banks and hence depends on the interest rate. Thus, the aggregate output (Y) at a given point of time is determined by planned aggregate demand corresponding to given level interest rate on credit (i). Now coming to the financial sector, consisting of credit/loan market geared at financing investments made by quality and non-quality borrowers, where the supply of credit essentiality owes to the saving held in form bank deposit sensitive to interest rate. Now on the demand side, the non-quality borrowers are rationed in the sense that at every point a given fraction of planned supply of new credit (L_S) is made available to MSME and is significantly depends on by the stock non-performing assets in the overall banking system. Thus, at every given point of time the interest rate in the credit market adjusts to the level where the planned supply of new loans net of the credit rationed to non-quality borrowers is matched the planned investment demand of quality borrowers forthcoming.

Real Sector:

The real sector manifestation of the determination of aggregate output from the goods market equilibrium condition given as:

$$Y = \overline{C} + c(Y - \theta Y) + I_{nq}(i) + \beta L_S + G, \quad 0 < c < 1 \qquad (3.1)$$

Now given that the amount of deficit that government can keep is regulated to a certain fraction (α) of aggregate output, we have, $G = (\alpha + \theta)Y$. Thus, overall goods market equilibrium reduces to:

$$Y = \overline{C} + c(Y - \theta Y) + I_{nq}(i) + \beta L_s + (\alpha + \theta)Y \qquad (3.2)$$

Financial Sector:

The financial sector is built on banking system which functions as intermediary between the net savers and net borrower through conversion savings to investments. Now as stated earlier, the aggregate savings are held only in bank deposits. Now banks are faced with the choice between credits extended to the private sector and excess reserves in keep their assets, whereas their liabilities are given as the stock outstanding deposits. Moreover, banks are to keep as fraction of total deposits as required reserves with central bank. Hence the balance sheet identity of entire banking sectors stands out to be:

$$\text{Asset} \equiv \text{CR(stock of outstanding credit)} + \text{ER(Excess Reserve)}$$
$$- \text{RR(Requires Reserve)} \equiv \text{Liability}$$
$$\equiv \text{D(Deposits)}, \text{ where } \text{RR} \equiv \sigma D, \text{ such that } 0 < \sigma < 1.$$

Now change in stock of deposits at a point time is given the magnitude of aggregate savings, therefore we have:

$$dD = (1-c)(1-\theta)Y \qquad (3.3)$$

Now, introducing the portfolio factor (say $\lambda \in (0, 1)$) in this context indicating the portfolio choice over credit and excess reserves the supply of new loan loans can be expressed as:

$$L_s = \lambda(i, r) \, dD = \lambda(i, r)(1-\sigma)(1-c)(1-\theta)Y,$$
$$\text{where } \frac{\partial \lambda}{\partial i} > 0, \frac{\partial \lambda}{\partial r} < 0 \qquad (3.4)$$

Here, it is emergent the proportion of total asset that banks keep in form of loans to the commercial sectors (non-financial in nature) varies directly with market interest rate while inversely with policy rate so since increase in market rate for given r enhances the scope for arbitrage gain to the banks while an increase in r for given i reduces the same.

Thus, we get the planned supply of new loans being extended to small business under credit rationing as, βL_s, where $\beta L_s \leq I_{nq}$ and thereof, its counterpart, $(1-\beta)L_s$, becomes the planned supply of new loans to the quality borrowers, which interacts with the respective investment demand (I_q) to determine the interest rate on credit. Now the primordial element herein is the interest treatment of non-quality borrowers, which is that the interest rate charged to them is pegged at premium above the risk-free one charged to the quality borrowers. Hence, we have the credit market equilibrium as given by:

$$(1-\beta)\lambda(i,r)(1-\sigma)(1-c)(1-\theta)Y = I_q(i) \qquad (3.5)$$

Moreover, in the light of the above dispensation, the goods market equilibrium reduces to:

$$Y = C(Y - \theta Y) + I_{nq}(i) + \beta\lambda(i,r)(1-\sigma)(1-c)(1-\theta)Y + (\alpha+\theta)Y \qquad (3.2')$$

Hence, it is possible to solve Eq. (3.5) and Eq. (3.2') for equilibrium Y and i as illustrated in Fig. 3.1. This can be proceeded with finding—(a) the adjustment in Y in response to change in interest rate to keep the goods market in equilibrium (as depicted by AA schedule) and (b) change in interest rate in response to Y to keep the credit market in equilibrium (as depicted by LL schedule). This in turn can be followed from Eq. (3.6) and Eq. (3.7), indicating the change in 'i' due to the unitary change in Y derived from each of Eq. (3.5) and Eq. (3.2').

$$\frac{di}{dY} = \frac{1 - [c(1-\theta) + \beta\lambda(1-\sigma)(1-c)(1-\theta) + (\alpha+\theta)]}{I'_q + \beta\lambda_i(1-\sigma)(1-c)(1-\theta)Y} < 0 \qquad (3.6)$$

$$\frac{di}{dY} = \frac{(1-\beta)\lambda(1-\sigma)(1-c)(1-\theta)}{I'_q - (1-\beta)\lambda_i(1-\sigma)(1-c)(1-\theta)Y} < 0 \qquad (3.7)$$

Let us now explain the intuitive underpinning of these results. To begin with (Eq. 3.6), we find that following a unitary increase in interest rate, ceteris paribus, the planned investment dips by $(-I'_q)$ units whereas, the supply of new loans will rise by $\lambda_i(1-\sigma)(1-c)(1-\theta)Y_0$ units and consequently the investment made by the non-quality borrowers will rise by $\beta\lambda_i(1-\sigma)(1-c)(1-\theta)Y_0$ units. Thus, the net impact of unitary interest rate on total planned investment becomes $(-I'_q) - \beta\lambda_i(1-\sigma)(1-c)(1-\theta)Y_0$ units which indicates a net fall in planned investment on having quality borrower being more interest sensitive than their non-quality counterparts in as much the latter is subject to credit rationing. Thus consequently, upon a ceteris paribus unitary rise in interest rate, planned aggregate demand will contract and hence, Y is required to fall to clear off the goods market. Now due to the

3 ROLE OF MICROFINANCE AS COUNTER-RECESSIONARY TOOL ...   37

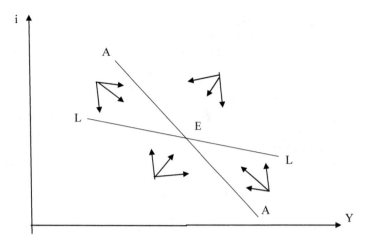

Fig. 3.1 Equilibrium analysis (*Source* Drawn by the authors)

unitary fall in Y, excess supply in goods market coming though the contraction of aggregate demand led by rise in interest rate will fall 1 unit. However, subsequent to the fall in Y by a unit, aggregate consumption demand will drop by $c(1-\theta)$ unit, government expenditure by $(\alpha+\theta)$ unit and planned investment demand by non-quality borrowers by $\beta\lambda(1-\sigma)(1-c)(1-\theta)$ due to fall in aggregate savings effective from the contraction of Y. Thus, in response to rise in i, Y has to fall by $\left[\frac{\{-I'_q\}+\beta\lambda_i(1-\sigma)(1-c)(1-\theta)Y}{1-[c(1-\theta)+\beta\lambda(1-\sigma)(1-c)(1-\theta)+(\alpha+\theta)]}\right]$ units or changes by $\left[\frac{I'_q+\beta\lambda_i(1-\sigma)(1-c)(1-\theta)Y}{1-[c(1-\theta)+\beta\lambda(1-\sigma)(1-c)(1-\theta)+(\alpha+\theta)]}\right](<0)$ to keep the goods market cleared. Now coming to the credit market, where there happens a ceteris paribus rise in Y by 1 unit. As a result, planned supply of new loans towards quality borrowers gets to rise by $(1-\beta)\lambda(1-\sigma)(1-c)(1-\theta)$ unit, thereby yielding excess supply in the credit market. Thus, interest is required to fall to equilibrate the credit market where for every unitary fall, the demand for credit by quality borrowers rises by $(-I'_q)$ units while the due to portfolio reallocation the planned supply of credit to quality borrowers, contracts by $(1-\beta)\lambda_i(1-\sigma)(1-c)(1-\theta)Y$ units. Hence the excess supply in credit market declines by $\{(-I'_q)+(1-\beta)\lambda_i(1-\sigma)(1-c)(1-\theta)Y\}$ units or net change in excess supply by $\{(I'_q) - (1-\beta)\lambda_i(1-\sigma)(1-c)(1-\theta)Y\}$ units which is negative. Thus, following unitary rise in Y, ceteris paribus, interest rate is required to fall so as to reinstate the credit market to equilibrium, by $\left[\frac{(1-\beta)\lambda(1-\sigma)(1-c)(1-\theta)}{-\{I'_q-(1-\beta)\lambda_i(1-\sigma)(1-c)(1-\theta)Y\}}\right]$ units or that the interest rate changes by $\left[\frac{(1-\beta)\lambda(1-\sigma)(1-c)(1-\theta)}{-\{I'_q-(1-\beta)\lambda_i(1-\sigma)(1-c)(1-\theta)Y\}}\right](<0)$. Moreover, to ensure the stability of the overall equilibrium it is necessary and sufficient to have the AA schedule to be steeper than LL schedule as what is emergent in Fig. 3.1.

Let us now overhaul the stability of equilibrium at E with reference to Fig. 3.1. To begin with, it is to be noted that any point to the right of AA indicates an excess in goods market while at point to the left goods market exhibits excess demand. The reason being that at a point to the right, the level of Y prevailing at that point is higher than what the level should be corresponding to the given interest to keep the goods market at equilibrium and likewise at a point the left, the level of Y is smaller than required to clear the goods market. Hence, from a point to the right of AA, Y tends to fall while it tends to rise from a point to the left. Now coming to LL schedule, any point to above it implies that for the given level of Y, interest rate is higher than what it is required to maintain equilibrium. Since a higher interest rate relative to the equilibrium level leads to the lower investment demand by quality borrowers, but a greater portfolio preference towards loans, at a point above LL, credit market experiences excess supply and therefore, interest rate will fall. On the other hand, at a point below LL, lower than equilibrium interest rate would yield higher investment demand by quality borrowers but a lower supply of credit, resulting in excess demand and consequently the interest will have a tendency to rise. Thus, as illustrated in the above diagram, no matter from whichever zone the system starts off with a disequilibrium, it will eventually make its way to the equilibrium at the point E, which therefore can be said to be stable in nature.

CREDIT RATIONING AND RECESSION

In this section, it has been pondered how a recession can emerge out of a sudden spike in non-performing asset in the banking system following the race of loan default among firm so much as it happens in case there is failure of the firm in fetching sale targets due to adverse in demand condition. To this end it remains to be seen how an exogenous rise in non-performing asset at beginning of a time period (however small) leads to cumulative contraction in aggregate output in form negative multiplier pushing the economy to recession. Herein, the exposition of the consequence of some adverse demand shock in contraction of credit flow to non-quality borrower due to flight in quality that happens in the wake on the spike in bad loan in the banking sector and thereby in the contraction of aggregate output has been based on making β being decreasing function of non-performing asset (N), as: $\beta = \beta(N)$, $\beta' < 0$.

The impacts of the sudden spike in N at the given point of time on equilibrium Y and I can be followed from the comparative static result on Y with respect to N, as what follow:

$$\frac{dY}{dN} = \frac{\beta' \lambda_i \{(1-\sigma)(1-c)(1-\theta)Y\} L_s}{D} < 0 \qquad (3.8)$$

where
where, $D = [1 - [c(1-\theta) + \beta\lambda(1-\sigma)(1-c)(1-\theta) + (\alpha+\theta)]] \cdot$
$[-\{I'_q - (1-\beta)\lambda_i(1-\sigma)(1-c)(1-\theta)Y\}]$
$- \begin{bmatrix} \{(1-\beta)\lambda(1-\sigma)(1-c)(1-\theta)\} \\ \{I'_q + \beta\lambda_i(1-\sigma)(1-c)(1-\theta)Y\} \end{bmatrix} > 0$,

since the AA is steeper than LL so as to ensure a stable equilibrium (a stable node).

Let us now explain the negative multiplier effect of an exogenous rise in bad loans in the banking system triggered by deterioration in demand condition leading to loan defaults by firms. Thus, consequent upon spike in NPA by dN units, ceteris paribus, the credit flow to the non-quality borrowers or MSME entities drops by $(-\beta' dN)$ units and so does the investment by non-quality borrowers by the same. This is what constitutes the flight to quality at the onset of this development leading to the supply of credit to quality borrowers by $[-\beta'\lambda\{(1-\sigma)(1-c)(1-\theta)\}Y]dN$ units and thereby, an excess in the credit market with respect to the demand for credit by quality borrowers comes up causing interest rate to fall. Now for unitary fall in interest rate, the demand for excess supply declines by $(-I'_q) + (1-\beta)\lambda_i(1-\sigma)(1-c)(1-\theta)Y$. Thus, interest rate falls by $\left[\frac{-\beta'\lambda\{(1-\sigma)(1-c)(1-\theta)Y\}dN}{(-I'_q)+(1-\beta)\lambda_i(1-\sigma)(1-c)(1-\theta)Y}\right]$ units to clear off the credit market. This in turn translates to rise in investment by $\left[(-I'_q)\left\{\frac{-\beta'\lambda\{(1-\sigma)(1-c)(1-\theta)Y\}dN}{(-I'_q)+(1-\beta)\lambda_i(1-\sigma)(1-c)(1-\theta)Y}\right\}\right]$ units and fall in investment by non-quality borrowers

$$\left[\{\beta\lambda_i(1-\sigma)(1-c)(1-\theta)Y\}\left\{\frac{-\beta'\lambda\{(1-\sigma)(1-c)(1-\theta)Y\}dN}{(-I'_q)+(1-\beta)\lambda_i(1-\sigma)(1-c)(1-\theta)Y}\right\}\right] \quad \text{units.}$$

Therefore, the ultimate change in aggregate demand in the aftermath of the exogenous rise in NPA by dN units becomes,

$$dAD = -[-\beta'\lambda\{(1-\sigma)(1-c)(1-\theta)Y\}]dN$$

$$+ \left[(-I'_q)\left\{\frac{-\beta'\lambda\{(1-\sigma)(1-c)(1-\theta)Y\}dN}{(-I'_q)+(1-\beta)\lambda_i(1-\sigma)(1-c)(1-\theta)Y}\right\}\right]$$

$$+ (-)\left[\begin{array}{c}\{\beta\lambda_i(1-\sigma)(1-c)(1-\theta)Y\} \\ \left\{\frac{-\beta'\lambda\{(1-\sigma)(1-c)(1-\theta)Y\}dN}{(-I'_q)+(1-\beta)\lambda_i(1-\sigma)(1-c)(1-\theta)Y}\right\}\end{array}\right].$$

$$dAD = \left[\frac{\{-\lambda_i(1-\sigma)(1-c)(1-\theta)Y\}\{\beta'\lambda(1-\sigma)(1-c)(1-\theta)Y\}dN}{I'_q - (1-\beta)\lambda_i(1-\sigma)(1-c)(1-\theta)Y}\right] < 0$$

(3.8′)

Hence, the aggregate demand sets for contraction following a exogenous spike in NPA, leading aggregate output to fall and thereof, an excess supply in goods market to emerge. Now for every unitary fall in Y, the excess supply drops by one unit. But the consumption expenditure and also the government expenditure plummet due to the fall in Y to cause the aggregate demand to decline by $[c(1-\theta)Y+(\alpha+\theta)]$ units. On other side there happens decline in aggregate savings and thereof the supply of deposits to the banking system leading to fall in the supply of credit. Now this straightway feeds through a drop in investment by non-quality borrowers by $[\beta\lambda(1-\sigma)(1-c)(1-\theta)]$. However, the cut in credit flow in turn creates an excess demand for credit of $[(1-\beta)\lambda(1-\sigma)(1-c)(1-\theta)]$ units vis-a-vis the quality borrowers, given the level of the respective investment and therefore, interest rate gets to shoot in the aftermath by $\left\{\frac{(1-\beta)\lambda(1-\sigma)(1-c)(1-\theta)}{(-I'_q)+(1-\beta)\lambda_i(1-\sigma)(1-c)(1-\theta)Y}\right\}$ units, leading to the fall in investment by quality borrowers by $(-I'_q)\left\{\frac{(1-\beta)\lambda(1-\sigma)(1-c)(1-\theta)}{(-I'_q)+(1-\beta)\lambda_i(1-\sigma)(1-c)(1-\theta)Y}\right\}$ units, but the rise in investment by non-quality borrowers, as the counterpart of the former, by $\left[\{\beta\lambda_i(1-\sigma)(1-c)(1-\theta)Y\}\left\{\frac{(1-\beta)\lambda(1-\sigma)(1-c)(1-\theta)}{(-I'_q)+(1-\beta)\lambda_i(1-\sigma)(1-c)(1-\theta)Y}\right\}\right]$ units. Therefore, we have the net fall in excess supply by:

$$\left[1-\left[\begin{array}{c}\left[\{c(1-\theta)Y+(\alpha+\theta)+\beta\lambda(1-\sigma)(1-c)(1-\theta)\}+(-I'_q)\right]\\ \left\{\dfrac{(1-\beta)\lambda(1-\sigma)(1-c)(1-\theta)}{(-I'_q)+(1-\beta)\lambda_i(1-\sigma)(1-c)(1-\theta)Y}\right\}\\ +\{\beta\lambda_i(1-\sigma)(1-c)(1-\theta)\}\\ \left\{\dfrac{(1-\beta)\lambda(1-\sigma)(1-c)(1-\theta)}{(-I'_q)+(1-\beta)\lambda_i(1-\sigma)(1-c)(1-\theta)Y}\right\}\end{array}\right]\right]$$

units, which has to be positive in order that goods market rebounds to equilibrium. Hence, the level of contraction in aggregate output that comes after the spike in NPA by dN units is:

$$dY = \dfrac{\left[\dfrac{\{-\lambda_i(1-\sigma)(1-c)(1-\theta)Y\}\{\beta'\lambda(1-\sigma)(1-c)(1-\theta)Y\}}{I'_q-(1-\beta)\lambda_i(1-\sigma)(1-c)(1-\theta)Y}\right]dN}{\left[1-\left[\begin{array}{c}\left[\{c(1-\theta)Y+(\alpha+\theta)+\beta\lambda(1-\sigma)(1-c)(1-\theta)\}\right.\\ +\{I'_q+\beta\lambda_i(1-\sigma)(1-c)(1-\theta)Y\}\\ \left\{\dfrac{(1-\beta)\lambda(1-\sigma)(1-c)(1-\theta)}{I'_q-(1-\beta)\lambda_i(1-\sigma)(1-c)(1-\theta)Y}\right\}\end{array}\right]\right]} < 0$$

(3.9)

It is worth noting at this juncture, in reference with (Eq. 3.9), an adverse demand shock would produce larger contraction of aggregate output under credit rationing in as much as it works to subdue the investments made by non-quality or small entities (MSME) to tune of.

Now from (Eq. 3.9), the impact of rise in NPA on interest rate can be elucidated as what follows:

$$di = \dfrac{(1-\beta)\lambda(1-\sigma)(1-c)(1-\theta)dY - \beta'\lambda(1-\sigma)(1-c)(1-\theta)YdN}{\{I'_q-(1-\beta)\lambda_i(1-\sigma)(1-c)(1-\theta)Y\}}$$

(3.10)

Now since dY is negative as for dN being positive, as in (Eq. 3.9), and the second term in (Eq. 3.10) negative for positive dN, di will be positive or zero or negative according as, $[(1-\beta)\lambda(1-\sigma)(1-c)(1-\theta)dY]$ is smaller or equal or greater than $[-\beta'\lambda(1-\sigma)(1-c)(1-\theta)YdN]$. This is what has been depicted in Fig. 3.2.

The revelation that comes up from Fig. 3.2 indicates in wake of a spike in NPA, the AA schedule shifts downward to reflect

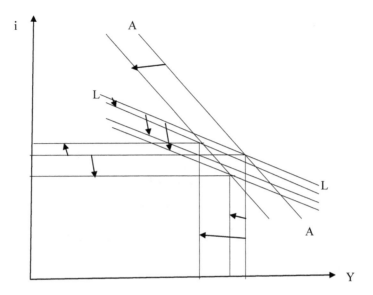

Fig. 3.2 Equilibrium analysis with parametric shifts (*Source* Drawn by the authors)

the fall in aggregate demand at given interest rate to the tune of $[-\beta'\lambda\{(1-\sigma)(1-c)(1-\theta)Y\}]dN$ units coming through the fall in investment by non-quality borrower under credit rationing due to the flight to quality by lenders. This in turn gives cue to the rise in planned supply of credit to the quality borrowers leading to excess supply to be cleared through fall in interest rate at given y. Hence, there happens a downward shift in LL schedule demonstrating the fall in interest rate by $\left[\frac{\beta'\lambda(1-\sigma)(1-c)(1-\theta)YdN}{I'_q-(1-\beta)\lambda_i(1-\sigma)(1-c)(1-\theta)Y}\right]$ units at given Y or equivalently, fall in Y by $\left[\frac{\beta'\lambda(1-\sigma)(1-c)(1-\theta)YdN}{(1-\beta)\lambda\{(1-\sigma)(1-c)(1-\theta)\}}\right]$ units at unchanged interest rate. Thus, the resultant changes in equilibrium Y and i follow from the magnitude of the downshift shift in AA schedule relative to that in LL. Hence, we have the following proposition.

Proposition: *An adverse demand shock leading to default on loan repayment by firms would manifest in contraction of aggregate output and consequently recession to be compounded by the presence of credit rationing of non-quality borrowers representing the small and micro business sector, while* *having its impact on interest rate being ambiguous and contingent upon the interest elasticity of investment demand by quality borrowers and interest elasticity of credit supply respective to the quality borrowers. However, the increase in interest rate as a consequence of demand crunch would lead to more poignant fall in aggregate output producing deeper recession.*

ADJUSTMENT PROCESS AND CUMULATIVE CONTRACTION OF AGGREGATE OUTPUT

Here in this section, it is being examined how the contraction of aggregate output in the aftermath of negative demand shock leading to an exogenous rise in NPA in the banking sector would take shape through a cumulative process. Following exogenous rise in NPA by dN units in period 1 will cause the aggregate demand to fall further owing to the investment by non-quality borrowers being comprising due to quality flight in credit extension by $[-\beta'\lambda\{(1-\sigma)(1-c)(1-\theta)Y\}]dN$, ceteris paribus. However, after taking into account the adjustment in interest rate in response to the demand–supply mismatch in quality credit, and in turn, its repercussion on gross investment, the aggregate demand is seen to decline by $\left[\frac{\{-\lambda_i(1-\sigma)(1-c)(1-\theta)Y\}\{\beta'\lambda(1-\sigma)(1-c)(1-\theta)Y\}dN}{I'_q-(1-\beta)\lambda_i(1-\sigma)(1-c)(1-\theta)Y}\right]$. Thus in period 1, the aggregate output will contract by:

$$dY_1 = \left[\frac{\{-\lambda_i(1-\sigma)(1-c)(1-\theta)Y\}\{\beta'\lambda(1-\sigma)(1-c)(1-\theta)Y\}dN}{I'_q-(1-\beta)\lambda_i(1-\sigma)(1-c)(1-\theta)Y}\right]$$

In the next period, on the back of falling private consumption and saving and government spending, aggregate demand will contract by $[c(1-\theta)Y+(\alpha+\theta)+\beta\lambda\{(1-\sigma)(1-c)(1-\theta)\}]dY_1$ units. However, owing to the rise interest rate in the wake of shortage of credit supply relative to its demand by quality borrowers, this negative adjustment in aggregate demand would be partly compounded by fall in investment by quality borrowers by $(I'_q)\left[\frac{(1-\beta)\lambda\{(1-\sigma)(1-c)(1-\theta)\}}{I'_q-(1-\beta)\lambda_i(1-\sigma)(1-c)(1-\theta)Y}\right]dY_1$ net of the rise in investment in non-quality borrowers by, $-\{\beta\lambda_i(1-\sigma)(1-c)(1-\theta)\}\left[\frac{(1-\beta)\lambda\{(1-\sigma)(1-c)(1-\theta)\}}{I'_q-(1-\beta)\lambda_i(1-\sigma)(1-c)(1-\theta)Y}\right]dY_1$.

Thus, in period 2, aggregate output dips by

$$dY_2 = c(1-\theta)Y + (\alpha+\theta) + \beta\lambda\{(1-\sigma)(1-c)(1-\theta)\}$$
$$+ (I'_q)\left[\frac{(1-\beta)\lambda\{(1-\sigma)(1-c)(1-\theta)\}}{\{I'_q - (1-\beta)\lambda_i(1-\sigma)(1-c)(1-\theta)Y\}}\right]$$
$$- \left[\begin{array}{c}-\{\beta\lambda_i(1-\sigma)(1-c)(1-\theta)\}\\ \left[\dfrac{(1-\beta)\lambda\{(1-\sigma)(1-c)(1-\theta)\}}{I'_q - (1-\beta)\lambda_i(1-\sigma)(1-c)(1-\theta)Y}\right]\end{array}\right]$$
$$= \left[\begin{array}{c}c(1-\theta)Y + (\alpha+\theta) + \beta\lambda\{(1-\sigma)(1-c)(1-\theta)\}+\\ (I'_q + \beta\lambda_i(1-\sigma)(1-c)(1-\theta))\\ \left[\dfrac{(1-\beta)\lambda\{(1-\sigma)(1-c)(1-\theta)\}}{I'_q - (1-\beta)\lambda_i(1-\sigma)(1-c)(1-\theta)Y}\right]\end{array}\right] dY_1$$

Similarly, on having to do with further adjustment in aggregate demand upon the fall in Y as indicated above, at the end of period 3, the aggregate output will decline by

$$dY_3 = \left[\begin{array}{c}c(1-\theta)Y + (\alpha+\theta) + \beta\lambda\{(1-\sigma)(1-c)(1-\theta)\}+\\ (I'_q + \beta\lambda_i(1-\sigma)(1-c)(1-\theta))\\ \left[\dfrac{(1-\beta)\lambda\{(1-\sigma)(1-c)(1-\theta)\}}{I'_q - (1-\beta)\lambda_i(1-\sigma)(1-c)(1-\theta)Y}\right]\end{array}\right] dY_2$$

$$= \left[\begin{array}{c}c(1-\theta)Y + (\alpha+\theta) + \beta\lambda\{(1-\sigma)(1-c)(1-\theta)\}\\ +(I'_q + \beta\lambda_i(1-\sigma)(1-c)(1-\theta))\\ \left[\dfrac{(1-\beta)\lambda\{(1-\sigma)(1-c)(1-\theta)\}}{\{I'_q - (1-\beta)\lambda_i(1-\sigma)(1-c)(1-\theta)Y\}}\right]\end{array}\right]^2 dY_2$$

so on.

This adjustment process goes on until there is convergence to yield the overall multiplier effect on Y as in (Eq. 3.9).

OUTPUT DYNAMICS DURING ECONOMIC DOWNTURN AND ITS STABILITY IMPLICATIONS

In this segment, we shall address the dynamic implication of the cumulative adjustment in aggregate output stemming from spike in NPA spurred by adverse demand shock to the firms. To this end, we shall adopt linear formulation of the model described earlier, as:

$$N_t = \emptyset(\overline{Y} - Y_{t-1}) + \mu_t, \quad \emptyset' > 0 \tag{3.11}$$

where, μ_t resembles random spike in NPA led by sudden downturn demand in condition

$$\beta_t = \gamma(N_t), \quad \gamma' < 0 \tag{3.12}$$

Rephrasing (Eq. 3.5) and (Eq. 3.2') having incorporated the (Eq. 3.11), (Eq. 3.12), we can have:

$$Y_t = F(Y_{t-1}, \mu_t), \frac{\partial F}{\partial Y_{t-1}} > 0, \frac{\partial F}{\partial \mu_t} > 0 \tag{3.13}$$

The logic underlying each partial derivative associated with (Eq. 3.13) being positive being that, an increase in Y_{t-1} ceteris paribus, lowers the stock of NPA coming up at the beginning of period t and thereof causes increase proportion of credit flowing to MSME, leading rise in investment by non-quality borrowers. This in turn results in the increase in aggregate demand in period t triggering off a rise in Y in the same period as what evident by from multiplier effect on Y discussed earlier. On the other hand, a positive demand shock in period t, denoted by $d\mu_t > 0$, ceteris paribus leads Y_t to shoot, whereas, a negative demand shock ($d\mu_t < 0$) does the reverse. Hence, we have following plane diagram in (Y_{t-1}, Y_t) plane indicating the steady state equilibrium coming up at the intersection of the phase graph with 45° line (0A) (Fig. 3.3).

In panel (a) phase lines (PP) are flatter than 0A, indicating each steady state equilibrium being stable. This essentially purports that following an adverse demand shock (to the tune of $d\mu_t$) in period 1, Y in that period declines for a given Y in period 0, as what is demonstrated by the downward shift in phase line. As a result, there emerges cumulative contraction in Y in the subsequent periods (as indicated by arrow heads staring from B heading towards B') until the economy gravitates at B'. However, in panel the phase lines are steeper than 0A yielding unstable steady state equilibrium and so much as, after diverging from initial equilibrium at B in the event demand contraction, the economy never gravitates to another steady state equilibrium and hence the cumulative contraction process keeps going on.

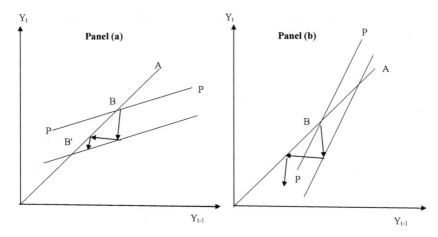

Fig. 3.3 Output dynamics with stability implications (*Source* Drawn by the authors)

CONCLUSION AND POLICY PERSPECTIVES

The essence of the present study lies in the argument that in the circumstance of credit market being imperfect, due to incomplete information about the debtor's diligence in the discharge of the liability of debt servicing and unforeseeable systemic disturbance, like sudden downturn in investment spree or consumption spending, there remains reasonable tendency on part of lenders towards the subjective classification of borrowers with respect to perceived risk profile, such as quality and non-quality entities, and this is further reinforced by the overarching regulatory regime facing the credit making institutions. At the backdrop of this dispensation, it seems warranted to contend that the rationing of non-quality borrowers in credit market serves to blight the resilience of the overall economic system to exogenous disturbance emanating demand-side factors like consumption spending and business and thereby acts as built-in destabilizer in face of recession. This therefore warrants instituting a counter-vailing mechanism to offset the destabilizing impact of inherent credit rationing regimen, which may take the form of the effective and implementation of implementation of priority sector lending ecosystem and additionally, the improve and expand the credit delivery mechanism of microfinance lending through creation of the necessary infrastructural network and backend support system. Moreover, it is imperative that there is substantial need to abandon the one-size-fits-all outlook on the supervision of credit lending institution in terms of asset recognition and application of prudential measures irrespective of nature of credit needs being served by them and rather, to put in place a differential regime in this regard to minimize the case of credit delivery mechanism being driven by single standard approach to perceived risk characterization and instead, having a more targeted and real time approach to evaluation of creditworthiness.

In India, some major strides are visible of late in regard to expediting the credit support to MSMEs and so, at an affordable cost. The first of such kind being the incorporation credit made by banks towards MSME into the purview of priority sector lending, which has further progressed to the incentivizing banks to dispense loan through NBFCs, as in what is vindicated by a provision of up to 20 lac worth of credit per borrower to be disbursed through registered NBFCs (RBI Bulletin, April 2020), which is in turn classifiable under priority sector lending. Followed by this, deserves mention a scheme of one-time debt restructuring for MSMEs registered in GSTN, without any downgrading of asset classification, which was floated out in 2019 for the MSME loan accounts which were in default but were rated standard as on 1 January 2020. This special vehicle was later on extended to the default account as on 1 January 2020 to widen the gamut debt restructuring for this particular sector and so far, this facility has benefitted 15 lac borrowers. From monetary side, some initiatives are well ostensive, as in enhancement of monetary transmission through the introduction of floating-rate loans to micro and small enterprises by linking them to external benchmarks. Besides, the monetary response is further graduated to exempting MSME loans from cash-reserve requirements, with effect from 31 January 2020 up to July 31, as per the Governor of RBI. This apart, the emergence of fintech companies and their networking with lending institutions by means of cutting-edge technologies has gone a long way in overcoming information constraint to the necessary credit appraisal and thereof has enabled expediting of credit flow towards this sector.

References

Ahlin, C., & Lin, J. (2006). *Luck or skill? MFIs' performance in macroeconomic context. An econometric analysis of MFI asset quality* (MIX Discussion Paper No. 1).

Annual Report CGAP. (2007). *Building financial system that work for the poor.*

Banerjee, S. B., & Jackson, L. (2016). Microfinance and the business of poverty reduction: Critical perspectives from rural Bangladesh. *SAGE Journals, 70*(1), 63–91.

Bernanke, B., Gertler, M., & Gilchrist, S. (1994). *Financial accelerator and flight to quality* (Working Paper No. 4789). National Bureau of Economic Research, Cambridge, MA.

Berthelemy, J. C., & Varoudakis, A. (1996). Economic growth, convergence clubs, and the role of financial development. *Oxford Economic Papers, New Series, 48*(2), 300–328.

Bella, G. D. (2011). *The impact of global financial crisis on microfinance and policy implications* (IMF working paper).

Mazumdar, D., Bisai, S., & Bhattacharjee, M. (2018). Performance of SHGs in the backward districts of West Bengal: An analysis. In R. C. Das (Ed.), *Microfinance and its impact on entrepreneurial development, sustainability, and inclusive growth* (chapter 13). IGI Global, USA.

Galema, R., Lensink, R., & Spierdijk, L. (2011). International diversification and microfinance. *Journal of International Money Finance, 30*(3), 507–515.

Khanam, D., Mohiuddin, M., Hoque, A., & Weber, O. (2018). Financing micro-entrepreneurs for poverty alleviation: A performance analysis of microfinance services offered by BRAC, ASA, and Proshika from Bangladesh. *Journal of Global Entrepreneurship Research, 27.*

Khandker, S. R. (2003). *Micro-finance and poverty—Evidence using panel data from Bangladesh* (The World Bank, Development Research Group, Policy Research Working Paper 2945).

Krauss, N., & Walter, I. (2009). Can microfinance reduce portfolio volatility? *Economic Development and Cultural Change, 58*, 85–110. https://doi.org/10.2139/ssrn.943786

Marconi, R., & Mosley, P. (2006). Bolivia during the global crisis 1998–2004: Macroeconomics of microfinance. *Journal of International Development, 18*, 237–261.

Llanto, G. M., & Fukui, R. (2003). Innovations in microfinance in Southeast Asia. *Philippine Institute for Development Studies Research Paper Series, 12*(2), 1–30.

Loncar, D., Novak, C., & Cicmil, S. (2009). *Global recession and sustainable development: The case of micro finance industry in Eastern Europe.* Microfinance Gateway.

Mecha, N. S. (2017). Effect of microfinance on poverty reduction: A critical scrutiny of theoretical literature. *Global Journal of Commerce & Management respective, 6*(3), 16–33. https://www.longdom.org/articles/effect-of-microfinance-on-poverty-reduction-a-critical-scrutiny-of-theoretical-literature.pdf

Mustafa, F., Khursheed, A., & Fatima, M. (2018). Impact of Global Financial Crunch on financially Innovative Microfinance Institutions in South Asia. *Financial Innovation, 4,* 13.

Patten, R. H., & Rosengard, J. K., & Johnston, Jr., J. R. (2001). Microfinance success amidst macroeconomic failure: The experience of Bank Rakyat Indonesia during the East Asian Crisis. *World Development, Elsevier, 29*(6), 1057–1069.

Silva, A. C., & Chavez, A. G. (2015). Microfinance, country governance, and the global financial crunch. *Venture Capital, 2*(1), 191–213.

Rodriguez, A. (2002). *Inter-American development bank, study on Bolivia.* www.seepnetwork.org/files/4720_file_Risk_in_a_Microfinance_Investment_Portfolio.pdf

Visconti, R. M. (2011). Global recession and microfinance risk governance in developing countries. *Virtus Inter Press, 1*(3). https://virtusinterpress.org/IMG/pdf/10-22495_rgcvli3art2.pdf

Visconti, R. M. (2012). *Global recession and microfinance risk governance in developing countries: Threats and opportunities.* Retrieved from SSRN: https://ssrn.com/abstract=1318581 or https://doi.org/10.2139/ssrn.1318581

CHAPTER 4

Performance of Microfinance Institutions Under Economic Growth and Fluctuations: Evidence from South Asian Countries

Ujjal Protim Dutta and Lipika Kankaria

Introduction

Over the last few years, microfinance has seen a rapid as well as successful growth especially in the developing nations. The microfinance institutions (MFIs) primarily emphasize on extending loans to the poorer section of the society, who are left out of the purview of traditional bank financing. The objective behind extending this credit is to encourage the creation of more small-scale business which will help in generating employment opportunities, thereby, alleviating poverty. Researchers, like Cull et al. (2009) have stressed on the fact that millions of people who were earlier

---

U. P. Dutta (✉)
Rangia College, Rangia, India
e-mail: ujjaldtt.06@gmail.com

L. Kankaria
Department of Humanities and Social Sciences, National Institute of Technology Durgapur, Durgapur, India

© The Author(s), under exclusive license to Springer Nature Singapore Pte Ltd. 2022
R. C. Das (ed.), *Microfinance to Combat Global Recession and Social Exclusion*, https://doi.org/10.1007/978-981-16-4329-3_4

not included in the formal financial circuit have been able to access finance owing to these MFIs.

Due to the immense potential that this form of financing holds, a number of studies have focused on MFIs. The focus of these studies has mainly been on analyzing its impact, outreach, and sustainability (Ahlin & Lin, 2006; Bogan, 2012; Hermes et al., 2011). Although at a glance, sustainability and outreach might seem to be competing factors but they may be seen as complementary forces, which indicates that sustainability is essential to accomplish outreach. Here, sustainability refers to the capability of a system to be financially feasible even when financial aids or subsidies are not extended. The focus of the studies that investigate the development of microfinance sector is generally on this variable. Out of these studies, a particular line of enquiry centers on analyzing the most favorable circumstances that promote the expansion of the microfinance sector (Adhikary & Papachristou, 2014; Vanroose & D'Espallier, 2013). The outcomes of these studies have underlined the fact that the macroeconomic environment of a given economy, specifically in the economic growth and the development of the financial structure, can influence the development of the microfinance sector.

In spite of the vital role played by the financial system and economic development as far as the microfinance sector is concerned, the outcomes of the various studies are not conclusive since different researchers have found contrasting relationships (Ahlin et al., 2011; Hermes & Lensik, 2011; Huijsman, 2011; Martinez, 2010; McIntosh & Wydick, 2005). Some of the previous studies have not found decisive evidence concerning the relationship between the development of the microfinance sector and economic growth. On one hand, few other studies have found evidence that the growth of an economy promotes the activity of MFIs while on the other few conclude that it slows down the activity (Ahlin et al., 2011; Wagner & Winkler, 2013). This inconsistency between the results may be triggered due to the fact that the existing studies have separately looked at the influence that the financial system and economic growth exerts on the microfinance sector.

Against this backdrop, the main aim of this study is to examine the impact of macroeconomic factors on the microfinance sector. For the empirical analysis, a sample of 7 countries ranging over the period of 2002–2018 was considered. Given the introduction, the rest of this chapter is organized in the given manner. The following section gives a brief review of previous studies. The third section proposes the model and elucidates the methodology adopted for this study. Finally, this paper ends with a summarization of main findings and proposes policy implications based on the conclusions.

Literature Review

The South Asian nations showcases a different scenario as far as financial insertion and the growth of financial market is concerned. The successful story of MFIs was initiated in Bangladesh almost forty years ago, and it still continues to thrive as a potential source of finance across the South Asian countries. Microfinance has grown into a recognized development strategy in many developing economies. In spite of this, the success of microfinance sector may vary as few initiatives fails while some other may thrive and successfully serve many people (Churchill, 2018). Therefore, a number of studies have started to examine the various factors which may influence the performance of the microfinance sector. This strand of literature has incorporated many institution-specific factors like governance, regulatory status and profit status, and social factors which includes religious and ethnic diversity (Christen & Drake, 2002; Hartarska, 2005; Hatarska & Nadolnyak, 2007).

A rather limited number of studies have focused on the how macroeconomic as well as institutional factors affect the MFIs (Ahlin et al., 2011; Imai et al., 2012). Nevertheless, the primary focus of these studies has been the role of macroeconomic and institutional factors in ascertaining influence over the financial performance of MFIs, with lesser stress on the outreach performance. For example, the previously mentioned studies have analyzed the macroeconomic variables affecting the financial performance of MFIs. Both these studies record that the economic development positively impacts the financial performance of MFIs. Likewise, a study concentrating on Latin America and the Caribbean by Janda and Zetek (2014) has shown that the different macroeconomic factors tend to affect the interest rates that the MFIs charge. Further, arguments have been put forth that shocks which are likely to impact macro-financial system in any economy will likely influence the MFIs, provided that these institutions are within the financial sector. Therefore, Patten et al. (2001) analyzed the impact of macroeconomic shocks on the performance of microfinance institutions following the Indonesian financial crisis of the 1990s chose an established MFI, Bank Rakyat Indonesia (BRI), to base their case study. This study showed that while Indonesian economy was facing a financial calamity, the performance of BRI was not significantly impacted although their interest rates were hiked due to the crisis. The resilient nature of the MFIs in the face of economic shocks has also been established by a study undertaken by Gonzalez (2007). In contrast to this, a study by Krauss and Walter in 2009 employed stock market indices as well as domestic income levels respectively as a proxy for the performance of the international and domestic capital market and find no existence of a relationship between the performance of MFI and capital markets. Their conclusion, however, underscore the effect of domestic GDP on the performance of MFI.

In contrast to this strand of literature that supports the resilience of MFI in the wake of institutional and macroeconomic shocks, another strand shows evidence pointing out that the performance of MFI is affected by different macroeconomic factors. The existing empirical literature exploring the relationship between the financial performance of the MFIs and the macroeconomy can be seen from a bi-causal perspective, which implies that the MFIs' financial performance impacts the macroeconomy (Imai et al., 2011; Krauss & Walter, 2009) and vice versa (Ahlin et al., 2011; Ahlin & Lin, 2006; Thapa, 2008). Ahlin et al. (2011) explored the determinants affecting the performance of the MFIs, employing variables like self-sufficiency, loan-size growth, or borrower growth are estimated through macroeconomic variables along with macro-institutional factors, like, corruption control utilizing the Microfinance Information Exchange data. They concluded that the performance of MFIs is not necessarily good or worse, in certain cases, in economies where the institutions are rather advanced. One of the limitations of this study is that the endogeneity of the main variables, including the macro-institutional variables, is not taken into consideration. In a study, Krauss and Walter (2009) investigated microfinance as a way of regressing the fundamental parameters, reducing portfolio volatility and the ratios of the important microfinance institutions against the S&P 500, MSCI Emerging Markets and MSCI Global indexes (as proxy for risks related to global market) and against domestic GDP (taken as proxy for domestic market risk). There are very few studies who have specifically concentrated on the major impacts of global financial crunch that is faced by the people who fall in low-income bracket and are aided by the MFIs in South Asia. Therefore, this study attempts to address this gap by studying the macroeconomic factors which might influence MFIs in the South Asian context.

Methodology

Model

This study tries to analyze the impact of financial development and economic growth on performance of microfinance institutions with the help of following model:

$$\ln\text{MFI}_{i,t} = \beta_0 + \beta_1 \ln y_{i,t} + \beta_2 \ln FD_{h,t} + \beta_3 \ln \text{Size}_{i,t} + \beta_4 \ln \text{FDI}_{i,t} + \beta_5 \ln \text{REM}_{i,t} + \varepsilon_{i,t} \quad (4.1)$$

where, MFI represent performance of micro finance institutions, FD is the financial development, $Size$ denotes size of the micro finance institutions. FDI represents foreign direct investment, and REM is the remittances. Except performance of MFIs and size of MFIs, data of above mentioned variables has been taken from the World Bank's database World Development Indicators (WDI), while data for size and performance of micro finance institutions have been obtained from Microfinance Information Exchange database.

Data and Variable Description

Performance of microfinance institutions has been taken as the dependent variable in this study. The number of active borrowers has been taken as a proxy for measuring the performance of microfinance institutions. GDP per capita has been used to measure economic growth of the country. A number of studies have found that the development of the MFIs is fostered by the economic growth. Martinez (2010) has found that the association amid the economic activities of a nation and the credit growth of MFIs to be increasingly pro-cyclical as an effect of the rising involvement of MFIs in the capital markets. Ahlin et al. (2011) and Constantinou and Ashta (2011) have found that in case of micro-entrepreneurs there is a rise in the per capita income and the cash flow of the business indicates a larger capacity to borrow and a higher capacity to repay the pending loans. Additionally, MFI funding sources improves with economic growth through subsidies from various sources like aid organizations, funds via capital market as well as public and private donors (Constantinou & Ashta, 2011). According to Wagner and Winkler (2013), economic growth might lead to the slowing down of the development of the microfinance system. This is due to the fact that economic growth results in more profits that can be further utilized by the microentrepreneur in the form of self-financing rather than going to a MFI. This is further reiterated by Schneider and Enste (2000) who found that when any economy improves, there is a reduction in the informal sector which leads to a reduction in the target market of the MFIs.

This study uses the ratio of domestic credit to the private sector expressed as percentage of GDP as a proxy for financial development. Existing literature recognized this as one of the standard measure of financial development (King & Levine, 1993; Levine et al., 2000). SIZE refers to the scale of the MFI, which is calculated as the logarithm of the total assets of the MFI. It can impact the development of the microfinance system by improving the sustainability and reach (Mersland & Strøm, 2010; Vanroose & D'Espallier, 2013) and also the financial efficiency (Gutiérrez-Nieto et al., 2009). The larger the size of the MFI, the greater is the prospect of financing and, therefore, the growth of the loan portfolio (Ahlin et al., 2011).

Net inflows of FDI as a percentage of GDP have been in this study to measure Foreign Direct Investment. As far as the MFI credit growth is concerned, a negative association is expected because FDI results in a rise in the number of workers employed in the formal sector thereby leading to a reduction in the potential demand of MFI (Ahlin et al., 2011; Vanroose & D'Espallier, 2013). The remittances received are represented by REM, and it is estimated as the remittances received by workers as a percentage of GDP. Here, a negative association is expected because it is implied that a rise in income would function as an alternative for microcredit financing (Wagner & Winkler, 2013).

Methods

Several methodologies have been applied to estimate the model. Initially, this study adopted fixed effect and random effect methods to carry out the preliminary estimation on the panel data. Subsequently, fixed effect and system Generalised Method of Moment (GMM) are used to check the robustness of the outcome. The panel data model is represented in the following equation

$$\Delta y_{it} = \rho y_{it-1} + X_{it}\beta + \vartheta_i + \gamma_t + \varepsilon_{it} \qquad (4.2)$$

where Δy_{it} is the first difference of the dependent variable, i.e., performance of microfinance institutions for country i and period t. X_{it} is the vector that captures all control variables. ϑ_i is the country specific effect, and γ_t is the time specific effect. ε_{it} is the error term that captures all other variables. This study estimated both fixed effect (FE) and random effect (RE) model and conducted Hausman test in order to make a consistent model choice between FE and RE models (Hausman, 1978). Though FE and RE models have the advantage over OLS because of its control of unobserved heterogeneity, yet they are not able to account for the problem of endogeneity. This study has taken into consideration of the problems of endogeniety by taking the lagged values of explanatory variable as an instrument in the Arellano–Bover (1995) and Blundell–Bond (1998) system GMM framework. Here, the lagged first differences of the variable are used as an instrument in the level Eq. 4.3 and lagged levels of the variables are used as an instrument for equation in first differences Eq. 4.4.

$$y_{i,t} = \rho y_{i,t-1} + X_{i,t}\beta + \vartheta_i + \gamma_t + \varepsilon_{i,t} \tag{4.3}$$

$$y_{i,t} - y_{i,t-1} = \beta_1(y_{i,t-1} - y_{i,t-2}) + \beta(X_{i,t} - X_{i,t-1}) + \gamma_t + (\varepsilon_{i,t} - \varepsilon_{i,t-1}) \tag{4.4}$$

The variables definition for Eqs. 4.3 and 4.4 are same as Eq. 4.2. The lagged values of the variables are now added in to the equation. It is assumed that the error terms are not serially correlated under GMM estimator. In addition to this, the explanatory variables are also not correlated with the future realization of the error terms. Thus, for the first difference estimator, the given moment condition holds:

$$E\big[y_{i,t-s}(\varepsilon_{i,t} - \varepsilon_{i,t-1})\big] = 0; \; E\big[X_{i,t-s}(\varepsilon_{i,t} - \varepsilon_{i,t-1})\big] = 0;$$

where $i = 1 \cdots n$, $t = 3 \cdots T$ and $s \geq 2$.

To check whether GMM estimator is consistent or not, this study applied both second order serial correlation test and Sargan test of over identifying restrictions for the validity of the instrumental variables. If the null hypothesis of this test is not rejected, then we can conclude that the model is correctly specified. This study applied both these tests to check whether the obtained results are valid or not.

Results and Analysis

Table 4.1 provides the results of FE and RE models. The outcome of both these models provides mix results. This study does not find a significant effect of GDP per capita of host country on remittances. The coefficient of GDP per capita is found to be negative and significant in both FE and RE model. However, the coefficient of Size is found to be positive in both the models. A one percentage point increase in size of the microfinance institutions of the selected countries leads to 0.867 percentage point increase in the performance of microfinance institutions. It is 0.849 percentage point rise in performance of microfinance institutions in random effect models. In contrast to this, financial development, FDI and remittances are not appearing to be significantly correlated with performances of microfinance intuitions in both fixed effect and random effect. Apart from all these, the table also provides the result of Hausman test, which is conducted in order to make a consistent model choice between fixed effect and random effect model. The result of the Hausman test prompted this study to choose fixed effect model, as the probability value of the Chi square test is less than 0.05. It implies that study reject

Table 4.1 Static models results

Dependent variable: Performance of microfinance institutions

Independent variables	Model: 1 Fixed effect	Model: 2 Random effect
GDP per capita	−0.4130*	−0.4042*
	(0.0923)	(0.0960)
Financial development	−0.1656	−0.0622
	(0.1381)	(0.1390)
Size	0.8677*	0.8497*
	(0.0319)	(0.0321)
FDI	−0.0141	−0.0269
	(0.0425)	(0.0443)
Remittances	−0.0523	−0.1161
	(0.0946)	(0.0944)
R^2	0.9479	0.9472
Hausman (χ^2)		−0.017
(*p*-value)		

One percent, five percent, and ten percent level of significance are denoted, respectively, by *, ** and ***
Source Authors' calculations

the null hypothesis that the empirical model is random effect. However, this study cannot rely on fixed effect model since it is not equipped to deal with the problem of endogeneity.

To deal with this problem, this study depends on the results of Arellano–Bover (1995) and Blundell–Bond (1998) system GMM panel estimator. Like FE and RE models, the coefficient of the GDP is negative and robust, meaning that the economic status of the country will negatively affect the performance of microfinance institutions. While the size of the microfinance institutions has positive effect on the performance of the microfinance institutions. The coefficient of the size variable is positive and statistically significant in all the models. Though this study did not find any significant effect of financial development of the country on the performance of MFIs, yet we cannot overlook the importance of financial development of the country on performance of microfinance institutions.

Similarly, this study did not find any significant effect of remittances and FDI on performance of microfinance institutions.

To check the validity of the results, this study also reported the value of the AR (2) test and Hansen test of over identifying restriction in Table 4.2. This study has performed these two tests to examine the serial correlation and validity of the instruments that are employed. In every specification, this study cannot reject the null hypothesis of valid over identifying restrictions. Thus, this study can conclude that the results of this study are valid and robust.

Conclusion

This study aims to explore the different macroeconomic variables which affects the performances of microfinance institutions. To attain this objective, this study initially estimated both FE and RE model and conducted Hausman test in order to make a consistent model choice between FE and RE model (Hausman, 1978). Though fixed effect and random effect models have the advantage over OLS because of its control of unobserved heterogeneity, yet they are unable to address the problem of endogeneity. This study has taken into consideration of the problems of endogeneity by taking the lagged values of explanatory variable as an instrument in the Arellano–Bover (1995) and Blundell–Bond (1998) system GMM framework. The findings of this study suggested that GDP is one of the significant variables that effect the performance of microfinance institutions as the GDP per capita of country goes up, the performance

Table 4.2 Dynamic models results

Dependent variable: Performance of microfinance institutions	
Independent variables	Model:3 System GMM
Performance of microfinance institutions$_{t-1}$	0.5271* (0.0715)
GDP per capita	−0.3540* (0.1217)
Financial development	0.0117 (0.0892)
Size	0.3193* (0.0907)
FDI	−0.0239 (0.0252)
Remittances	0.0512 (0.0564)
AR(1) test	0.001
AR(2) test	0.966
Hansen test	0.240

One percent, five percent, and ten percent level of significance are denoted, respectively, by *, ** and ***
Source Authors' calculations

of microfinance institutions comes down. The coefficient of the GDP per capita of home country is negative and statistically significant. In contrast to this, the coefficient of size of the microfinance institutions is found to be positive. It implies that size of the microfinance institutions will positively impact the functioning of the MFIs. In addition to this, this study didn't find any significant effect the variables namely financial development, FDI, and remittances.

The outcome of this study implies that the governments have a vital role to play in boosting the outreach of MFIs by developing effective policies and by ensuring a financially secure environment for the MFIs and the people availing the services from them. Keeping in view the increased integration of the MFIs with the formal financial system and the consequently increased vulnerability to the global financial crunch, the results of this study recommend effective as well as innovative features in the microfinance sector, and robust political practices have become more significant now than before.

REFERENCES

Adhikary, S., & Papachristou, G. (2014). Is there a trade-off between financial performance and outreach in South Asian microfinance institutions? *The Journal of Developing Areas, 48*, 381–402.

Ahlin, C., & Lin, J. (2006). *Luck or skill? MFI performance in macroeconomic context* (Vol. 132, BREAD working paper).

Ahlin, C., Lin, J., & Maio, M. (2011). Where does microfinance flourish? Microfinance institution performance in macroeconomic context. *Journal of Development Economics, 95*(2), 105–120.

Arellano, M., & Bover, O. (1995). Another look at the instrumental variable estimation of error-components models. *Journal of Econometrics, 68*(1), 29–51.

Awaworyi Churchill, S. (2018). The macroeconomy and microfinance outreach: A panel data analysis. *Applied Economics, 51*(21), 2266–2274.

Blundell, R., & Bond, S. (1998). Initial conditions and moment restrictions in dynamic panel data models. *Journal of Econometrics, 87*(1), 115–143.

Bogan, V. L. (2012). Capital structure and sustainability: An empirical study of microfinance institutions. *Review of Economics and Statistics, 94*(4), 1045–1058.

Christen, R. P., & Drake, D. (2002). Commercialization. The new reality of microfinance. In D. Drake & E. Rhyne (Eds.), *The commercialization of microfinance: Balancing business and development* (pp. 2–22). Kumarian Press.

Constantinou, D., & Ashta, A. (2011). Financial crisis: Lessons from microfinance. *Strategic Change: Briefings in Entrepreneurial Finance, 20*(5/6), 187–203.

Cull, R., Demirgüç-Kunt, A., & Morduch, J. (2009). Microfinance meets the market. *Journal of Economic Perspectives, 23*(1), 167–192.

Gonzalez, A. (2007). *Resilience of microfinance institutions to national macroeconomic events: An econometric analysis of MFI asset quality.*

Gutiérrez-Nieto, B., Serrano-Cinca, C., & Mar Molinero, C. (2009). Social efficiency in microfinance institutions. *Journal of the Operational Research Society, 60*(1), 104–119.

Hartarska, V. (2005). Governance and performance of microfinance institutions in Central and Eastern Europe and the newly independent states. *World Development, 33*(10), 1627–1643.

Hartarska, V., & Nadolnyak, D. (2007). Do regulated microfinance institutions achieve better sustainability and outreach? Cross-Country evidence. *Applied Economics, 39*(10), 1207–1222.

Hausman, J. A. (1978). Specification tests in econometrics. *Econometrica: Journal of the Econometric Society, 46*, 1251–1271.

Hermes, N., Lensink, R., & Meesters, A. (2011). Outreach and efficiency of microfinance institutions. *World Development, 39*(6), 938–948.

Hermes, N., & Lensink, R. (2011). Microfinance: Its impact, outreach, and sustainability. *World Development*, *39*(6), 875–881.

Huijsman, S. (2011). *The impact of the economic and financial crisis on MFIs*. Planet Finance: Stuttgart.

Imai, K., Gaiha, R., Thapa, G., Annim, S. K., & Gupta, A. (2011). Performance of microfinance institutions: A macroeconomic and institutional perspective. School of Social Sciences, University of Manchester.

Imai, K. S., Gaiha, R., Thapa, G., Annim, S. K., & Gupta, A. (2012). Financial performance of microfinance institutions-A macroeconomic and institutional perspective (Research Institute for Economics & Business Administration, Kobe University, Discussion Paper Series: DP2012, 4).

Janda, K., & Zetek, P. (2014). Macroeconomic factors influencing interest rates of microfinance institutions in the Latin America and the Caribbean. *Agricultural Economics*, *60*(4), 159–173.

King, R. G., & Levine, R. (1993). *Financial intermediation and economic development* (Vol. 156189). Cambridge University Press.

Krauss, N., & Walter, I. (2009). Can microfinance reduce portfolio volatility? *Economic Development and Cultural Change*, *58*(1), 85–110.

Levine, R., Loayza, N., Beck, T. (2000). Financial intermediation and growth: Causality and causes. *Journal of Monetary Economics*, *46*, 31–77.

Martinez, R. (2010). *Latin America and the Caribbean 2009: Microfinance analysis and benchmarking report*. Microfinance Information Exchange.

McIntosh, C., & Wydick, B. (2005). Competition and microfinance. *Journal of Development Economics*, *78*(2), 271–298.

Mersland, R., & Strøm, R. Ø. (2010). Microfinance mission drift? *World Development*, *38*(1), 28–36.

Patten, R. H., Rosengard, J. K., & Johnston, D. E. (2001). Microfinance success amidst macroeconomic failure: The experience of Bank Rakyat Indonesia during the East Asian crisis. *World Development*, *29*(6), 1057–1069.

Schneider, F., & Enste, D. H. (2000). Shadow economies: Size, causes, and consequences. *Journal of Economic Literature*, *38*(1), 77–114.

Thapa, G. (2008, August 21). *Sustainability and governance of microfinance institutions: Recent experiences and some lessons for Southeast Asia* (Working Paper No: 07-11). IFAD.

Vanroose, A., & D'Espallier, B. (2013). Do microfinance institutions accomplish their mission? Evidence from the relationship between traditional financial sector development and microfinance institutions' outreach and performance. *Applied Economics*, *45*(15), 1965–1982.

Wagner, C., & Winkler, A. (2013). The vulnerability of microfinance to financial turmoil: Evidence from the global financial crisis. *World Development*, *51*, 71–90.

CHAPTER 5

Microfinance as a Strategy to Curb the Global Recession

Suman Chakraborty, Arpita Chaudhury, and Riddhima Panda

Introduction

Global recession is a buzz phrase on this gift era. It is the principal barrier in the back of the socio-financial improvement of any financial system. It may be stated that the worldwide recession has hit remittances that's one of the crucial types of earnings for the poorest families.

S. Chakraborty (✉)
Department of Economics, Raja N. L. Khan Women's College (Autonomous), Midnapore, West Bengal, India
e-mail: sc_economics@rnlkwc.ac.in

A. Chaudhury
General Studies, University of Engineering and Management, Kolkata, West Bengal, India

R. Panda
Department of Economics & Commerce, Syamaprasad College, Kolkata, West Bengal, India

© The Author(s), under exclusive license to Springer Nature Singapore Pte Ltd. 2022
R. C. Das (ed.), *Microfinance to Combat Global Recession and Social Exclusion*, https://doi.org/10.1007/978-981-16-4329-3_5

Because close to approximately 80% of remittances to beneath advanced and growing nations come from advanced or excessive earnings nations, this supply of sales is liable to financial crisis (Cali & Dell'Erba, 2009). The principal results of worldwide recession are poverty, excessive fee of unemployment, fall of common earnings, monetary crisis, inequality and better authorities borrowing etc. Here we've used poverty as a logo for the worldwide recession. Micro credit score or Microfinance have these days emerged as a crucial device to slash the threat of poverty with inside the growing nations via micro-financing the entrepreneurs. Microfinance is an approach for offering higher get right of entry to finance to the unbanked human beings of a financial system, might also additionally have effect on financial increase inside territory. In this context, microfinance can assist the financial system via way of means of its numerous affects. The affects may be defined in diverse elements or regions along with family stage, person stage, corporation stage, activity advent etc. Poverty and sustainable improvement are one of the parameters of a wholesome financial increase. Microfinance impacts on poverty via ways. Economic increase may be reached via growing monetary offerings. There are varieties of microfinance establishments. The first one is especially focused on upliftment of the terrible and the second one kind ambition at monetary sustainability (Weber, 2013). Microfinance promotes appropriate functioned monetary quarter of the financial system that's crucial for correct allocation of assets which thereby main to boom in productivity, better funding and better financial increase. From literature survey it's been determined that there exists an advantageous dating among monetary quarter and financial increase. According to researchers get right of entry to finance is the maximum crucial part. An get right of entry to finance is needed to have sustainable financial increase, in order that low-earnings families, that also represent a majority, have probabilities to break out from poverty (Alimukhamedova, 2013; Aziz & McConaghy, 2014). While analyzing the transmission channels of microfinance to financial increase, Alimukhamedova (2013) reveals that microfinance envisages the mixing of the monetary necessities of families right into a usa's monetary device and it's miles predicted to have an effect on the increase in an advantageous manner. Although it's miles notion that via decreasing earnings inequality and poverty there may be a right away impact of microfinance, however, this effect is in long-term. Several empirical evidences along with Hossain (1984); Amin et al. (2003); Irobi (2008); Johnson and Rogaly (1997) and Bakhtiari (2011) have proven that microfinance financial institution is a crucial device for poverty eradication and socio-financial improvement in some of the growing nations throughout the globe. Even the look at of Hossain (1988) in Bangladesh determined that the terrible and landless contributors of Grameen banks have common family of forty three percentage better than the ordinary landowners. It is argued that over 112 million Nigerians are presently dwelling beneath poverty stage, at the same time as the mixture wide variety of the terrible is near a billion globally (Obayagbona, 2018). Since Yunus acquired Nobel Peace Prize award in (2006), numerous investigations are occurring to look at the effect of microfinance banks on poverty remedy globally. In a study of recent part, Khanam et al. (2018) discuss the performance of microfinance institutions such as BRAC, the Association for Social Advancement ASA and PROSHIKA in relation to the poverty alleviation in the context of Bangladesh. Results show that the variables such as amount of cultivable land, amount of fixed asset, number of earning persons, number of male persons, number of female person and amount of loan, except the amount of fixed assets and the number of female family members have a significant impact on poverty alleviation in the country.

BACKGROUND OF THE STUDY

The Sustainable Development Goals (SDG) is one of the programs also known as global goals adopted by UN as a universal call to action to end poverty and hunger (UN 2015).

In Nigeria, the version of microfinance isn't always idiot evidence of a success version like in different nations like Bangladesh. With recognize to poverty remedy and microfinance banks nexus, several researches found within side the empirical literature as to how microfinance banks may be correctly used to limit the poverty stage in nations throughout the globe. For instance, the look at of Jegede et al. (2011) empirically tested the impact of microfinance credit score on poverty discount in Nigeria. Oladejo (2013) examines the effect of the usage of credit score and different precise microfinance financial institution's associated variables on decided on SMEs positioned in Osun State of Nigeria. Using the descriptive facts on number one and secondary records, the empirical evaluation shows giant advantageous effect of microcredit transport offerings on SMEs performance. In every other associated look at, Okezie et al. (2013) tested the efficiency of microfinance financial institution in removing poverty in Nigeria, the usage of descriptive facts on number one records regarding 382 respondents for three Senatorial districts in Imo state. The empirical outcomes discovered that excessive earnings magnificence has the capacity to shop the terrible dwelling with inside the rural regions. Akosile and Ajayi (2014) take a look at the impact of microfinance financial institution's credit score centers on micro small and medium firms in decreasing poverty stage and reaching speedy financial increase in Nigeria. Employing the survey and descriptive studies designs on 5 microfinance banks and three (CICSs) with inside the rural, semi-city and concrete centers, the empirical outcomes discovered a robust advantageous effect of microfinance credit and monetary offerings on poverty discount or low-earnings institution in addition to micro, small and medium scale firms in Nigeria. Kasali et al. (2015) look at microfinance financial institution and poverty discount nexus with inside the South-West Zone of Nigeria. The look at of Kamel and Jalel-Eddine (2015) examines the impact of microfinance on poverty discount for approximately 596 microfinance banks in fifty seven rising economies for the length 2005 to 2011. Employing the panel records evaluation, the empirical findings discovered that a financial system with better microfinance establishments' gross mortgage portfolio according to capita has a tendency to lessen poverty stage the various human beings. Thus, this shows that microfinance banks have the capacity to correctly alleviate poverty in those nations. Financial improvement via microfinance takes place in 4 ways. Firstly, financially sustainable MFIs can sell marketplace deepening that during flip advances monetary improvement. Secondly, microfinance as a effective device in nations with terrible developmental applications. Thirdly, microfinance may want to facilitate monetary marketplace adulthood in each advanced and growing nations. Finally, microfinance can assist to guide home monetary reforms via way of means of breaking down constraining elements. On the opposite hand, Adonsou and Sylwester (2015) argue that the boom in intermediation via way of means of microfinance establishments comes at a value to the borrower. Empirically, Adonsou and Sylwester (2015) reveal that the boom in microfinance loans has an advantageous and giant impact on financial increase and general issue productivity. Buera et al. (2012) say that microfinance may have appropriate results on output, capital, wages, hobby charges and general issue productivity. Ahlin and Jiang (2008) and Yusupov (2012) determined that microfinance has appropriate macroeconomic results. Microfinance incorporates each monetary and social tools. Microcredit is part of microfinance which presents micro-loans for a specific tenure. The compensation time is ready as weekly and monthly. About seventy percent and thirty percent microfinance institutions out of 707 microfinance institutions are working in rural and urban sectors respectively in Bangladesh (MRA, 2018). Overall MFIs have less than twenty percent city debtors who're the slum dwellers (CDF, 2016a, b). Urban surroundings have a few dangers elements almost about credit score disbursements. From 2011 to 2017 periods, the wide variety of city microfinance contributors grew via way of means of 45.61%, which changed into better than the corresponding rural wide variety of 11.82% (CDF, 2017). In the recent past 2017, the entire disbursement of city microfinance mortgage loan was into USD 2.2 billion and the financial savings of the contributors reached USD 0.47 billion. Moreover, the common wide variety of contributors according to MFI with inside the city grew greater than the corresponding wide variety of rural regions (Hossain & Wadood, 2020). Every year common increase of quantity of city microfinance changed into additionally better than that of the primary sector (CDF, 2016a, b). Equal distribution of earnings among populace can result in uniform earnings upward push and as a consequence will result in financial increase (Berthélémy & Varoudakis, 1998; De Grégori & Guidotti, 1995; King & Levine, 1993). It has been cited that if monetary offerings are geared toward terrible, earnings inequality will decline with inside the populace (Beck et al., 2007; Bigsten & Levin, 2000; Bourguignon, 2004; Datt & Ravallion, 1992; McKenzie & Woodruff, 2008; Ravallion, 2001). The cap potential useful merchandise from microfinance ends in development in get right of entry to health, schooling which can be once more the parameters of appropriate financial health. Microfinance may be the important thing to a progressed financial situation and social welfare because it enables to slash inflation, extended meals' costs thereby stabilizing the buying electricity of the terrible (Littlefield et al., 2003). In the phrases of Clarke et al. (2006) and Beck et al. (2007), inequality in regard to terrible's get right of entry to offerings associated with finance in society is especially because of marketplace imperfections. It is in which microfinance performs a crucial function with inside the discount of inequality with inside the society. Thus, microfinance and sustainability are noticeably connected. The monetary sustainability of a micro-monetary organization is depending on whether or not the organization is capable of keeping enterprise with guide from donors. The non-economic dreams like upliftment of terrible and empowering them also are ascertained.

The altogether results of financial, environmental and societal also are ascertained to recognize the efficiency of microfinance and sustainability.

In this chapter, we are trying to analyze microfinance as an effective instrument to curb the impact of global recession or crisis. Here to address the issue of global recession, we have taken poverty as an allegory for global recession. We have selected three different countries namely India, Bangladesh and Nigeria to analyze the entire chapter.

Objective of the Study

Our major objective of the chapter is to find out the impact of activities of microfinance on poverty through the per capita expenditure of the households.

Hypothesis of the Study

It has been assumed that a positive and significant relationship exists between poverty (Per Capita expenditure of households) and activities of microfinance (i.e., loans from microfinance institutions and deposit in the microfinance institutions).

Database and Methodology

To bring about the concerned objectives of our study, we have collected per capita expenditure of households (as a proxy of poverty), loan from microfinance institutions and deposit in the microfinance institutions as secondary data from NABARD, IMF and Microcredit Regulatory Authority (MRA) of Bangladesh, Central Bank of Nigeria (CBN) and World Bank data for three different countries such as India, Bangladesh and Nigeria to analyze the chapter.

Important statistical techniques have been used to analyze and interpret the data. The various tools such as compound annual growth rate, regression analysis have been used.

Regression

To examine the factor relationship of dependent and explanatory (independent) variables, regression analysis is used wherever it is necessary. Regression analysis is the most important way to estimate the exact relationship between dependent variable and explanatory (independent) variables. Now, an equation of the linear regression line can be written as, Y = (a + bX); here Y is the dependent variable and X is the explanatory variable. The adjusted R^2 and F of the estimated regression equation of this model are such that the relevant regression model is fitted to the data set.

The Compound Annual Growth Rate (CAGR)

The compound annual growth rates (CAGR) of different heads of value such as, microfinance institution (MFL), deposit of the microfinance institution (MFD) for the selected countries and also investment from microfinance institutions or microfinance bank (INVMF) for Nigeria have been calculated with the help of log linear equation as follows:

ln Y = α + βt, where α and β are the regression coefficients.

The slope coefficient β of 't' in the above growth model gives the instantaneous rate of growth. The compound annual growth rate (CAGR) can be found by taking the antilog of regression coefficients i.e., β, subtracting unity (1) from it and multiplying the difference by 100.

Status of Activities of Microfinance

The microfinance industry has tremendously increased its intermediation activities over the last decade, particularly in developing countries.

According to Microfinance Outlook 2015, the global microfinance market achieved growth of 15–20% in 2015. Asia displayed the strongest growth momentum. According to the International Monetary Fund (IMF), the growth rate in the micro financed countries will be double than that of the rate of developed countries (Etzensperger, 2014).

Data on assets and liabilities of microfinance Banks/Institute has been collected from 2008 to 2017 for the countries like Nigeria, India and Bangladesh. The establishment of Microfinance banks because of the inability of the informal microfinance institutions to satisfy the needs of small business operators. Microfinance banks made available, credit to low income earners and rural areas and also financially empower those areas. Now the status of microfinance of the selected countries can be explained one after another.

Nigeria

The data of Nigeria shows that in 2008 the amount of loans and advances Nmillion 42,753.06, which is recorded Nmillion 58,215.66 in 2009. Hence there was an increase in loans and advancement (15,462 Nmillion) but then for the next two years (2010 and 2011) there was a significant drop in the amount of loans and advancement made by the microfinance institutes of the country. In 2012 the lending amount increased significantly from 50,928.30 Nmillion dollars in 2011 to 90,422.25 Nmillion dollars (Central Bank of Nigeria). Thereafter a continuous growth in the lending amount was seen till 2016 after which a slight decrease in the amount of loans and advancement was noticed in 2017 from 196,194.99 Nmillion dollars in 2016 to 194,024.94 Nmillion dollars (Central Bank of Nigeria). The significant compound annual growth rate (CAGR) of disbursement of loans was 8.4% in our study periods. There is a steady rise in the amount of total investment done by the microfinance institutes of the country throughout the years (2008–2017). The significant compound annual growth rate (CAGR) of investment from the microfinance institutes was 6.3% in the study periods. There was a significant rise in the deposit amounts of these institutes in the first two years of the study (2008 and 2009). There was a slight decrease in the deposits next year in 2010 after which there was a dramatic fall in the number of deposits in the year 2011. The deposit amount with the microfinance bank in 2008 was 61,568.10 Nmillion dollars which has increased to 76,662 Nmillion dollars but fell to 59,375.90 Nmillion dollars in the year 2011 (Central Bank of Nigeria). Thereafter there was a continuous growth in the number of deposits with the microfinance institutes of the country which was around 159,453.52 Nmillion dollars in 2015. The amount fell in 2016 to 149,798.38 Nmillion dollars. In 2017, the deposits with the microfinance institute jumped to 186,405.86 Nmillion dollars (Central Bank of Nigeria). The significant compound annual growth rate (CAGR) of savings or deposits was 5.5% in our study periods.

India

During this time the amount of lending by microfinance institutions in India has increased more than ever before. It is recorded that average loan size per customer has raised from 10,364 rupees in 2014 to 16,394 rupees in 2016 (NABARD, IMF Report). Indian Microfinance is mainly a rural-focused sector. At present, MFIs are also interested about urban areas. In urban sector, their customers are increasing. Large MFIs are already started to provide the loans in urban sectors.

It is seen that loans disbursement by MFIs shows a positive trend since 2012–13. In 2015–16, the amount increased to 72,345 crore, but in 2016–17 due to demonetization the amount declined. It can be seen from the data, the lending amount by the microfinance institutions has increased over the years from 2008 to 2017. The asset and liabilities were around 3732.33 crores in 2008 which increased continuously every year and was seen to be 47,185.88 crores in 2017 (NABARD, IMF Report). The deposits with the MFIs increased from 5545.62 crores in 2008 to 7016.30 crores in 2010, then it fell slightly in the year 2011 (NABARD, IMF Report). The compound annual growth rates (CAGR) of Savings and disbursement of loans are 6.3% and 11.3% respectively of India in our study periods. Both are statistically significant.

Bangladesh
In Bangladesh, microfinance Loans are well targeted in the sense that their ultimate objective is to gradually alleviate the poverty from the society. Of the total microcredit and microenterprise loan disbursed in 2017–18 was 1,201.91 billion BDT which was in excess 14.91% (Microcredit Regulatory Authority (MRA) of Bangladesh) than the previous years. The number of borrowers rose to 25.40 million and 93% of them is women. It covers 15.88% of the total population of Bangladesh. Other large microcredit programs in Bangladesh include Grameen Bank which disburses 207.85 billion BDT, BRDB 13.96 billion BDT and Jubo Unnayan Adhidoptor 1.44 billion BDT (Microcredit Regulatory Authority (MRA) of Bangladesh). This microcredit especially microenterprise directly affects people as a benefit for the source of working capital. There are different types of loan in this sector including general microcredit, ultra poor loan, microenterprise loan, house loan etc. In 2013–14, all the MFIs totally disbursed BDT 432.28 billion which was BDT 217.06 billion in 2008–09. In 2015–16, total loan disbursement was BDT 634 billion (Microcredit Regulatory Authority (MRA) of Bangladesh). Total amount of savings also been increasing for last 8 years in a smooth trend from BDT 47.38 billion to BDT 135.41 billion in 2015 and over the years loan disbursement was BDT 634 billion in 2015 which was 217.06 in 2008 (Microcredit Regulatory Authority (MRA) of Bangladesh). The amount was more than doubled by 8 years. The significant compound annual growth rate of savings and disbursement of loans are 7.03 and 6.33 of

Bangladesh respectively in our study periods 2008 to 2015. Microfinance is a strategy for providing better access to finance to the unbanked people of an economy, may have impact on economic growth within territory as evidenced for Bangladesh (Sultan et al., 2016).

Microfinance as an Instrument of Alleviation of Poverty

Global Financial Crisis as a worldwide economic slump. It is a time of general turn down in economic activity characterized by general fall in income, expenditure, savings, investment, conditions of different types of business declines and mass unemployment (Bernanke, 1995). Hence, poverty is one of the major consequences of global recession. Here we have used poverty as a metaphor for the global recession. To deal with by any effective program related to sustainable development poverty alleviation plays a vital role (Chokor, 2004; Duraiappah, 1998).

Roughly, one fifth of the world population lives in severe and extreme poverty (Hermes & Lensink, 2007b) and since 1990s, (Develtere & Huybrecht, 2005), eradication of poverty is one of the top priorities for worldwide economic development. Livelihood of about 2.5 billion people is on less than $2 a day (Bruton et al., 2011). Enhanced access to finance is needed for the low-income households to escape from poverty and to ensure sustainable economic growth. (Alimukhamedova, 2013; Aziz & McConaghy, 2014). Access to financial services of regulated financial organizations is yet to arrive at more than half of the world's working-age adults (Fouillet et al., 2013). Because of this reason there is dependence on informal moneylenders for getting loans for maintaining a microenterprise. To lift more than hundred million customers out of poverty credits are provided to them by more than three thousand microfinance institutions globally. (Cull et al., 2011; Epstein & Yuthas, 2011; Hartarska & Nadolnyak, 2007). Few effective policies to tackle the problem of poverty alleviation by financing small, collateral free loans to micro-entrepreneurs are promising (Baklouti, 2013). To eradicate poverty, microfinance services have now become an efficient means by financing micro-entrepreneurs. Thus, since the 1970s, development theorists believe non-governmental microfinance institutions (MFIs) as the most vital runners of achieving sustainable development by financing micro-entrepreneurial activities (Muhumuza, 2005).

The Model

To analyze microfinance is a useful tool to poverty alleviation, we can use regression model. Here we have taken per capita consumption expenditure of households (as a proxy of poverty) (PCCE) as dependent variable and loan disbursement from microfinance bank and institutions (MFL), deposits in microfinance bank and institutions (MFD) as explanatory variables for the selected countries India, Bangladesh and Nigeria.

In this model, we have got the data from several periods due to unavailability of the essential data. Thus, for India, Bangladesh and Nigeria, the study periods are 2008 to 2017, 2008 to 2015 and 1997 to 2017 respectively.

In our analysis we can write the regression model as,

$$PCCE = \beta_0 + \beta_1 \, MFL + \beta_2 \, MFD + e$$

(β_0 is the constant & β_1, β_2 are the coefficients of the variables loan disbursement from microfinance bank and institutions (MFL) and deposits in microfinance bank and institutions (MFD) respectively). Above equation is estimated by Ordinary Least Squad (OLS) method. The estimated results of the regression model for the countries India, Bangladesh and Nigeria are presented in Tables 5.1, 5.2 and 5.3 respectively.

India

The Regression equation concerning per capita consumption expenditure of households (PCCE) as dependent variable and loans from microfinance institution (MFL) deposit of the microfinance institution (MFD) as independent variables shows that the variation in per capita consumption expenditure of households (PCCE) is significantly explained by the value of loans from microfinance institution (MFL) and deposit of the microfinance institution (MFD) to the extent of 98% this means that the model has a very high predictive ability. It is also observed that coefficient of the variables value of loans from microfinance institution (MFL) and deposit of the microfinance institution (MFD) are significant at 1% and 10% level of significance for the nation India respectively. The whole model's significance level is at 1% level of significance. Hence it can be stated that, the combined effects of the value of loans from microfinance

Table 5.1 Regression equation between per capita consumption expenditure of households (PCCE) (proxy of poverty) as dependent variable and loan disbursement (MFL), deposits in microfinance bank and institutions (MFD) as explanatory variables for the selected country India (2008–2017)

Regression equation	R^2	$AdjR^2$	F
$PCCE = \dfrac{0.007\,MFL**}{(4.64)} + \dfrac{0.009\,MFD*}{(1.84)} + 598.75$	99%	98%	343.98**

**Indicates significant at 1% level, *Indicates significant at 10% level. The values of parentheses are 't' Values. *Sources* Data From NABARD, World Bank open data sources and IMF
Source Author's own computation of results

institution (MFL) and deposit of the microfinance institution (MFD) are in the model have significant effects on poverty alleviation in India in our study period (Table 5.1).

Bangladesh

The Regression equations concerning per capita consumption expenditure of households (PCCE) as dependent variable and loans from microfinance institution (MFL) deposit of the microfinance institution (MFD) as independent variables show that the variation in per capita consumption expenditure of households (PCCE) is explained by the value of loans from microfinance institution (MFL) and deposit of the microfinance institution (MFD) to the extent of 93% this means that the model has a very high predictive ability. It is also observed that coefficient of the variable, deposit of the microfinance institution (MFD) is significant at 10% level of significance. Another coefficient of the variable value of loans from microfinance institution (MFL) is not significant but positively related to the dependent variable. The whole model's significance level is at 1% level of significance for both the cases in Bangladesh. Hence it can be stated that, both the variables in the model are explaining poverty alleviation significantly in Bangladesh in our study period (Table 5.2).

Table 5.2 Regression equation between per capita consumption expenditure of households (PCCE) (proxy of poverty) as dependent variable and loan disbursement (MFL), deposits in microfinance bank and institutions (MFD) as explanatory variables for the selected country Bangladesh (2008–2015)

Regression equation	R^2	$AdjR^2$	F
$PCCE = \dfrac{0.102\,MFL}{(0.5)} + \dfrac{1.23\,MFD*}{(2.3)} + 484.5$	95%	93%	49.65**

**Indicates significant at 1% level, *Indicates significant at 10% level. The values of parentheses are 't' Values. *Sources* Data MRA-MIS Database, 2014 & 2018 of Bangladesh for Bangladesh, & World Bank open data sources
Source Author's own computation of results

Nigeria

The Regression equation concerning per capita consumption expenditure of households (PCCE) as dependent variable and loans from microfinance institution (MFL) deposit of the microfinance institution (MFD) as independent variables shows the following that the variation in per capita consumption expenditure of households (PCCE) is significantly explained by the value of loans from microfinance institution (MFL) and deposit of the microfinance institution (MFD) to the extent of 57% this means that the model has a high predictive ability. It is also observed that coefficient of the variable value of deposit of the microfinance institution (MFD) is significant at 1% level of significance. On the other hand, the explanatory variable loans from microfinance institution (MFL) does not hold the expected positive signs. The coefficient of loans from microfinance institution (MFL) is negatively signed. But it is significant at 5% level of significance. This means that, in the determination of the overall poverty rate, this variable, i.e., loan from microfinance institution (MFL) is an important factor to be considered. However, the negative sign is an indication that either the borrowers are not utilizing the amount of loans for their betterment or the borrowers are not under poverty conditions.

The whole model's significance level is at 1% level of significance. Hence it can be stated that, the combined effects of the value of loans from microfinance institution (MFL) and deposit of the microfinance institution (MFD) are in the model have significant effects on poverty alleviation in Nigeria in our study period (Table 5.3).

Table 5.3 Regression equation between per capita consumption expenditure of households (PCCE) (proxy of poverty) as dependent variable and loan disbursement (MFL), deposits in microfinance bank and institutions (MFD) as explanatory variables for the selected country Nigeria

Regression equation	R^2	$AdjR^2$	F
$PCCE = \dfrac{0.012\,MFD**}{(3.56)} - \dfrac{0.007\,MFL*}{(-2.53)} + 980.43$	61%	57%	14.2**

**Indicates significant at 1% level , *Indicates significant at 5% level . The values of parentheses are 't' Values. *Sources* Data From CBN (1997–2017) for Nigeria & World Bank open data sources
Source Author's own computation of results

According to the results, the diagnostic indicators are very much notable. These above findings agree in all respect with our hypothesis and those of (Jegede et al., 2011; Kamel & Jalel-Eddine, 2015; Kasali et al., 2015; Oladejo, 2013) who variously submitted that microfinance banks or microfinance institutions have significant impact on poverty reduction or alleviation of poverty. Hence activities of microfinance can combat the global recession.

Conclusion

The study empirically investigates how much the microfinance system is effective to curb the global recession. Here we have used poverty as an allegory for the global recession. According to the estimation of United Nation, the worldwide recession has pushed 100 million more people below the poverty line (UN, 2009). Hence poverty is one of the major consequences of global recession. To investigate the effectiveness of microfinance we have analyzed the impact of microfinance institutions or microfinance banks on poverty alleviation in India, Bangladesh and Nigeria. Poverty alleviation is one of the most important factors of Sustainable development goal (SDG) of United Nation (UN). Financing of micro-entrepreneurs for creation of job and other income generating activities shows some success in many developing countries. The compound annual growth rate of loans from microfinance or microfinance banks deposits in microfinance Institutions or banks is positive and significant. The explanatory variables of the model i.e., loans from microfinance institutions and deposits in the microfinance institutions are very much effective for poverty alleviation. There is positive and significant impact of financial activities of microfinance institutions (i.e., loans from microfinance institutions and deposit in the microfinance institutions) on poverty alleviation for the selected nations except Nigeria. The negative result of microfinance loans clearly supports the view of Dr. Yunus regarding microfinance in Nigeria that the nature of Nigerian microfinance is contrary to that espoused in Bangladesh. An expansion of gross loans by microfinance institutions leads to higher youth unemployment as loans are provided to the wrong persons.

Thus, our findings agree in all respect with our hypothesis, i.e., the impacts of microfinance activities are effective to curb poverty condition which is one of the major impacts of global recession. Hence, we can combat the poverty which is a metaphor of global recession through microfinance activities.

There's no doubt that microfinance institutes have a positive impact on poverty alleviation but without proper monitoring of these institutions our objective will get blurred out eventually. Hence to use microfinance as an instrument to boost the socio-economic development of a nation and to alleviate poverty condition as well as to restrict or curb the global recession in the economy we need to take care of the proper and efficient functioning of microfinance institutions.

REFERENCES

Ahlin, C., & Jiang, N. (2008). Can micro-credit bring development? *Journal of Development Economics, 86*, 1–12.

Alimukhamedova, N. (2013). Contribution of microfinance to economic growth: Transmission channel and the ways to test it. *Business and Economic Horizons* (BEH), *9*(4), 27–43.

Akosile, A. I., & Ajayi, O. A. (2014). The impact of microfinance institutions on poverty reduction in Nigeria. *European Journal of Business and Management, 6*(35), 1–8.

Amin, S., Rai, A., & Topa, G. (2003). Does microcredit reach the poor and vulnerable? Evidence from northern Bangladesh. *Journal of Development Economics, 70*, 59–82.

Aziz, T. A., & McConaghy, P. (2014). Promoting financial inclusion for growth and development in Iraq (No. 18154). The World Bank.

Bakhtiari, S. (2011). Microfinance and poverty reduction: Some international evidence. *International Business & Economics Research Journal* (IBER), *5*(12).

Baklouti, I. (2013). Determinants of microcredit repayment: The case of Tunisian Microfinance Bank. *African Development Review*, 25(3), 370–382.

Beck, T., Demirgüç-Kunt, A., & Levine, R. (2007). Finance, inequality, and the poor. *Journal of Economic Growth*, 12, 27–49.

Bernanke, B.So. (1995). The macroeconomics of the grat depression: A comparative approach. *Journal of Money, Credit and Banking*, 27.

Bertelemy, J. -C., & Varoudakis, A. (1998). Développement financier, réformes financières et croissance: une approche en données de panel. *Revue Économique*, 49(1), 195–206.

Bigsten A., & Levin, J. (2000). Growth, income distribution and poverty: A review. Working Paper in Economics no 32, Goteborg University.

Bourguignon, F. (2004). Trade exposure and income volatility in cash-crop exporting developing countries. *European Review of Agricultural Economics, Foundation for the European Review of Agricultural Economics*, 31(3), 369–387.

Bruton, G., Khavul, S., & Chavez, H. (2011). Micro-lending in emerging economies: Building a new line of inquiry from the ground up. *Journal of International Business Studies*, 42, 718–739. https://doi.org/10.1057/jibs.2010.58.

Buera, F. J., Kaboski, J. P., & Shin, Y. (2012). The macroeconomics of microfinance, NBER Working Papers 17905, National Bureau of Economic Research, Inc.

Cali, M., & Dell'Erba, S. (2009). The global financial crisis and remittances: What past evidence suggests. ODI Working Paper 303.

Clarke, G., Colin, Xu. L., & Zou, H.-F. (2006). Finance and income inequality: What do the data tell us? *Southern Economic Journal*, 72, 578–596.

CDF statistics 2015 & 2016 (2–6), development of microfinance sector, credit and development Forum web site. Retrieved April 20, 2019, from http://www.cdfbd.org/new/Chapter%201.doc (2016a).

CDF statistics 2015 & 2016 (14–19), trends and growth of microfinance programs of MFIs, credit and development Forum web site, Retrieved April 20, 2019, from http://www.cdfbd.org/new/Chapter%202.doc (2016b).

CDF Bangladesh microfinance statistics 2016–2017, credit and development Forum web site.

Chokor, B. (2004). Perception and response to the challenge of poverty and environmental resource degradation in rural Nigeria: Case study from the Niger Delta. *Journal of Environmental Psychology*, 24, 305–318.

Cull, R., Demirgüç-Kunt, A., & Morduch, J. (2011). Does regulatory supervision curtail microfinance profitability and outreach? *World Development*, 39(6), 949–965.

De Gregori J., & Guidotti P. (1995). Financial development and economic growth. *World Development*, FMI, 23, 433–448.

Datt, G., & Ravallion, M. (1992). Growth and redistribution components of changes in poverty measures: Decomposition with applications to Brazil and India in the 1980s. *Journal of Development Economics, 38*, 275–295.

Donou-Adonsou, F., & Sylwester, K. (2015). Macroeconomic effects of microfinance: Evidence from developing countries. *Journal of Economics* (J ECON).

Duraiappah, A. (1998). Poverty and environmental degradation: A review and analysis of the Nexus. *World Development, 26*(12), 2169–2179.

Develtere, P., & Huybrecht, A. (2005). The impact of microcredit on the poor in Bangladesh. *Alternatives: Global, Local, Political, 30*(2), 165–189.

Donor Brief No. 13, July 2003, CGAP (Consultative Group to Assist the Poor), World Bank.

Epstein, M., & Yuthas, K. (2011). The critial role of trust in microfinance success: Identifying problems and solutions. *Journal of Developmental Entrepreneurship, 16*(4), 477–497.

Etzensperger, C. (2014). Microfinance Market Outlook 2015. *ResponsAbility Investments AG.*

Fouillet, C., Hudon, M., Harriss-White, B., & Copestake, J. (2013). Microfinance studies: Introduction and overview. *Oxford Development Studies, 42*, 1–16. https://doi.org/10.1080/13600818.2013.790360.Hermes,

Hossain, M. (1988). Credit for the alleviation of rural poverty: The Grameen bank in Bangladesh (W/P No. 65). IFPRI.

Hermes, N., & Lensink, R. (2007). The empirics of microfinance: What do we know? *The Economic Journal, 117*(517), F1–F10. https://doi.org/10.1111/j.1468-0297.2007.02013.x.

Hartarska, V., & Nadolnyak, D. (2007). Do Regulated microfinance institutions cchieve better sustainability and outreach? Cross-country evidence. *Applied Economics, 39*, 1207–1222.

Hossain, M. (1984). *Credit for the rural poor; the experience of Grameen bank in Bangladesh.* BIDS.

Hossain, B., & Wadood S. N. (2020). Impact of urban microfinance on the livelihood strategies of borrower slum dwellers in the Dhaka city, Bangladesh. *Journal of Urban Management*, Elsevier. www.elsevier.com/locate/jum.

Irobi, N. C. (2008). Microfinance and poverty alleviation: A case study of Obazu Progressive Women Association Mbieri, (Master's thesis, Imo State–Nigeria, 1–25). Retrieved from https://stud.epsilon.slu.se/10927/1/irobi_n_170920.pdf.

Johnson, S., & Rogaly, B. (1997). Microfinance and poverty reduction. Oxfam Publication.

Jegede, C. A., Kehinde, J. A., & Akinlabi, B. H. (2011). Impact of micro finance on poverty alleviation in Nigeria: An empirical investigation. *European Journal of Humanities and Social Sciences, 2*(1), 97–111.

Kasali, T. A., Ahmad, A. S., & Lim, H. E. (2015). The role of microfinance in poverty alleviation: Empirical evidence from South-West Nigeria. *Asian Social Science, 11*(21), 183–198.

Kamel, B. H. M., & Jalel-Eddine, B. R. (2015). Microfinance and poverty reduction: A review and synthesis of empirical evidence. *Procedia—Social and Behavioral Sciences, 195*, 705–712.

Khanam, D., Mohiuddin, M., Hoque, A., et al. (2018). Financing microentrepreneurs for poverty alleviation: A performance analysis of microfinance services offered by BRAC, ASA, and Proshika from Bangladesh. *Journal of Global Entrepreneurship Research, 8*(27).

King, R.-G., & Levine, R. (1993). Finance and growth: Schumpeter might be right. *Quarterly Journal of Economics, 108*(3), 717–738.

Littlefield, E., Murdurch, J., & Hashemi, S. (2003). *Is microfinance an effective strategy to reach the Millennium development goals?* CGAP Focus Note.

Mckenzie, D., & Woodruff, C. (2008). Experimental evidence on returns to capital and access to finance in Mexico. *World Bank Economic Review, 22*, 457–482.

Microfinance Outlook 2014.

Microfinance Outlook 2015.

MRA-MIS Database, 2014 of Bangladesh.

MRA-MIS Database, 2018 of Bangladesh.

Muhumuza, W. (2005). Unfulfilled promises? NGOs' micro-credit programmes and poverty reduction in Uganda. *Journal of Contemporary African Studies, 23*(3), 392–416. https://doi.org/10.1080/01426390500273858

Oladejo, M. (2013). Evaluation of the Nigerian microfinance banks credit administration on small and medium scale enterprises operations. *International Review of Management and Business Research, 2*(2), 505–517.

Okezie, A. I., Bankoli, B., & Ebomuche, N. C. (2013). The impact of Nigerian microfinance banks on poverty reduction: Imo state experience. *Mediterranean Journal of Social Sciences, 4*(6), 97–114.

Obayagbona, J. (2018). Microfinance Bank and poverty alleviation in Nigeria: An impact assessment. *Amity Journal of Finance, 3*(2), 1–12. ©2018 ADMAA. Retrieved April 20, 2019, http://www.cdfbd.org/new/Bangladesh_Microfinance_Statistics_2016-17.pdf (2017).

Ravallion, M. (2001). Growth, inequality and poverty: Looking beyond averages. *World Development, 29*(11), 1803–1815.

Sultan, Y., & Masih, M. (June 2016). *Does microfinance affect economic growth? Evidence from Bangladesh based on ARDL approach.* INCEIF.

United Nations. (2009). *Voices of the vulnerable: The economic crisis from the ground up.* GIVAS (UN).

Weber, O. (2013). Impact measurement in microfinance: Is the measurement of the social return on investment an innovation in microfinance? *Journal of Innovation Economics, 11*, 149–171.

Yusupov, N. (2012). Microcredit and development in an occupational choice model. *Economics Letters*, Elsevier, *117*(3), 820–823.

CHAPTER 6

Developing Strategies to Improve Microfinance System in Turkey with Fuzzy Logic

Hasan Dinçer, Serhat Yüksel, Çağatay Çağlayan, and Gözde Gülseven Ubay

INTRODUCTION

If a country's economic performance indicators are at a desirable level, it means that sustainable economic growth is achieved. Therefore, this situation is very important in terms of both social welfare and politics

H. Dinçer · S. Yüksel (✉) · Ç. Çağlayan · G. G. Ubay
The School of Business, İstanbul Medipol University, İstanbul, Turkey
e-mail: serhatyuksel@medipol.edu.tr

H. Dinçer
e-mail: hdincer@medipol.edu.tr

Ç. Çağlayan
e-mail: cagatay.caglayan@std.medipol.edu.tr

G. G. Ubay
e-mail: gozde.ubay@std.medipol.edu.tr

© The Author(s), under exclusive license to Springer Nature Singapore Pte Ltd. 2022
R. C. Das (ed.), *Microfinance to Combat Global Recession and Social Exclusion*, https://doi.org/10.1007/978-981-16-4329-3_6

because it provides opportunities, such as preventing unemployment and increasing the income of citizens within the borders of the country. At the same time, it is also essential to prevent poverty by distributing revenues properly for sustainable economic growth and national development. In order to prevent poverty, provide welfare and distribute income properly with using the earnings of economic growth, a country's current financial system needs to be constructed completely and work efficiently (Gerard & Johnston, 2019).

Microfinance is the provision of financial services to poor people who cannot access the credit services of banks and various financial supports (Zamore et al., 2019). In order to increase social welfare, achieve economic growth by maximizing the level of in-country production and spread financial support to all segments of the society, the concept of microfinance has gained great importance. Microfinance activities based on a strong legal basis and a strict audit mechanism that has become the roof of microfinance institutions provides several advantages, such as mobilization of saving that will provide economic efficiency, credit unions that finance each other regularly, sector-based system diversity and education programs covered in many areas.

Although there are many advantages of the microfinance system, it is also possible to talk about some solvable disadvantages that must be overcome. As it is known, the institutions that provide microcredit are non-profit institutions. Donators are one of the most important factors to sustain the microfinance system (Schulte & Winkler, 2019). In this process, each donator is equal to a minimum of one person who must be saved from poverty. The microfinance institution, which cannot get enough donations, will not be able to cover operational costs. Additionally, it will not be able to provide credit services to the poor people (Golesorkhi et al., 2019).

Being based on voluntariness is one of the disadvantages of the microfinance system. For this reason, microfinance mobilization should be initiated, and potential donors should be directed to institutions and donations should be explained to people by gaining means of social responsibility. When the disadvantages of microfinance are mentioned, it should be said that operational costs are very high. The target group in microfinance is those in the low-income class (D'Espallier et al., 2017) and this group has problems with access to finance and some of them have remained in long-term unemployment. They may also have fallen into poverty for various reasons, for example, illnesses, accidents. They need more information because the education levels of this group may also be low (Möllmann et al., 2020).

Due to the problems of the target audience such as these, even the cost of a single customer may be too high for the institution. In addition, microfinance institutions offer many low-budget loans to many customers as they do not work like banks. These factors increase operational costs and are one of the disadvantages of the microfinance system. Another point is that for microfinance customers to form groups, entrepreneurial women or men should find five people. It is very difficult to find people with the same level of education and maturity, and it is possible that some people who do not have entrepreneurship qualifications to form a group can be included in these groups. Finally, group-based microfinance institutions deal with more people and examine their financial standing one by one. This means that operational costs have increased considerably. For all these reasons, such as negatively affecting the performance of group members, problems in repayment of finance, and increased operational costs, the group approach should be revised while conducting microfinance studies.

In every country and region where the importance of the microfinance system is understood, various ideas about how this system can be developed are generated. First, legal arrangements should be made in which microfinance institutions and people receiving loans can operate freely. An audit mechanism that controls microfinance institutions and can gather all institutions under one roof is required for the irregularities in the market. Different needs of each sector should be approached differently by providing sector-based system diversity. Sectoral or regional credit unions should be established separately, and advisory and support units should be supported. In order for poor people to be more involved in the financial system, flexible payment opportunities should be provided by institutions. Savings mobilities should be provided to help poor people better manage and protect their assets. In order for this whole system to work properly, to maintain it and to gather information, a broad training program should be implemented.

In Turkey, microfinance activities have been started to be implemented in the recent past, and these activities have made positive contributions in preventing poverty. When comparing with developed countries, the number of poor individuals in developing countries such as Turkey is understood to be much more (Yas et al., 2018). That's why it can be said that microfinance studies have been getting greater importance, and the impact of the application is more effective in Turkey. Based on the 2018 data, Turkey's population, the number of immigrants and the number of tourists coming every year show that Turkey has a huge power consumption what is generated approximately 150 million people. This feature also shows that Turkey strong economic potential and offers an environment were taken quite understandable and effective results for microfinance studies. Differences between lower, middle and upper-income people have been increasing, number of people who have middle income have been decreasing, in Turkey. Increasing on the lower level of income shows that practices of microcredit also have been getting more importance day by day, in Turkey.

Especially microfinance system in Turkey should have a wide variety of sector-based system because the economic activities and the needs of every town, every region are different (Dincer et al., 2018). Therefore, the approach to the target audience of each region should be different. For example, working sectors and problems of people who live in Turkey Southeastern Anatolia Region are quite different from the situation of people who live in the Marmara Region. While Southeastern Anatolia Region carries out more activities in agriculture, Marmara Region carries out more activities in technology. In addition, while the Southeastern Anatolia Region may have adverse conditions such as terrorism, education and climate, the situation is generally more positive for the Marmara Region. Therefore, there is a need of sector-based systems' variety that responds differently to each region and each person of each region. A financial system with this system diversity will be effective and efficient in solving problems and ensuring sustainability. At the same time, microfinance institutions will be able to integrate the poor people into the system more easily by providing different trainings to the people of each region thanks to the diversity. Microfinance institutions can strengthen the solidarity among the poor entrepreneurs by establishing and financing various credit unions and can ensure the continuity of the system by offering flexible payment opportunities. When the system is maintained, microfinance institutions will reach more donators and provide the opportunity to offer credit services to poor people more.

This chapter aims to focus on the ways to improve microfinance system in Turkey. For this purpose, a detailed literature review is conducted firstly regarding microfinance system. As a result of this analysis, seven different factors are identified that can have an influence on the improvement of microfinance system. The main reason of selecting Turkey is that it is a developing country. Additionally, it aims to develop its economy to reach the status of developed economy. In this framework, an effective financial system is necessary to have sustainable economic growth. Hence, microfinance system can be an opportunity for this situation. In the analysis process, fuzzy DEMATEL methodology is considered in order to find which criteria play more significant role to have more effective microfinance system. This methodology has many advantages over similar approaches in the literature. For instance, the causality relationship can be identified by using this approach. In addition to this issue, impact relation map can be created between the items with the help of fuzzy DEMATEL methodology. With the help of this analysis, it can be possible to generate strategies to improve microfinance system in Turkey.

General Information About Microfinance

Microfinance history can be based on the oldest religious texts, civilization rituals and tribes when considering the purpose of microfinance system and its applications. From an economic perspective, the history of microfinance can also be associated Lysander Spooner, who is antislavery and basically defends the idea of "slavery is unconstitutional." Briefly, the beginning of microfinance history can be based on the aims of poor people to get rid of poverty and misery. German cooperative and mayor Friedrich Wilhelm Raiffeisen, who lived in the 1800s, also should be referred in the history of microfinance since he pioneered rural credit associations and established banks (Mia et al., 2019).

Microfinance's modern ground and the beginning of the concept goes back to the 1970s, Bangladeshi Mohammed Yunus. He is an economics professor who claims that the economic laws cannot find the equivalent in real life and he is one of those who found and developed the concept of microcredit in line with this idea. He is the founder of the Grameen Bank of Bangladesh (Gold, 2019). Yunus and his bank were awarded the Nobel Peace Prize in 2006 in response to efforts to create improvements in the field of social and economics. Although the history of modern microfinance is based on Muhammed Yunus, Pakistani Akhtar Hameed Khan is also included among the pioneers of microfinance. He promoted participatory rural development in Pakistan and other developing countries and studied about that.

Microfinance is the provision of financial services to low-income customers or groups who cannot access banking and similar services.

Microfinance institutions are non-profit organizations, and their client portfolio is usually female entrepreneurs and their groups. Microfinance has a wide variety of services, but the most well-known is microcredit. Microcredit aims to provide credit support to poor customers. Although microfinance and microcredit are used together, the microfinance system has an insurance program called micro insurance, a program applied to protect the life and labor of customers who receive microcredit against unexpected accidents and situations (Mushtaq & Bruneau, 2019). Micro insurance program can cover many situations, including natural disasters, various accidents, terrorist attacks, funeral expenses. Microfinance customers can ensure their labor by paying a very low premium to have a micro insurance policy. In addition, microfinance customers are subjected to a training program in which they learn the system to benefit from the system in the most efficient way. This training program supports communication and agreement between microfinance institutions and customers (Li et al., 2019).

Another important issue to know about the microfinance system is the obligation to provide some conditions required by the microfinance institutions to get microcredit. First, it is necessary to have a business idea to access microcredit service. In some cases, having a business idea is not enough to access this service. Therefore, another issue to be known is which model the microfinance institution adopts. An institution that implements a group-based model wants its customers to establish a micro entrepreneur group consisting of 5 people and non-kin relationship between 5 microcredit customers, to provide microcredit service. Today, microfinance services are very diverse and influenced by different disciplines. Therefore, it is difficult to assess the full effect of microfinance and there are few studies evaluating this (Haile et al., 2015).

It is thought that there is a link between poverty and dependency. Hence, to fight poverty, the economic dependencies of the poor should be resolved. A large proportion of the society is formed of poor people. The word "poor" is used for people, communities, countries that have the property, money, low or no income, and which have many difficulties to make a living. Therefore, profit banks do not see poor people as the target customer base because poor people have little money. That situation means that a large proportion of the society cannot access banking services. Persons with very low income or no income need to have security deposits or guarantors to access credit opportunities. Access to loans for the poor, who do not have any mortgage assets, is theoretically and practically impossible. The purpose of microfinance is to overcome this gap in the financial system, to contribute to making credit access a fundamental human right, and to provide participation of many people as possible to the market. In order to achieve this goal, microfinance institutions try to deliver unsecured, guarantor less and low interest loans (Drori et al., 2019).

There are dozens of advantages in the direction of the purposes of the microfinance system. The framework of all the advantages can be identified as that will occur is to reduce poverty as much as possible. In addition, microfinance enlivens the production by enabling the poor people to participate in the market and accelerate the production and consumption in the market. Microcredit takers are converted into small entrepreneurs, enabling them to earn both income and repay debts, thus returning the money they receive back to the system. The entrepreneurs who take microcredit create employment by creating new work areas. Therefore, it cannot be denied that the concept of microfinance has an important place in the entrepreneurial ecosystem. These micro activities at the micro level have positive macro results for the states. Macro results such as decreasing unemployment, controlling inflation and increasing national income per capita are positive economic results that can be described as state oriented. The fact that the economic indicators are at a good and rising level also causes the concepts that are very important such as prosperity and happiness, which means the development of the society, to increase in the society (Kassim et al., 2019). As the welfare and happiness of the citizens of a country increases, it has positive results about the future of the political actors of the country. On the other hand, poor women entrepreneurs who are included in the microfinance system and who receive micro credits will be able to get rid of their economic dependencies by achieving their economic freedoms and will go a long way toward preventing gender inequality.

Although the basic advantages of the microfinance system are in this direction, different advantages will be possible with the suggestions given to the establishment of the system. For example, making legal arrangements, tax reductions and similar political movements makes the microfinance system more attractive, and it has been possible to reach a large part of the poor entrepreneurs (Morduch, 2000). When the poor people who make up a large part of the society, see incentives and feel the support of the state for the participation of the poor entrepreneurs to the market, that situation strengthens the relation between the society and the state. However, the establishment of a supervision mechanism and the linking of microfinance institutions to this mechanism will ensure the control and efficiency of the economic activities of institutions and, entrepreneurs who receive credit. The control mechanism is essential to prevent abuse, injustice and for protecting and increasing people's beliefs in the system. The supervision mechanism is obliged not to put pressure on the market and the rules of the free market, but to ensure control and operability of the market. Another area of interest of the microfinance system is the issue of spending the assets of the poor. A saving mobilization should be initiated to protect and maintain the economic situation of the poor who receive credit. Thereby, poor people can transform their assets into profits without unnecessary expenses by meeting their basic needs and making necessary investments.

Literature Review

There are many articles on the development process of countries in the literature. In a large part of these articles, especially the subjects to include low-income people in the financial system are covered. Microfinance is also one of the useful topics in this area. Investigation of microfinance issues in developing countries was evaluated in the literature by many different researchers. Making the necessary legal arrangements for microfinance institutions by policy makers plays an important role for the development of the system (Chen et al., 2019). For example, if microfinance institutions (MFIs) are not limited to the legal restriction that prohibits them to offer various microcredit products other than microcredit, these institutions may develop in future (Kassim et al., 2019).

The flexible movement area brought by the legal regulations requires a control mechanism that will serve as the roof of microfinance institutions. For instance, the weakness of self-regulation of MFIs has been proven in practice, which requires independent regulation and supervision to minimize the sector's exploitative tendencies, including excessive indebtedness, profiteering and control fraud (Awaworyi Churchill, 2019; Butcher et al., 2019). They should provide sector-based system diversity by considering the different sectors that each different geography has. Although current empirical studies do not have certainty about the necessity of diversity, diversification is not bad if advanced monitoring and control mechanisms are available (Zamore et al., 2019).

Sectoral and regional credit unions should be established. Studies show that credit unions in the country play an important role in supporting financial inclusion (Adusei & Obeng, 2019). Micro-finance institutions should provide flexible payment opportunities, considering that their customers have different time periods in their income cycles. For example, the income cycles of borrowers engaged in agricultural activities have different time periods. Therefore, MFIs need to reassess financial programs to reduce the burden of borrowers to repay loans (Kassim et al., 2019). In order to better explain the microfinance system, training of existing credit recipients will increase their access to the system, the willingness of customers, and the income from investments. As an example, when micro entrepreneurs receive higher loans, training on issues such as business, nutrition and health or women's empowerment and increasing use of other auxiliary microfinance services of people, may lead to more income in the medium term after investments (Fan et al., 2019; Lacalle et al., 2019).

The results of the literature review show that the microfinance system is a topic that is evaluated in detail among researchers and as a promising system as a method of reducing poverty. It is understood that there are many different problems and needs in each country, and that each country should develop methods specific to its geography.

An Evaluation for Microfinance System in Turkey

Firstly, selected indicators based on the literature review will be explained under this section. After that, the significance of these factors will be identified by fuzzy DEMATEL approach.

Selected Indicators

Similar studies in the literature are analyzed to understand the significant issues of an effective microfinance system. Hence, 7 factors are identified. The details of these factors are given on Table 6.1.

Table 6.1 indicates that first of all, it is defined that legal arrangements (C1) play a very key role to improve the effectiveness of this system. The robust legal infrastructure will increase investors' confidence in the microfinance system. This situation is also directly related to an effective control mechanism (C2). Another important point in this process is the application's need to be system based (C3). On the other hand, credit unions

Table 6.1 The Details of the criteria

Criteria	References
Legal Arrangements (C1)	Chen et al. (2019), Kassim et al. (2019)
Audit Mechanism (C2)	Awaworyi Churchill (2019), Butcher et al. (2019), Yang et al. (2021)
Sector-based System Diversity (C3)	Adusei and Obeng (2019), Zamore et al. (2019)
Sectoral or Regional Credit Unions (C4)	Fan et al. (2019), Jun et al. (2021), Lacalle et al. (2019)
Flexible Payments (C5)	Drori et al. (2019), Morduch (2000)
Saving Mobility (C6)	Gold (2019), Haile et al. (2015)
Training Program (C7)	Mia et al. (2019); Möllmann et al. (2020)

Source Authors' calculations

(C4) will also play an important role in choosing the right customer. This will contribute to increasing the efficiency of the microfinance system. In addition to the issues mentioned, another important issue in this process is the existence of the flexible payment system (C5). The high saving of mobilization on a country basis (C6) is also important in this process. Finally, providing the necessary training for the microfinance system (C7) will increase awareness of this issue.

Methodology

DEMATEL approach is considered to define the weights of different factors (Zhao, Cheng et al., 2021; Zhao, Xu et al., 2021). In other words, it is very beneficial to understand which factors are more important to reach the objective (Dinçer et al., 2017; Yuan et al., 2021). The main novelty of this methodology is that impact relation map can be developed between the criteria (Haiyun et al., 2021). This situation is not possible while making analysis with similar methods (Dinçer & Yüksel, 2019; Li et al., 2021). In the first stage of the analysis, expert opinions are obtained, and they are converted to the fuzzy numbers (Zhou et al., 2021). With the help of the average values of them, average fuzzy matrix is created (Liu et al., 2021). In the next stage, this matrix is normalized (Xie et al., 2021). After that, the total relation fuzzy matrix is created (Zhao, Cheng et al., 2021; Zhao, Xu et al., 2021). In the final part, defuzzification process is performed, and the weights of the criteria can be calculated (Dinçer et al., 2021).

Analysis of Results

In the analysis process, the evaluations of 3 different experts are considered. These people have at least 15-year experience in this area. Hence, it is believed that their opinions lead the way to improve microfinance system. Their opinions are firstly converted to the fuzzy numbers. After that, the calculation process of fuzzy DEMATEL is performed, such as initial direct relation matrix, normalized direct relation matrix, total influence matrix and total relation matrix. Just then, the defuzzification process is performed and the weights of the criteria are calculated. The details are given on Table 6.2.

Table 6.2 indicates that legal arrangements (C1) play the most significant role to improve the microfinance system in Turkey. On the other side, it is also obvious that sectoral or regional credit unions (C4) is the second most important factor for this situation. In addition to these issues, audit mechanism (C2) and sector-based system diversity (C3) are also other significant criteria in this framework. Nevertheless, it is also determined that flexible payments (C5), saving mobility (C6) and training program (C7) have the weakest weight in the improvement of microfinance system in Turkey.

Table 6.2 Weights of the criteria

Criteria	D_i	R_i	$D_i + R_i$	$D_i - R_i$	Weights
Legal Arrangements (C1)	1.265	0.289	1.554	0.976	0.164
Audit Mechanism (C2)	1.025	0.346	1.371	0.680	0.145
Sector-based System Diversity (C3)	0.419	0.966	1.385	−0.548	0.146
Sectoral or Regional Credit Unions (C4)	0.525	0.941	1.465	−0.416	0.155
Flexible Payments (C5)	0.365	0.770	1.134	−0.405	0.120
Saving Mobility (C6)	0.576	0.734	1.310	−0.158	0.139
Training Program (C7)	0.554	0.683	1.237	−0.129	0.131

Source Authors' calculations

Conclusion and Discussion

It is aimed to evaluate the influencing factors of the effective microfinance system in Turkey. For this purpose, 7 different criteria are defined as a result of the literature review. These criteria are weighted by using fuzzy DEMATEL methodology. It is concluded that legal arrangements and credit unions are the most significant criteria to improve microfinance system in Turkey. In addition to them, it is also identified that audit mechanism and sector-based system diversity are other important items for this situation. On the other side, it is also determined that flexible payments, saving mobility and training program play a lower role in this condition by comparing with other factors.

While considering these issues, it is understood that primarily in Turkey it is necessary to establish the legal infrastructure related to the microfinance system. It is obvious that the microfinance system, whose legal processes have been clarified, will attract the attention of both investors and users. In this context, details of this topic in Turkey clearly stated that the law urgently needs to be prepared. In this way, investors in the country will feel more secure. On the other hand, with the establishment of credit unions regionally, it will be possible to select the people to be loaned more effectively. Therefore, the risk of selecting inappropriate people to give loans can be minimized. This situation will provide a significant contribution to the development of the microfinance system in Turkey.

The main limitation of this study is that analysis is also performed for Turkey. Therefore, in future studies, new country groups can be taken into consideration. For instance, a comparative analysis can be conducted to see the leading indicators of an effective microfinance system in both developing and developed economies. Another limitation is that only one evaluation is performed to see the weights of criteria. Nevertheless, another analysis can be made to understand which countries have better performance with respect to the microfinance system. In this context, fuzzy TOPSIS, fuzzy MOORA or fuzzy VIKOR methods can be used. It is thought that these studies have an important contribution to the microfinance literature.

References

Adusei, M., & Obeng, E. Y. T. (2019). Board gender diversity and the capital structure of microfinance institutions: A global analysis. *The Quarterly Review of Economics and Finance, 71*, 258–269.

Awaworyi Churchill, S. (2019). The macroeconomy and microfinance outreach: A panel data analysis. *Applied Economics, 51*(21), 2266–2274.

Butcher, W., & Galbraith, J. (2019, January). Microfinance control fraud in Latin America. In *Forum for Social Economics* (Vol. 48, No. 1, pp. 98–120). Routledge.

Chen, J. I., Foster, A., & Putterman, L. (2019). Identity, trust and altruism: An experiment on preferences and microfinance lending. *European Economic Review, 120*, 103304.

D'Espallier, B., Goedecke, J., Hudon, M., & Mersland, R. (2017). From NGOs to banks: Does institutional transformation alter the business model of microfinance institutions? *World Development, 89*, 19–33.

Dincer, H., & Yuksel, S. (2019). IT2-based fuzzy hybrid decision making approach to soft computing. *IEEE Access, 7*, 15932–15944.

Dinçer, H., Hacıoğlu, Ü., & Yüksel, S. (2017). Balanced scorecard based performance measurement of European airlines using a hybrid multicriteria decision making approach under the fuzzy environment. *Journal of Air Transport Management, 63*, 17–33.

Dinçer, H., Hacıoğlu, Ü., & Yüksel, S. (2018). Evaluating the effects of economic imbalances on gold price in Turkey with MARS method and discussions on microfinance. In *Microfinance and its impact on entrepreneurial development, sustainability, and inclusive growth* (pp. 115–137). IGI Global.

Dinçer, H., Yüksel, S., Gökalp, Y., & Eti, S. (2021). SERVQUAL-based evaluation of service quality in Turkish health industry with fuzzy logic. *Interdisciplinary Perspectives on Operations Management and Service Evaluation*, 213–233.

Drori, I., Manos, R., Santacreu-Vasut, E., & Shoham, A. (2019). How does the global microfinance industry determine its targeting strategy across cultures with differing gender values?. *Journal of World Business*, 100985.

Fan, Y., John, K., Liu, F. H., & Tamanni, L. (2019). Security design, incentives, and Islamic microfinance: Cross country evidence. *Journal of International Financial Markets, Institutions and Money, 62*, 264–280.

Gerard, K., & Johnston, M. (2019). Explaining microfinance's resilience: The case of microfinance in Australia. *Globalizations, 16*(6), 876–893.

Gold, T. B. (2019). Becky Yang Hsu, borrowing together: Microfinance and cultivating social ties.

Golesorkhi, S., Mersland, R., Piekkari, R., Pishchulov, G., & Randøy, T. (2019). The effect of language use on the financial performance of microfinance banks: Evidence from cross-border activities in 74 countries. *Journal of World Business, 54*(3), 213–229.

Haile, H. B., Osman, I., Shuib, R., & Oon, S. W. (2015). Is there a convergence or divergence between feminist empowerment and microfinance institutions' success indicators? *Journal of International Development, 27*(7), 1042–1057.

Haiyun, C., Zhixiong, H., Yüksel, S., & Dinçer, H. (2021). Analysis of the innovation strategies for green supply chain management in the energy industry using the QFD-based hybrid interval valued intuitionistic fuzzy decision approach. *Renewable and Sustainable Energy Reviews, 143*, 110844.

Jun, Q., Dinçer, H., & Yüksel, S. (2021). Stochastic hybrid decision-making based on interval type 2 fuzzy sets for measuring the innovation capacities of financial institutions. *International Journal of Finance & Economics, 26*(1), 573–593.

Kassim, S. H., Kassim, S. N., & Othman, N. (2019). Islamic Microfinance in Malaysia: Issues and Challenges. In *Proceedings of the Second International Conference on the Future of ASEAN (ICoFA) 2017-Volume 1* (pp. 367–377). Springer.

Lacalle-Calderon, M., Larrú, J. M., Garrido, S. R., & Perez-Trujillo, M. (2019). Microfinance and income inequality: New macrolevel evidence. *Review of Development Economics, 23*(2), 860–876.

Li, L. Y., Hermes, N., & Meesters, A. (2019). Convergence of the performance of microfinance institutions: A decomposition analysis. *Economic Modelling, 81*, 308–324.

Li, Y. X., Wu, Z. X., Dinçer, H., Kalkavan, H., & Yüksel, S. (2021). Analyzing TRIZ-based strategic priorities of customer expectations for renewable energy investments with interval type-2 fuzzy modeling. *Energy Reports, 7*, 95–108.

Liu, Y., Gong, X., Yüksel, S., Dinçer, H., & Aydın, R. (2021). A multidimensional outlook to energy investments for the countries with continental shelf in East Mediterranean Region with hybrid decision making model based on IVIF logic. *Energy Reports, 7*, 158–173.

Mia, M. A., Lee, H. A., Chandran, V. G. R., Rasiah, R., & Rahman, M. (2019). History of microfinance in Bangladesh: A life cycle theory approach. *Business History, 61*(4), 703–733.

Morduch, J. (2000). The microfinance schism. *World Development, 28*(4), 617–629.

Möllmann, J., Buchholz, M., Kölle, W., & Musshoff, O. (2020). Do remotely-sensed vegetation health indices explain credit risk in agricultural microfinance?. *World Development, 127*, 104771.

Mushtaq, R., & Bruneau, C. (2019). Microfinance, financial inclusion and ICT: Implications for poverty and inequality. *Technology in Society, 59*, 101154.

Schulte, M., & Winkler, A. (2019). Drivers of solvency risk—Are microfinance institutions different? *Journal of Banking & Finance, 106*, 403–426.

Xie, Y., Zhou, Y., Peng, Y., Dinçer, H., Yüksel, S., & an Xiang, P. (2021). An extended pythagorean fuzzy approach to group decision-making with incomplete preferences for analyzing balanced scorecard-based renewable energy investments. *IEEE Access, 9*, 43020–43035.

Yang, F., Kalkavan, H., Dinçer, H., Yüksel, S., & Eti, S. (2021). Gaussian-based soft computing approach to alternative banking system for sustainable financial sector. *Complexity, 2021*.

Yas, M., Aslan, H., & Ozdemir, M. (2018). Modern history of Islamic finance and a strategic roadmap for its development in Turkey. In *Turkish Economy* (pp. 213–238). Palgrave Macmillan.

Yuan, G., Xie, F., Dinçer, H., & Yüksel, S. (2021). The theory of inventive problem solving (TRIZ)-based strategic mapping of green nuclear energy investments with spherical fuzzy group decision-making approach. *International Journal of Energy Research*.

Zamore, S., Beisland, L. A., & Mersland, R. (2019). Geographic diversification and credit risk in microfinance. *Journal of Banking & Finance, 109*, 105665.

Zhao, Y., Cheng, F., Yüksel, S., & Dinçer, H. (2021). Integer code series enhanced IT2 fuzzy decision support system with alpha cuts for the innovation adoption life cycle pattern recognition of renewable energy alternatives. *IEEE Access*.

Zhao, Y., Xu, Y., Yüksel, S., Dinçer, H., & Ubay, G. G. (2021). Hybrid IT2 fuzzy modelling with alpha cuts for hydrogen energy investments. *International Journal of Hydrogen Energy, 46*(13), 8835–8851.

Zhou, P., Luo, J., Cheng, F., Yüksel, S., & Dinçer, H. (2021). Analysis of risk priorities for renewable energy investment projects using a hybrid IT2 hesitant fuzzy decision-making approach with alpha cuts. *Energy, 224*, 120184.

CHAPTER 7

Efficiency of Microfinance Institutions and Financial Inclusion in West Bengal: A DEA Approach

Tarak Nath Sahu, CMA Sudarshan Maity, and Srimoyee Datta

INTRODUCTION

The Government considers the monetary inclusion program as an critical step to carry financially excluded human beings with inside the fold of formal monetary sectors (Maity & Sahu, 2021). To carry financially excluded human beings to the monetary inclusion institution, each principal and nation governments promoted microfinance establishments (MFIs). Microfinance thru MFI is an powerful tool for terrible human beings to get admission to monetary offerings with none collateral safety

---

T. N. Sahu
Department of Commerce, Vidyasagar University, Midnapore, West Bengal, India

C. Sudarshan Maity (✉)
Deputy Director, The Institute of Cost Accountants of India, 12, Sudder Street, Kolkata, West Bengal, India
e-mail: sudarshan.maity@gmail.com

© The Author(s), under exclusive license to Springer Nature Singapore Pte Ltd. 2022
R. C. Das (ed.), *Microfinance to Combat Global Recession and Social Exclusion*, https://doi.org/10.1007/978-981-16-4329-3_7

and enhance their trendy of residing. The escalating social and monetary improvement war confronted via way of means of sure financially excluded populace international nowadays raised new questions in addition to expectancies approximately social duties and roles of monetary establishments lively globally. There are versions of monetary establishments to cater the want as consistent with requirement however in sure regions or among sure populace agencies conventional varieties of Financial Institutions (FIs) couldn't penetrate. The motives can be because of operating patterns, organizational structure, regulatory policies, notion in the direction of the groups etc. In this context, a unique form of FIs i.e., MFIs was given get admission to and helps the formal financially excluded institution to be protected with inside the mainstream. The primary targets of microfinance that distinguish it from the preceding modes of credit score shipping are small quantities of loan, loss of bodily safety however highlighting on social safety or peer tracking and recognition on girls borrowers. The reason of an MFI is to offer finance to folks that aren't protected. It might be secure to mention that monetary inclusion now will become a customary time table and microfinance's function in it's miles an eminent one. The Asian Development Bank initiated method 2020 for sustainable monetary increase, developing a high quality surroundings for monetary inclusion, decorate MSMEs for making poverty unfastened Asia and Pacific. Apart from that, different tasks like monetary literacy campaign, creation of agent device, schooling program, technology-pushed device, social sports had been carried out via way of means of diverse monetary establishments to make monetary inclusion greater viable. But still, the monetary inclusion fame stays challenging. Now the overall performance of MFI is wanted to evaluate as it's miles without delay related with the effectiveness and destiny angle of the focused populations or economy. India has been taken into consideration as the largest rising marketplace for MFIs (Ferdousi, 2013). From 2004 onwards, in conjunction with the Reserve Bank of India and the Government greater specific, centered and custom designed method has been observed in India to decorate micro-monetary sports. In case of MFIs, sustainability and methods of operation pass hand on hand. This

---

S. Datta
Department of Business Administration, Sidho Kanho Birsha University, Purulia, West Bengal, India

results in the inducement to head similarly and try and recognize wherein quantity the MFIs are acting with inside the economy. Our nation, West Bengal is in a mild function in phrases of outreach and penetration of micro-monetary sports even though the call for is high. There are 38 MFIs working on this nation as consistent with the Association of Microfinance Institution (AMI), West Bengal. Considering the function of MFIs in micro-monetary sports, researchers have approached the lively MFIs on this nation and their performance size to decide their contribution in the direction of monetary inclusion. As the overall performance of MFIs is blended with each quantitative and qualitative measures so a non-parametric check is needed on this case. Data Envelopment Analysis (DEA) is used to degree the performance degree of choice Decision making Units (DMUs). There are sure enter and output variables decided on this examine for studying performance of MFIs in the direction of monetary inclusion which might be lively in West Bengal for 3 consecutive years.

Literature Review

Microfinance is an effective device for sustainable enlargement and assists in accomplishing inclusive increase via way of means of developing dynamic employment, lowering gender and geography distinction which cause the enlargement of the economy, thereby contributing to the increase of the economy (Sahu & Datta, 2017; and Datta & Sahu, 2018). Microfinance has tiled the manner to create a center for inclusive increase via way of means of figuring out and digital the excellent practices and fashions which are low in cost and sustainable.

Pandey (2008) in his a examine entitled microfinance gives extra promise and potential to cope with poverty as it's miles centered on constructing social capital thru supplying get admission to monetary carrier. In a examine, Pillai and Nadarajan (2010) recommended that microfinance has delivered higher social empowerment and mental than monetary empowerment. Further, in any other examine, Tenaw and Islam (2009) have located that microfinance performs a totally crucial function in enhancing and keeping a trendy of rural human beings in Bangladesh and Ethiopia. The monetary device that becomes originated via way of means of the neighborhood populace proved a high quality device in selling self-assist and independence. The predominant downside of this domestically originated monetary device becomes the guidelines and regulations. The predominant region of earnings in Bangladesh and Ethiopia is agriculture, however, depending on infrastructure, unreliable climate, and terrible technology, small and fragile marketplace creates troubles with inside the improvement of this region. Microfinance is the handiest approach thru which this trouble may be overcome. When the agriculture region will become strong in those countries, poverty might be removed mechanically. Further, Anuradha and Ganesan (2010) of their examine concluded that microfinance now advanced into an critical shipping tool for attaining the terrible and reaching monetary inclusion. Swain and Nayak (2008) have located that the failure of formal credit score establishments in assembly the credit score wishes agricultural terrible has been the main purpose for the innovation in micro-financing. To enhance the same old of residing of the terrible and the downtrodden, the idea of microfinance has been initiated. Bargal (2016) has proven how microfinance has helped in growing the slum regions in Indore, a town located with inside the nation of Madhya Pradesh in India.

So in this regards overall performance fame of those establishments gambling an critical function with inside the monetary improvement of a nation. Performance size has unique processes in unique literatures from time to time. The overall performance size of MFIs isn't the same as different establishments because it has the particular nature of handling each monetary and social performances (Gutiérrez-Nieto et al., 2009). So, literature approximately performance size of MFIs both entails SFA (Stochastic Frontier Analysis) or DEA approach (Haq et al., 2010; Hermes et al., 2011; Oteng-Abayie et al., 2011). According to Oteng-Abayie et al. (2011), SFA has been implemented to a hundred thirty five MFIs of Ghana to discover the monetary performance attractive 4 years of facts. It has been located that the monetary performance of the chosen MFIs is depending on mobilizing and high-satisfactory of carrier in conjunction with different parameters like value consistent with borrower, diverse financial savings product, heightens the quantity of social commitments etc. In the examine of Haq et al. (2010), 39 microfinance establishments had been taken into consideration for performance checks the usage of DEA. The end result indicates that non-governmental establishments are green in phrases of poverty comfort in conjunction with monetary sustainability. Studies had been completed incorporating DEA evaluation for overall performance size of MFIs on global (Bassem, 2008; Hassan & Sanchez, 2009) in addition to the country wide foundation with diverse enter and output variables. In unique literatures, unique factors have an impact on the monetary and social performance of MFIs. Keeping all of the mistakes in attention it's been located that the dimensions of MFIs may have a bad impact on performance (Bassem, 2008), someday it is able to be the age of MFIs (Widiarto & Emrouznejad, 2015), outreach (Hermes et al., 2011) or now no longer generating enough outputs (Hassan & Sanchez, 2009). On the alternative hand, research on universal MFIs working in India also is available (Kar & Deb, 2017; Singh et al., 2014). With the utility of 3 enter and 3 output variables twenty MFIs had been analyzed and ranked accordingly. This end result throws mild at the variables that can have an impact on performance in the direction of positivity in destiny (Singh et al., 2014). Considering facts of thirty Indian MFIs for 7 years it's been located that they may be greater technically green via way of means of dealing with their unproductive output (Kar & Deb, 2017).

The above literatures support the statement that assessment of efficiency measurement especially in case of MFIs is different from the traditional one (Zerai & Rani, 2012). So while considering efficiency measurement of MFIs, selective variables have been chosen to reflect outreach and financial sustainability simultaneously. Different literatures consider different input–output variables (Hermes et al., 2011; Singh et al., 2014; Widiarto & Emrouznejad, 2015). The analysis reflects the different elements responsible for efficiency or inefficiency of the particular MFIs and leads the way to future improvement.

Objectives of the Study

The performance of any institution is often evaluated in terms of its efficiency in the use of its resources (Maity & Sahu, 2017; Saha & Ravisankar, 2000). This study tries to capture efficiency level related to financial inclusion of the existing MFIs which are active in West Bengal. Depending on the performance level efficiency of each MFI can be predicted for the selected region. The specific objective as follows:

- To investigate the overall technical efficiency in terms of financial inclusion of active MFIs operated in West Bengal.
- To classify the inefficient MFIs and further to rank the MFIs according to their efficiency level.
- To investigate the trend of efficiency scores of MFIs.

Based on the previous discussion and research objectives, the following testable hypotheses are developed for the study.

Hypothesis (H_{01}): The ranks and efficiency scores of MFIs are not normally distributed.

Hypothesis (H_{02}): There is no significant difference in efficiency scores between the period of study.

Research Methodology

Sample Design

The study concentrates only on those MFIs which are operating in West Bengal during last three financial years (2016–17 to 2018–19) consecutively. There are total of 38 registered MFIs. Out of them, 11 MFIs are active in last three financial years with the selective variables. These MFIs are Ashirvad Microfinance Ltd.; Arohan Financial Services Ltd.; Annapurna Microfinance Pvt. Ltd.; Belgharia Jana Kalyan Samity (BJKS); Uttarayan Financial Services Pvt. Ltd.; Sarala Women Welfare Society; Satin Credit Care Network Ltd.; Grameen Shakti Microfinance Services Pvt. Ltd.; Fusion Microfinance Pvt. Ltd.; Spandana Sphoorty Financial Ltd.; and Muthoot Microfin Ltd.

Methodology

Efficiency is the ratio between an output and the factors that made it possible. In the present study, researchers have applied DEA under CCR (Charnes, Cooper and Rhodes) model. Here researchers have considered two input and two output models. DEA has been carried out with three years of average data under study period from 2016–17 to 2018–19. DEA approach using CCR model is applied for homogeneous units (rather than organizations). The outputs of an organization depend on many extraneous factors and they are not within our control. Setting targets for outputs, therefore, is not feasible. Hence, input-oriented constant return to scale (CCR model) measuring the overall technical efficiency (OTE) was found more feasible (Maity, 2020; Maity & Sahu, 2020).

Further, Shapiro Wilk test rather than Kolmogorov—Smirnov test is used to check normality of efficiency ranks and efficiency scores (for <50 samples). Further, Friedman test and Wilcoxon signed-rank test are used to compare between the period of study and pair-wise comparison respectively. Other than above, other tests like mean, medium, quartile values, standard deviation etc. have been determined.

Input and Output Variable

The specifications are selected so that financial inclusion measures such as sustainability and outreach are included. To fulfill the objective of the study, researchers have considered two output variables both from supply side and demand side. The study considered number of branches and numbers of borrowers as outputs. Input variables include, finance cost (i.e., interest expenses on borrowings and other) and employee cost (i.e., employee benefit expenses of the MFI).

Analysis of Results

Many MFIs are currently working to attain the desired goal and to reach the mission to outreach people. Microfinance is to provide basic facilities of financial services to increase productivity, earning capacity and employment rate. Microfinance will have much impact on people by reducing poverty, and other social impacts. Descriptive statistics of the variables are presented in Table 7.1. Researchers have also run Pearson Correlation among all variables to check assumptions of "isotonicity" relationship. And the results satisfy isotonicity test due to positive correlations among all (Table 7.1).

MFIs are categorized as efficient whose technical efficiency (TE) score is 100% and whose TE score <100% those MFIs are termed as inefficient. To classify inefficient MFIs this study uses quartile values of OTE scores obtained from CCR model (Maity & Sahu, 2018). By applying the quartile values researchers have classified them into 4 categories viz., marginally inefficient, above average, below average and most inefficient. If efficiency score varies from third quartile value to <100%, the MFI concerned is taken as moderately efficient or marginally inefficient. If efficiency score varies from median value to < third quartile value, the MFI concerned is taken as above average. Following this, if efficiency score varies from first quartile value to < median value, the MFI concerned is taken as below average. We have identified an MFI as most inefficient if its technical score is < first quartile value.

Table 7.2 presents efficiency scores of the eleven selected MFIs and

Table 7.1 Descriptive statistics and correlation matrix among the variables (2016–17 to 2018–19)

MFI	Finance cost (₹)	Employee cost (₹)	Active borrowers	Branch
Ashirvad	2,136,347,000	903,657,333	1,500,582	846
Arohan	1,586,521,256	767,971,601	1,206,813	433
Annapurna	1,785,501,418	869,090,448	4,507,909	265
BJKS	47,632,021	21,888,364	28,508	26
Uttarayan	167,180,291	56,408,050	124,644	73
Sarala	120,949,789	50,782,928	130,463	66
Satin Creditcare	5,372,258,198	2,275,897,404	1,718,333	725
Grameen Shakti	5,481,645	4,318,450	10,373	8
Fusion	1,594,162,632	1,012,982,717	1,103,357	368
Spandana	2,553,296,125	4,780,325,764	1,085,300	1025
Muthoot	899,592,142	1,052,481,075	1,190,107	474
Mean	1,478,992,956	1,072,345,830	1,146,035	392
Minimum	5,481,645	4,318,450	10,373	8
Maximum	5,372,258,198	4,780,325,764	4,507,909	1025
Std. Deviation	1,580,613,755	1,402,991,308	1,279,836	351
Finance Cost	1			
Employee Cost	0.6433	1		
Active borrowers	0.4644	0.232	1	
Branch	0.7463	0.84	0.3108	1

Source Authors' Calculation based on AMIs' information

their classification. Among the sample MFIs, Annapurna and Grameen Shakti are efficient with 100% efficiency scores. According to quartile values, Sarala is marginally inefficient or moderately efficient ones among the sample MFIs. Uttarayan, BJKS and Muthoot are above average; Ashirvad, Arohan and Fusion are below average; whereas Satin Creditcare and Spandana are most inefficient.

Table 7.2 also demonstrates benchmark and ranking of efficient and inefficient MFIs. Ranking for efficient MFIs has given based on benchmark no. of another DMU. Benchmark DMUs are those whose TE is highest. The first rank of efficient MFI is given to Grameen Shakti with a maximum of 9 times and second rank to Annapurna with 7 times. Ranking for inefficient MFIs has been given based on efficiency score. Accordingly, Satin Creditcare is most inefficient MFI and ranked eleventh among the selected MFIs consider in this study. Further, Sarala is the least inefficient after the benchmark and ranked third.

Table 7.2 MFI-wise efficiency scores with their classification and ranking (2016–17 to 2018–19)

DMU	2016–19 CCR model—input	Benchmark	Times as benchmark	Rank	2016–17 CCR model	2017–18 CCR model	2018–19 CCR model
Annapurna	1.0000	Annapurna	7	II	0.4140	1.0000	0.4636
Arohan	0.4510	Annapurna; Grameen Shakti	–	VIII	0.5802	0.3696	0.6449
Ashirvad	0.5831	Annapurna; Grameen Shakti	–	VII	0.6474	0.5192	0.6452
BJKS	0.6412	Grameen Shakti	–	V	0.7693	0.5997	0.5440
Fusion	0.3094	Annapurna; Grameen Shakti	–	IX	0.2135	0.3626	0.5887
Grameen Shakti	1.0000	Grameen Shakti	9	I	1.0000	1.0000	1.0000
Muthoot	0.6075	Annapurna; Grameen Shakti	–	VI	0.4145	0.3487	0.4787
Sarala	0.8577	Annapurna; Grameen Shakti	–	III	0.8475	0.8384	1.0000
Satin Creditcare	0.2316	Annapurna; Grameen Shakti	–	XI	0.2444	0.2052	0.3617
Spandana	0.2752	Grameen Shakti	–	X	0.6094	0.5338	0.5701
Uttarayan	0.7894	Annapurna; Grameen Shakti	–	IV	0.8193	0.7264	0.9899
Average	0.6133				0.5963	0.5912	0.6625
Efficient MFIs	2				1	2	2
1st Quartile	0.3094						
Median	0.6075						
3rd Quartile	0.8577						

Notes RTS = Returns to Scale; CRS = Constant Returns to Scale; DRS = Decreasing Returns to Scale
Source Authors' calculation

This study further suggests that Sarala has a scope of producing 1.17 times (i.e., 1/0.8577) and Satin Creditcare has 4.32 times (i.e., 1/0.2316). Alternatively, the same interpretation of rest inefficient MFIs can be extended. The connotation of this finding is that the magnitude of OTE in selected MFIs is to the tune of 38.67% (1−0.6133). This suggests that, by adopting best practice technology, MFIs can, on average, reduce their inputs of finance cost and employee cost by at least 38.67% and still generate the identical level of outputs. However, the potential reduction in inputs from adopting best practices varies from MFI to MFI. OTE scores among the inefficient MFI range from 0.2316 for Satin Creditcare to 0.8577 for Sarala. This indicates Satin Creditcare and Sarala can potentially reduce their input by 76.84 and 14.13% respectively. The study finds that among the 11 MFIs, four MFIs are operating below 50% efficiency level and five MFIs are between 50% to below 100%.

The results of Shapiro—Wilk test specify that, MFIs efficiency scores follow a normal distribution ($p > 0.05$). In second part of Table 7.2 presents the OTE scores for 2016–17, 2017–18 and 2018–19 to understand the trend and MFIs working at an efficient level during these periods toward financial inclusion. Among the 11 MFIs, only Grameen Shakti is efficient in 2016–17, while Annapurna and Grameen Shakti are efficient in 2017–18. Further, Grameen Shakti and Sarala are efficient in 2018–19. So Grameen Shakti running efficiently throughout the years of study. Average efficiency scores increased from 0.5963 (2016–17) to 0.6625 (2018–19). This indicates that overall their performances are improving. Though, they have scope to increase TE by 1.01% (Uttarayan i.e., 1−0.9899) to 83.83% (Satin Creditcare i.e., 1−0.3617).

Researchers have further compared the TE scores between 2016–17, 2017–18 and 2018–19. The mean rank decreases from 2.18 in 2016–17, to 1.55 in 2017–18 and then to 2.55 in 2018–19. Further, Friedman test reveals efficiency scores of 2016–17, 2017–18 and 2018–19 are not same as $\chi^2 = 6.200$ which is significant as the p-value <0.05 (Table 7.3).

Although the result suggests that there is at least one statistically significant change between the three years, it does not tell us where the difference lies. To find the significant change between any two years, three Wilcoxon signed-rank tests need to be performed for the pairs of 2016–17, 2017–18 and 2018–19.

The null hypothesis is that there is no significant change from one-time point to another. The result as presented in Table 7.3 indicates that

Table 7.3 Detailed results of Friedman test and Wilcoxon signed-rank tests

Total N	11		
Test statistic	6.2		
Degrees of freedom	2		
Asymptotic Sig. (2-sided test)	0.045*		
Pair-wise combinations	Z		Asymp. Sig. (2-tailed)
Y_2-Y_1	−1.539		0.124
Y_3-Y_1	−0.973		0.331
Y_3-Y_2	−2.251		0.024*

Note *Significance level is 5%
Source Authors' calculation

Asymp. Sig. (2-tailed) value for Y_3-Y_2 is 0.024 (i.e., *p*-value) i.e., significantly differ from 2017–18 to 2018–19 (Y_3-Y_2) at 5% significance level, as the *p*-value <0.05. The results are insignificant in respect of the other two combinations (Y_2-Y_1 and Y_3-Y_1).

The strategy matrix of DEA identifies those DMUs which need to be closed down. Benchmark DMUs are those, whose technical efficiency is highest i.e., Annapurna and Grameen Shakti are the benchmarks that fall under the benchmark DMUs group. And further, Satin Creditcare, Spandana and Fusion are the problem DMUs with low profit which resulted in low efficiency. It must be noted that the problem DMUs are not the ones that need to be closed down. Rather these are the DMUs that, with management interventions, can be potentially increasing their performance (Maity et al., 2020).

Discussion

Based on factual analysis the study finds that among the selected eleven MFIs, two are efficient (technically) and one is moderately efficient. Further, three MFIs are above average, three MFIs are below average and two MFIs are most inefficient. Other than the two efficient MFIs, the rest nine MFIs have a scope of producing more output than the present level. During 2016–17 the selected MFIs operating at 59.63% efficiency level, whereas in 2017–18 they operate at 59.12% and in 2018–19 they operating at 66.25% level. This concludes that overall they enhance their performance. Though the level of mean efficiency scores during the study period, not at a significant level. To achieve their target, MFIs must have collective strategies beyond micro-credit to empower the poverty-stricken. The result of Friedman test shows there is significant difference in mean ranks between 2016–17, 2017–18 and 2018–19. The study further indicates year 2017–18 and 2018–19 are significantly different. With mean value of these two years, we found positive growth of efficiency level from 2017–18 to 2018–19.

The efficiency scores explicit that the MFIs operating in West Bengal have a larger scope to enhance output level. These additional outputs if achieved will help to escalate financial inclusion status which ultimately will help to uplift Gross State Domestic Product. Among the 11 DMUs, two are efficient i.e., these two have no benchmark, whereas rest nine have a benchmark. So these nine inefficient MFIs should follow their benchmark to improve technical efficiency level. According to DEA strategy matrix, Satin Creditcare, Spandana and Fusion are the problem DMUs. Further, Annapurna and Grameen Shakti are the benchmarks of the rest nine inefficient MFIs. The problem DMUs needs intervention to upgrade their efficiency level at per benchmark.

The present Indian economic scenario shows a fall in real GDP. To avoid this recession there may be a requirement in an increase of aggregate demand of consumer spending, investment, etc. In the Indian context, as a large share of the population is living in a rural-based Indian region, microfinance has a great role in this region by providing tiny finance for escalating socio-economic development. The demand for investment and consumer spending can be improved in rural-based Indian regions by the escalating number of MFIs' loan borrowers and their operational points. So, while efficiency will improve, the economy of the region and social development will also improve.

Conclusion and Recommendations

To accelerate the economic growth rate, investment and savings are two pillars. Increasing credit necessities have emphasized more on the mobilization of deposits. But inculcation of financial habit among households is to be the ultimate priority. Therefore, to cover most households into bank ambit, an innovation of products and processes must be ensured worldwide (Maity & Sahu, 2021). It is needless to say that DEA is a wonderful method for benchmarking and for computing efficiency of DMUs. This study investigates OTE by using DEA of MFIs operating in West Bengal, India. DEA has been used as an efficiency measurement tool of MFIs with respect to service provision and branch coverage. Based on the DEA model (under CRS assumptions), the results on efficiency measures observed that two MFIs are efficient and rest sample MFIs are inefficient. All these inefficient MFIs have the scope of producing more output i.e., they have a scope of expansion of more branches and enhancement of more borrower so that financial inclusion may be achieved and their efficiency level also maximize. To conclude, it may be said that the fulfillment of social objectives thrust on the MFIs, may be the root cause of inefficiency of the MFIs. However, due to enormous differences in efficient and most inefficient MFIs from 14.2 to 76.8% level, it is suggested the inefficient MFIs adopt all such measures which are applying by the benchmark. This will increase their efficiency level which ultimately enhances their financial performance and financial stability and escalate socio-economic development. It has been postulated that by making policy toward income generation and development, ultimately to eradicate poverty and improve the health status through time.

References

Anuradha, P. S., & Ganesan, G. (2010). Sustainable development and fostering inclusive growth through microfinance in the Indian economy. *Indian Journal of Finance, 4*, 3–7.

Bargal, P. (2016). Effectiveness of microfinance in development os slum areas of Indore. The thesis submitted to the Department of Commerce, Vidyasagar University. https://shodhganga.inflibnet.ac.in

Bassem, B. S. (2008). Efficiency of microfinance institutions in the Mediterranean: An application of DEA. *Transition Studies Review, 15*(2), 343–354.

Datta, S., & Sahu, T. N. (2018). Role of microfinance institutions on the empowerment of female borrowers: Evidence from West Bengal. *The Journal of Indian Management & Strategy, 23*(1), 32–39.

De Crombrugghe, A., Tenikue, M., & Sureda, J. (2008). Performance analysis for a sample of microfinance institutions in India. *Annals of Public and Cooperative Economics, 79*(2), 269–299.

Ferdousi, F. (2013). Performance of microfinance institutions in Asia: DEA based efficiency analysis. In *International conference on the Modern Development of Humanities and Social Science* (MDHSS 2013) (pp. 91–94). Atlantis Press.

Gutiérrez-Nieto, B., Serrano-Cinca, C., & Mar Molinero, C. (2009). Social efficiency in microfinance institutions. *Journal of the Operational Research Society, 60*(1), 104–119.

Haq, M., Skully, M., & Pathan, S. (2010). Efficiency of microfinance institutions: A data envelopment analysis. *Asia-Pacific Financial Markets, 17*(1), 63–97.

Hassan, K. M., & Sanchez, B. (2009). *Efficiency analysis of microfinance institutions in developing countries* (Networks Financial Institute Working Paper).

Hermes, N., Lensink, R., & Meesters, A. (2011). Outreach and efficiency of microfinance institutions. *World Development, 39*(6), 938–948.

Kar, S., & Deb, J. (2017). Efficiency determinants of microfinance institutions in India: Two stage DEA analysis. *The Central European Review of Economics and Management, 1*(4), 87–116.

Maity, S. (2020). Are private sector banks really more efficient than public sector banks?—A comparative analysis using DEA. *NMIMS Management Review, 38*(2), 82–92.

Maity, S., & Sahu, T. N. (2017). Pre-merger performance measures of State Bank of India and its associate banks using data envelopment analysis. *Business Spectrum, 7*(2), 16–26.

Maity, S., & Sahu, T. N. (2018). Role of public and private sector banks in financial inclusion in India—An empirical investigation using DEA. *SCMS Journal of Indian Management, 15*(4), 62–73.

Maity, S., & Sahu, T. N. (2020). Role of public sector banks towards financial inclusion during pre and post introduction of PMJDY: A study on efficiency review. *Rajagiri Management Journal, 14*(2), 95–105.

Maity, S., Sahu, T. N., & Biswas, D. (2020). Assessing efficiency of private sector banks in India—An empirical investigation using DEA. *International Journal of Financial Services Management, 10*(2), 138–155.

Maity, S., & Sahu, T. N. (2021). How far the Indian banking sectors are efficient?: An empirical investigation. *Asian Journal of Economics and Banking.* https://doi.org/10.1108/AJEB-02-2021-0016

Oteng-Abayie, E. F., Amanor, K., & Frimpong, J. M. (2011). The measurement and determinants of economic efficiency of microfinance institutions in Ghana: A stochastic frontier approach. *African Review of Economics and Finance, 2*(2), 149–166.

Pandey, D. P. (2008). Inclusive financing through microfinance. *Indian Journal of Finance, 1*, 8–12.

Pillai, T., & Nadarajan, S. (2010). Impact of microfinance—An empirical study on the attitude of SHG leaders in Kanyakumari District—Tamil Nadu. *International Journal of Enterprise and Innovation Management Studies, 1*(3), 89–95.

Saha, A., & Ravisankar, T. S. (2000). Rating of Indian commercial banks: A DEA approach. *European Journal of Operational Research, 124*, 187–203.

Sahu, T. N., & Datta, S. (2017). An empirical study on the impact of microfinance on women empowerment: Evidence from West Bengal. *Indian Journal of Commerce & Management Studies., 8*(3), 53–62.

Singh, R., Mahapatra, B., Mukherjee, K., & Bhar, C. (2014). Application of DEA for performance evaluation of Indian microfinance institutions. *Asian Journal of Management Research, 4*(3), 597–605.

Swain, K., & Nayak, G. (2008). *Micro credit through SHGs*. New Century Publications.

Tenaw, S., & Islam, K. M. Z. (2009). *Rural financial services and effects of micro-finance on agricultural productivity and on poverty* (Discussion Papers Series) (pp. 1–28). University of Helsinki Department of Economics and Management.

Widiarto, I., & Emrouznejad, A. (2015). Social and financial efficiency of Islamic microfinance institutions: A data envelopment analysis application. *Socio-Economic Planning Sciences, 50*, 1–17.

Zerai, B., & Rani, L. (2012). Is there a trade-off between outreach and sustainability of micro finance institutions? Evidence from Indian microfinance institutions (MFIs). *European Journal of Business and Management, 4*(2), 90–98.

CHAPTER 8

Effects of Financial Widening Activities on Self-Employment Opportunities in Nigeria: Implications on Global Recession and Social Exclusion

Ezebuilo Romanus Ukwueze and Henry Thomas Asogwa

Introduction

Financial inclusion has been adjudged a very important policy framework both developing and developed countries. It is because it provides access to, use of available and affordable, financial services and products to those poor, the underserved, the unbanked, individuals, households, and businesses. There has been a growing consensus that when the youths increase

---

E. R. Ukwueze
Department of Economics, University of Nigeria, Nsukka, Nigeria
e-mail: ezebuilo.ukwueze@unn.edu.ng

H. T. Asogwa (✉)
Institute for Development Studies, University of Nigeria, Enugu Campus, Nsukka, Nigeria
e-mail: henry.asogwa@unn.edu.ng

access to and use of financial products and services and providing the opportunity for them to use these services and products would change their future life needs and would transform their chances for employment and better livelihoods (Sykes et al., 2016). Financial inclusion can also cover the financially included youth by providing access to and use of formal financial services and other mobile money facilities, banks, microfinance institutions, and insurance companies. There could be other sources of finance which are not formal which could also be available to people to make use of. These may include village money lenders, pawn shops, village savings and loan association, the *isusu* saving strategies, etc. Triki and Faye (2013) assert that informal financial mechanisms are critical resources for millions of adults and youth globally, especially in Africa.

Financial inclusion may be assessed by the quality and nature of its products and services available to people. Many communities, particularly in remote and rural areas, have resorted to relying on other informal financial services because either that accessibility to or affordability of their formal services are difficulty or they are totally absent. There seems to be a growing consensus that accessibility to and use of informal financial services, like village saving and loan associations (*isusu*), etc., would provide a leeway to added to the formal financial services. However, there is evidence, both in the development parlance and in the literature, that because informal services are more limited in scope, expensive, and insecure, they cannot be assumed to capable of facilitating the process of full financial inclusion (Sykes et al., 2016: 4).

It has been shown that developing countries, especially Africa, lag behind other regions in the development and management of financial services. Available data from the Global Findex shows that estimate of youths (aged 15–24) who have account with banking institution is 46%, which is very low as compared with adults (aged 25 and above) with 66%. The data also shows that only 5% of youths have ever borrowed from these institutions while adults are about 12%, globally. These data show that in sub-Saharan countries about 20% youths have account with financial institutions whereas 33% of adults have account; similarly, only 3% of youths have ever borrowed from formal sources of financial services, compared with 8% adults. This exposition implies that the youths have no full access to and use of financial services, especially in SSA (sub-Saharan Africa) and most of other less developed countries.

The ILO has a robust hobby in gaining a better view and clearer perception on the linkage among children monetary inclusion and employment consequences, as employment advent is an important task in the 4 pillars of its "respectable work" targets, which is embedded into Goal eight of the United Nations 2030 Agenda for Sustainable Development (Sykes et al., 2016). Unfortunately, even though an increasing number of identified in studies circles, the linkage among children monetary inclusion and employments consequences is presently now no longer sufficiently well-documented. To ILO, worldwide children unemployment charges have remained consistently excessive at thirteen according to cent in 2014 (ILO, 2015) and ought to be better with the aid of using now because of worldwide pandemic which has ravaged the world.

In Nigeria, numerous efforts were made by the government to improve economic inclusion through some of public-quarter-led loan schemes and poverty comfort programs inclusive of the Microfinance Institutions (MFIs); Subsidy Reinvestment and Empowerment Programme or SURE-P; National Economy Reconstruction Fund (NERFUND); Community Banking Models, the Bank of Industry (BOI); Youth Enterprise with Innovation in Nigeria (YouWin) Programme; National Poverty Eradication Programme; the People's Bank; the Small and Medium Enterprises Equity Investment Scheme (SMEEIS); National Enterprise Development Programme (NEDEP), and numerous others (Njoku & Odumeru, 2013; Raimi, 2017; Siano et al., 2020).

In 2012, the government of Nigerian made a specific dedication to improving economic inclusion withinside the country through its country wide economic inclusive strategic plan. The fundamental goal of this plan is to lessen the wide variety of adults who cannot get entry to economic provider withinside the economy from 46.3 to 20% and boom the formal sector's percentage of economic inclusion from 30 to 70% with the aid of using the year 2020 (Babajide et al., 2020). The record also shows that the percentage of Nigerian adults not included in the financial system which was 36.9% in 2014 rose to 40.1% in 2016, due to the substantial decline of contributions of MFIs as a result of economic downturn experienced in the economy in 2016. This figure averaged 36.8% in 2018 as the economy started recovering. The percentages of financial system's share of inclusive program stood at 30%, 36.3%, 38.3%, and 39.6%, in 2010, 2014, 2016, and 2018, respectively, due to the steadfastness of deposit money banks and their drive to improve inclusive motive throughout the period of downturn (CBN, 2018; EFINA, 2018).

Several attempts have been made at reducing exclusion in financial system through efforts to build, expand, and introduce new banking policies into the system. For example, a rural banking program, which was introduced in 1977, made it compulsory for the money deposit banks in Nigeria to extend branches rural areas, and from then several policies and programs were introduced and implemented, including, the People's Bank, which was meant to take banking services closer to people. Further, government introduced community banking system which were should be owned by community members, and to be able to function effectively, were supported by the Government, in 1990; other policies like bank reforms of 2005, massive financial literacy campaign by Central Bank of Nigeria (CBN), an electronic payment system, and cashless policy, and framework for mobile banking, approved an agent banking scheme, and putting in place a financial service consumer protection policy, which were implemented to ensure financial inclusion.

In spite of these efforts, there are still failures to achieve the objectives of the efforts and plans because of weak institutional framework, the government's failure to properly nurture its development programs, dysfunctional structures, endemic poor program implementation, and weak reward system (Amuda & Embi, 2013; Ihugba et al., 2014; Raimi, 2017; Rjoub et al., 2017). In 2000s, Nigeria's adoption of mobile banking emerged; this was made possible by information technology (IT)-driven innovative technology, and the use of mobile phones and other internet-based gadgets, which greatly improved the degree of financial inclusiveness in Africa (Asuming et al., 2019).

This has created a rift between the supply of funds to unbanked, unserved, and underserved individuals, households and businesses who would utilize these funds and create jobs for themselves and others, hence this study. This study aims at estimating the effects of financial widening activities (inclusion) on self-employment opportunities in Nigeria.

Literature Review

Some scholars like Dupas and Robinson (2009) and Caskey et al. (2006), applying household data, show that having access to financial products and facilities such as credits, savings and payments are likely to influence and improve greatly the poor people's lives and welfare. It has been asserted that financial deepening has a lot of impact on poverty alleviation and structural transformation in developing countries (Beck,

2016). Demirguc-Kunt and Levine (2009) and other researchers have developed models to show where exclusion from financial services shapes the dynastic transmission of investment opportunities, human capital, and wealth, which eventually produce persistence inequality.

Financial inclusion is capable of influencing entrepreneurial ability of individuals, which affects inequality and income distribution (Banerjee & Newman, 1993; Piketty, 1997, 2000). As a result of imperfection in markets for financial services, and in the face of fixed nature of costs of being entrepreneurs, the distribution of wealth determines who can obtain finance from external sources and startup businesses. The initial distribution of income and wealth determines the distribution of income and total output in future. Imperfections in financial market permeate hindrances and obstacles of becoming an entrepreneur, thus leading to higher inequality in income and increasing poverty. Low income and wealth prohibit entrepreneurship, thus continuing the dynasty of poverty (low-income level) and thereby reducing overall level of efficiency in the economy.

The unique channels through which economic inclusion can have an effect on inclusive boom relies upon on some of factors, such as the extent of economic development, documentation, infrastructure, location (rural or city dwellers), and fees (Fowowe & Folarin, 2019; IFC, 2011).

First, financial inclusion allows in facilitating financial transactions. Households dwelling in far flung or rural regions or regions bereft of fee offerings and in lots of cases, they need to journey lengthy distances to get admission to such offerings. This imposes a number of expenses in multiple ways, namely touring expenses, time expenses; and some concerns about protection. Furthermore, in lots of such cases, such expenses and protection problems discourage such people and families from having access to economic offerings, thereby inhibiting financial activities. Second, economic inclusiveness helps families in enhancing their welfare. Access to financial widening facilitates openings for families to get admission to education, housing products, and health care, thereby enhancing better life for them. Third, economic inclusion allows to guard families in opposition to vulnerabilities. Poor families are especially at risk of vulnerabilities, shocks, and vicissitudes of changes in household conditions, such as theft, illness, and get admission to economic offerings consisting of financial savings, credit score, and coverage assist to mitigate those shocks (Fowowe & Folarin, 2019). Fourth, and carefully associated with the preceding channel, economic inclusion can assist families to resist volatility and unpredictability in earnings. Most rural dwellers are characterized by seasonal earnings, with swings in their earnings, which negatively affecting their welfare. Availability of credits and savings, due to prevalence of economic inclusion, allows families to smooth consumption, hence enhancing their welfare. Above all, financial inclusion facilitates entrepreneurship within the household and creates opportunities for productivity-enhancing investments. In addition to having savings and obtaining credit for household use, the financial products and services could also an also be directed and put to investment in productive assets, thus generating employment, income, and boosting inclusive economic growth.

It has been acknowledged by some scholars that use of and access to financial products and services are sources of and agents to the development of (MSMEs) globally (Beck & Honohan, 2009; Godwin, 2011; Onaolapo & Odetayo, 2012; Pallavi & Bharti, 2013; Stephen & Sibert, 2014). The Nigerian apex bank identifies the act of microfinance in providing financial admittance to the operators of MSMEs that are generally omitted from or incompetently aided by the existing financial institutions (Ibor et al., 2017).

In a study of the linkage between financial inclusion and agent banking in Kenya, using descriptive survey research method, Waihenya (2012) investigated the factors facilitating financial exclusion, with emphasis on both human-caused barriers like limited access due to limited bank branches, natural barriers such as rough terrains and high charges on financial services. This researcher found that agent banking is continuously growing and improving the level of financial inclusion. Comparing financial inclusion in the UK and Nigeria, Ibeachu (2010), using survey questionnaires for data collection, found that economic inclusion was more market driven when customer satisfaction and consumer behavior are of interest.

Also, Bertram et al. (2016) employed questionnaires distributed to banks, regulators, insurance, and Telecom firms to collect data on financial inclusion and asserted that inclusion people financially is fundamental for inclusive economic growth and development of Nigeria, because they provide households with savings, insurance, credits, payments, supports, and educating them in good decision making. The researchers were able to conclude that all efforts and ideas which could avail formal financial products and services affordable, available, and accessible to the people of all categories of the population would be designed, encouraged, and implemented to achieve inclusive economic growth.

Nandru and Anand (2015) identified the correlates of financial inclusion as, gender ratio, population size, branch penetration, deposit to credit penetration ratio, and literacy rate in Andhra Pradesh State of Indian. Another study reaffirmed that branch penetration, credit to deposit penetration ratio, size of population, and gender ratio have statistically significant influence on financial inclusion program in south Indian states (Nandru et al., 2016).

Abdinoor and Ulingeta (2017) also tried to explore the influence of socioeconomic and demographic variables of respondents from a survey, such as age, sex, and income level, on households' participation in financial inclusion programs and observed that the variables are statistically significant factors influencing adoption of mobile financial services. Abdulsalam and Nurudeen (2019) investigated whether economic factors such as gender, income level, literacy rates, and income sources affect financial inclusion for 41 African countries. Their results show that income level and literacy rates significantly affect financial inclusion, but gender and income sources did not establish any significant effect.

Soyemi et al. (2020) have shown that developing countries have economic structures (mainly agriculture) which are akin to financial exclusion and which are also characterized by dominance of rural sector (majority of population located at the rural areas) with and low spread of money deposit bank branches and poor banking intermediation at various parts of the country. Soumaré et al. (2016) also identified of other factors which inhibit inclusion in financial programs for the population, as bureaucracy, distance, and high costs of banking products and services.

The development of telecommunication infrastructure has helped very much in opening many rural and remote villages and has also helped in accessing funds by individuals and households through their mobile phones. The revolution brought by digital phones is at the foundation of the changes in the lives and behaviors of many Africans, and other developing countries by providing not just telecommunications and their allied services, but also access to, use and application of basic financial products and facilities in the form of mobile money—money transfer and storage (Demombynes & Thegeya, 2012; Johnson & Upadhyaya, 2015; Jonathan & Camilo, 2008; Nguena, 2012, 2015; Ondiege, 2010). The revolution in telecommunication industry has created an in-depth penetration rates of mobile telephony which are changing and transforming cell phones into pocket banks in Africa (Tchouto & Nguena, 2015). According to them, mobile telephony has been found to create opportunities for countries on the continent to increase cost-effective means and affordable service, hence including a large part of the population who hitherto has been excluded from formal financial services for a long time. More interestingly, the use of mobile banking in the WAEMU zone contributed significantly to raising the rate of access to financial services for the population, which was established in 2013 at 49.5% with a banking coverage rate of exactly 12.2% (Tidiani, 2015).

This shift is a good development for microfinance institutions (MFIs), deposit money banks, as well as governments, financial regulators, and development partners who have worked hard to improve the lives of Africans through policies that promote long-term growth and poverty reduction. "A technology that was once a yuppie toy has suddenly become a weapon for economic progress in the world's poorest countries," according to *The Economist* (2008). At the Connect Africa meeting in 2007, Rwandan President Paul Kagame declared: "In ten short years, what was once a luxury and privilege, the mobile phone, has become a basic requirement in Africa" (Aker & Mbiti, 2010). Asongu (2013) investigated these phenomena and discovered that mobile phone adoption reduces African inequality due to its beneficial impact/correlation with the development of the informal finance sector.

Mobile money is currently a widely used platform in banks, serving both the unbanked and underserved. According to Porteous (2009), the acceptability of mobile money is heavily dependent on how users perceive innovative features such as simplicity, security, convenience, flexibility, cost, and accessibility. The many perspectives on an innovation have a direct impact on the intention to utilize and actual use of the innovation (Venkatesh & Davies, 2000). Mobile banking, according to Ngugi et al. (2010), is a new technology in many countries that can be adopted or rejected by consumers based on the elements that influence their perceptions.

Though these advancements in telecommunication infrastructure have aided in a variety of ways, they have not demonstrated a high level of access to, usage of, or credit penetration. Even in nations with significant credit penetration and other financial services, Dabla-Norris et al. (2015) show that huge amounts of credit do not necessarily indicate complete use of financial services because credit is always concentrated among the largest enterprises. When it comes to financial outreach, most financial institutions have been fairly conservative over the years. Even in the face of those who are intended to service the unbanked, banks have resorted to adopting a risk-averse mentality, with some notable exceptions, to simply give to the general good.

The main issue is that, despite all of the legislation, efforts, technological improvements, and so on, there is still a significant gap in the benefits that SMEs and MSMEs obtain from financial institution services. This raises the important topic of the impact of financial inclusion/widening on small firms in the self-employed sector. This is the study's main purpose.

Methodology

Financial widening activities which many literatures have also termed financial inclusion have created many arguments among scholars. Generally, it has been argued that this mechanism has huge importance especially in creating job opportunities among households. Though not very clear yet, but one research argument clearly agrees that the democratization of credit, the decentralization of services, financial penetration, greater range of financial services, and access to finance among different income group have helped to mitigate many risks as well as employment opportunities.

Furthermore, Clamara et al. (2014) stated that the number of people and businesses who utilize financial services has risen in most industrialized nations, affecting specific levels of small company activity. However, few empirical studies in Nigeria have supported this trend, owing to the fact that most people who use multiple financial services live in cities, while others who have access to affordable financial services but choose not to use certain financial services live in both urban and rural areas. However, due to regulatory and legal hurdles, a large number of people in rural areas still lack access to a variety of financial possibilities.

It is against this backdrop that this study uses Rogers' 1962 innovation diffusion theory as its theoretical framework, which argues that people are more likely to adopt an innovation if they believe it will, among other things, improve their utility and thus yield some relative advantage over the idea it supersedes, as well as have a strong positive effect on financial inclusion, which should be initiatives by banks to meet households' needs.

Therefore, to investigates the effect of financial widening activities on self-employment opportunities, this study adopts the logit estimation techniques.

Where *selfeml* represents self-employment opportunity in agricultural value chain, trading through electronic transaction; where 1 stand for such means and 0 otherwise. The parameter coefficient, marginal effects, and odd ratio were used for easy interpretation.

$$\text{Logit(selfeml)} = \ln\left[\frac{P}{1-p}\right] = \alpha_0 + \delta_1 \text{sex} + \delta_2 \text{age} + \delta_3 \text{educ} + \delta_4 \text{mobilemoney} + \delta_5 \text{etrac} + \delta_6 \text{mobilagric} + \mu_{it}$$

Because cross-sectional variables are rarely continuous and fully observed, evidence from theoretical studies provides a strong foundation for this paradigm. They can be censored (e.g., household expenditure), discrete (e.g., death), durational (e.g., time to die), or integer counts (e.g., visits to doctor). Nonlinear estimation is required for multivariate analysis of such dependent variables. The researchers in this study look at the most important (parametric) nonlinear estimators for analyzing financial broadening actions that create chances for small companies among households.

The study makes use of secondary data from the World Bank's Financial Inclusion Survey (2014). The Global Findex database contains detailed information on financial inclusion in households. It is the world's most comprehensive database on financial inclusion, measuring people's use of financial services across nations and over time in a consistent manner. Over 100 indicators are included in the 2014 Global Findex, which may be sorted by gender, income, and age.

The Global Findex is based on 150,000 nationally representative and randomly selected adults (age 15+) in over 140 countries. Mobile money accounts, as seen in sub-Saharan Africa, can help people gain access to financial services. While only 1% of adults worldwide say they exclusively use a mobile money account, in sub-Saharan Africa, 12% of adults (64 million adults) have mobile money accounts (compared to only 2% internationally), and 45% of them solely use a mobile money account. For the analysis, STATA 13 econometric software was employed.

Presentation of Results and Discussion

Table 8.1 presents the level of significant differences existing among different income groups access on mobile money in Nigeria.

The findings of this study demonstrate that not all parameters met a prior expectation as expected. The result showed that mobile money and households' level of education have significant and positive impact on self-employment opportunity and poverty reduction. In other words, for every unit increase in mobile money, it is expected that a 0.0881301 increase in the log-odds of self-employment opportunity, holding all other independent variables constant. This is also demonstrated among household level of education. As every unit increase in household level of education, it is expected that 2.213026 rise in the log-odds of self-employment opportunity, holding all other independent variables constant. One interesting finding in this result is the role households' level education play in self-employment opportunity through technology adoption in small businesses. It is clear how mobile transfer (mobile money) seems to have supported self-employment opportunity as well as sustaining small businesses. The rising economic hardship in Nigeria demonstrated by the rise of unemployment rate to 33.3% appears to be leading factor pushing so many school leavers to self-employment opportunity as supported by education level. This reveals the connection in the result. This evidence is

Table 8.1 Estimated results of effect of financial widening activities on self-employed Nigerians

Selfeml	*Coeff*	*Marginal effects*	*Odd ratio*	$|z|$	$P > |z|$
Constant	0.3111296			0.13	0.895
Sex (female)	−0.0306674	−0.0048622	0.969798	−0.09	0.928
Age	0.0143397	0.0022735	1.014443	1.30	0.193
Education	0.794361	0.1259418	2.213026	2.31	0.021
Mobilemoney	2.428942	0.3850962	0.0881301	2.96	0.003
E-transaction	−0.0743364	−0.0117857	0.9283593	−0.10	0.919
Mobileagric trade	0.6800033	0.107811	1.973884	0.92	0.358
Number of obs = 533					
Log likelihood = −122.03406	Prob > χ^2 = 0.0000			Pseudo R^2 = 0.0731	

Source Computation by the authors

also, supported by Cámara and Tuesta (2015) who adopted correlations analysis to identify socioeconomic characteristics that have influenced small businesses through the support of financial inclusion (or exclusion) of households. Studies by Jonathan and Camilo (2008), Ondiege (2010), Demombynes and Thegeya (2012), Nguena (2012, 2015), Johnson and Upadhyaya, (2015) among others have demonstrated the rate at which telecommunication infrastructure has helped very much in opening many rural and remote villages and has also helped in accessing funds by individuals and households through their mobile phones thereby providing opportunities for countries on the continent to increase affordable and cost-effective means of small businesses.

Conclusion

The study investigated the effect of financial widening activities on self-employment opportunities using World Bank Financial Inclusion Survey (2014) data and the logit estimation techniques. Interestingly, the findings showed that mobile money, and households' level of education have significant and positive impact on self-employment opportunity and poverty reduction. Hence, in examining the effect financial widening options like mobile money, banking services, e-payment options, savings, access to financial institutions outlets among mobile money, and households' level of education demonstrates huge connection to self-employment opportunities, and as such, the need for strengthened policies that widen financial channels is strongly encouraged and advocated in Nigeria so as to reduce the increasing movement of paper money and to have positive influence in the reduction of unemployment through self-employment by the teeming population of youths.

Appendix A: Output of Estimation Using Stata 13 Software

Selfeml	Coef	Marginal effects (dy/dx)	Odd ratio	z	P > |z|
Sex (female)	−0.0306674	−0.0048622	0.969798	−0.09	0.928
Age	0.0143397	0.0022735	1.014443	1.30	0.193

(continued)

(continued)

Selfeml	Coef	Marginal effects (dy/dx)	Odd ratio	z	P > |z|
Educ	0.794361	0.1259418	2.213026	2.31	0.021
Mobile money	2.428942	0.3850962	0.0881301	2.96	0.003
Etransaction	−0.0743364	−0.0117857	0.9283593	−0.10	0.919
Mobile agric trade	0.6800033	0.107811	1.973884	0.92	0.358
_cons	0.3111296			0.13	0.895
Number of obs = 533					
Log likelihood = −122.03406	Prob > χ^2 = 0.0000			Pseudo R^2 = 0.0731	

References

Abdinoor, A., & Ulingeta, M. O. (2017). Factors influencing consumers' adoption of mobile financial services in Tanzania. *Cogent Business & Management, 4*(1), 1392273.

Abdulsalam, M., & Nurudeen, A. Z. (2019). Economic factors and financial inclusion in African States. *Dutse Journal of Economics and Development Studies (DUJEDS), 7*(1).

Aker, J. C., & Mbiti, I. M. (2010). Mobile phones and economic development in Africa. *Journal of Economic Perspectives, 24*(3), 207–232.

Amuda, Y. J., & Embi, N. A. C. (2013). Alleviation of poverty among OIC countries through Sadaqat, CashWaqf and public funding. *International Journal of Trade Economics and Finance, 4*, 405–407.

Asongu, S. A. (2013). How has mobile phone penetration stimulated financial development in Africa. *Journal of African Business, 14*(1), 7–18.

Asuming, P. O., Osei-Agyei, L. G., & Mohammed, J. I. (2019). Financial inclusion in sub-Saharan Africa: Recent trends and determinants. *Journal of African Business, 20*(1), 112–134.

Babajide, A. A., Lawal, A. I., Amodu, L. O., Ewetan, O. O., Esowe, S. L., & Okafor, T. C. (2020). Financial institutions concentration and financial inclusion penetration in Nigeria: A comparative analysis. *Journal of Contemporary African Studies, 38*(4), 610–626. https://doi.org/10.1080/02589001.2020.1822991

Banerjee, A. V., & Newman, A. F. (1993). Occupational choice and the process of development. *Journal of Political Economy, 101*(2), 274–298.

Beck, T. (2016). *Finance, institutions and development: Literature survey and research agenda* (EDI Working Paper Series No. 16). Economic and Development Institutions.

Beck, T., & Honohan, P. (2009). Access to financial services measurement, impact and policies. *World Bank Research Observer, 24*(1), 119–145.

Bertram, O. A., Nwankwo, S. N. P., & Onwuka, I. O. (2016). Full financial inclusion (Ffi): A pre-requisite for inclusive economic development in Nigeria. *Advances in Social Sciences Research Journal, 3*(9), 65–78. https://doi.org/10.14738/assrj.39.2128

Cámara, N., & Tuesta, D. (2015). Factors that matter for financial inclusion: Evidence from Peru. *The IEB International Journal of Finance, 10*, 10–31.

Caskey, J., Duran, C. R. & Solo, T. M. (2006). *The urban unbanked in Mexico and the United States* (Policy Research Working Paper 3835). World Bank, Washington, DC.

CBN. (2018). *National financial inclusion strategy* (Revised). Abuja: Central Bank of Nigeria. https://www.cbn.gov.ng/out/2019/ccd/national%20financial%20inclusion%20strategy.pdf

Clamara, N., Pena, X., & Tuesta, D. (2014). *Factors that matter for financial inclusion: Evidence from Peru*(BBVA Working Paper 09).

Dabla-Norris, E., Ji, Y., Townsend, R., & Filiz Unsal, D. (2015). *Identifying constraints to financial inclusion and their impact on GDP and inequality: A structural framework for policy* (IMF Working Paper 15/22). International Monetary Fund, Washington, DC.

Demirguc-Kunt, A., & Levine, R. (2009). *Finance and inequality: Theory and evidence* (NBER Working Paper 15275). National Bureau of Economic Research, Cambridge.

Demombynes, G., & Thegeya, A. (2012). *Kenya's mobile revolution and the promise of mobile savings* (World Bank Policy Research Working Paper, No. 5988).

Dupas, P., & Robinson, J. (2009). *Savings constraints and microenterprise development: Evidence from a field experiment in Kenya* (NBER Working Paper 14693). National Bureau of Economic Research, Cambridge, MA.

EFInA. (2018). EFInA access to financial services in Nigeria 2018. Accessed at https://www.efina.org.ng/wp-content/uploads/2019/01/A2F-2018-Key-Findings-11_01_19.pdf

Fowowe, B., & Folarin, E. O. (2019). The effects of fragility and financial inequalities on inclusive growth in African countries. *Review of Development Economics, Special Issue,.* https://doi.org/10.1111/rode.12594

Global Findex Data. (2014). *The Global Findex Database*. International Bank for Reconstruction and Development/The World Bank.

Ibeachu, E. H. (2010). *Comparative analysis of financial inclusion: A study of Nigeria and the UK*. International Business, Leeds Metropolitan University.

Ibor, B. I., Offiong, A. I., & Mendie, E. S. (2017). Financial inclusion and performance of micro, small and medium scale enterprises in Nigeria. *International Journal of Research—Granthaalayah*, 5(3), 104–122. https://doi.org/10.29121/Granthaalayah.v5.i3.2017.1758

Ihugba, O. A., Odii, A., & Njoku, A. (2014). Theoretical analysis of entrepreneurship challenges and prospects in Nigeria. *International Letters of Social and Humanistic Sciences*, 5, 21–34.

International Finance Corporation. (2011). *Toward universal access: Addressing the global challenge of financial inclusion*. International Finance Corporation.

International Labour Organization (ILO). (2015). *Global employment trends for youth 2015: Scaling up investments in decent jobs for youth* (Geneva).

Johnson, S., & Upadhyaya, R. (2015), Transformation of Kenya's banking sector 2000–2012. In A. Heyer & M. King (Eds.), *Kenya's financial transformation in the 21st Century* (17 p.). Financial Sector Deepening Kenya.

Jonathan, D., & Camilo, T. (2008). Mobile banking and economic development: Linking adoption, impact and use. *Asian Journal of Communication*, 18(4), 318–322.

Nandru, P., & Anand, B. (2015). Determinants of financial inclusion—Evidence from Andhra Pradesh. *Jamal Academic Research Journal*, Special Issue, 172–179. ISSN: 0973-0303.

Nandru, P., Anand, B., & Rentala, S. (2016). Determinants of financial inclusion: Evidence from account ownership and use of banking services. *International Journal of Entrepreneurship and Development Studies*, 4(2), 141–155.

Nguena, C. L. (2012). Rethinking pro growth monetary policy in Africa: Monetarist versus Keynesian approach. *Africa Economic Brief*, 4(6), 1–8.

Nguena, C. L. (2015). *Boosting investment and business environment in Africa today: Mobile Banking as an optimal strategy for financial inclusion*. http://nguena.blogspot.com/2015/02/boosting-investment-and-business_13.html

Ngugi, B., Pelowski, M., & Ogembo, J. G. (2010). M-Pesa: A case study of the critical early adopters. Role in the rapid acceptance of mobile money transfer in Kenya. *The Electronic Journal on Information Systems in Developing Countries*, 43(3), 1–16.

Njoku, A. C., & Odumeru, J. A. (2013). Going cashless: Adoption of mobile banking in Nigeria. Niger. Chapter Arab. *Journal of Business Management Review*, 6, 1–9.

Onaolapo, A. A., & Odetayo, T. A. (2012). Financial inclusion and microfinance banks in Nigerian. *American Journal of Business and Management*, 1(4), 241–247.

Ondiege, P. (2010). Mobile banking in Africa: Taking the bank to the people. *Africa Economic Brief*, 1(8), 1–16.

Pallavi, G., & Bharti, S. (2013). Role of literacy level in financial inclusion in India: Empirical evidence. *Journal of Economics, Business and Management, 1*(3), 272–276.

Piketty, T. (2000). Theories of persistent inequality and intergenerational mobility. In A. B. Atkinson & F. Bourguignon (Eds.), *Handbook of income distribution* (pp. 429–476). Elsevier.

Piketty, T. (1997). The dynamics of wealth distribution and the interest rate with credit rationing. *Review of Economics Studies, 64*(2), 173–189.

Porteous, D. (2009). *Beyond financial inclusion: The promise and practice of inclusive cash lite.* https://center4affordablehousing.org/wp-content/uploads/2019/01/Beyond-financial-inclusion-David-Porteousv1.11.pdf

Raimi, L. (2017). Imperative of meta-study for research in the field of corporate social responsibility and emerging issues in corporate governance. In D. Crowther & L. M. Lauesen (Eds.), *The handbook of research methods on corporate social responsibility.* Edward Edgar.

Rjoub, H., Aga, M., Abu-AlRub, A., & Bein, M. A. (2017). Financial reforms and determinants of FDI: Evidence from landlocked countries in sub-Saharan Africa. *Economics, 2017*(5), 1.

Siano, A., Raimi, L., Palazzo, M., & Panait, M. C. (2020). Mobile banking: An innovative solution for increasing financial inclusion in Sub-Saharan African countries: Evidence from Nigeria. *Sustainability, 12*, 10130. https://doi.org/10.3390/su122310130

Soumaré, I., Tchana, F. T., & Kengne, T. (2016). Analysis of the determinants of financial inclusion in Central and West Africa. *Transnational Corporations Review, 8*(4), 231–249. https://doi.org/10.1080/19186444.2016.1265763

Soyemi, K. A., Olowofela, O. E., & Yunusa, L. A. (2020). Financial inclusion and sustainable development in Nigeria. *Journal of Economics Management, 39*, 105–131.

Stephen, M., & Sibert, C. (2014). The impact of mobile banking on financial inclusion in Zimbabwe: A case for Masvingo province. *Mediterranean Journal of Social Sciences, 5*(9), 221–230.

Sykes, J., Elder, S., Gurbuzer, Y., & Principi, M. (2016). *Exploring the linkages between youth financial inclusion and job creation: Evidence from the ILO school-to-work transition surveys.* International Labour Organization (ILO).

Tchouto, L., & Nguena, C. L. (2015). *Innovation financière et développement durable au Cameroun: pourquoi le développement du mobile banking est-il important?* (AAYE Policy Research Working Paper Series, No. 15/029). Association of African Young Economists, Yaounde.

The Economist. (2008). *Halfway there: How to promote the spread of mobile phones among the world's poorest.* http://www.economist.com/node/11465558?story_id=11465558

Tidiani, S. (2015). *Mobile banking and mobile money: A highly instrument against corruption* (MPRA Paper No. 66634).
Triki, T., & Faye, I. (Eds.). (2013). *Financial inclusion in Africa*. African Development Bank.
Venkatesh, V., & Davis, F. D. (2000). A theoretical extension of the technology acceptance model: Four longitudinal field studies. *Management Science, 45*(2), 186–204.
Waihenya, H. (2012). *The effect of agent banking on financial inclusion in Kenya* (Unpublished Masters project). University of Nairobi, Kenya.

CHAPTER 9

Role of Microfinance to Promote the Growth of Unorganized Manufacturing Enterprises in India: An Analysis

Akash Dandapat and Pinaki Das

INTRODUCTION

In the wake of global recession, governments throughout the world including that of India are trying to boost their own economies by different fiscal and monetary measures. Indian government has also taken many steps so far to keep the growth rate of Indian GDP higher than the exiting rate. To revive and stimulate Indian economy, employment generation of poor and middle-income group people is crucial. Enhancing access to finance for micro, small and medium enterprises is crucial for the development of an economy like India where unorganized sector is

---

A. Dandapat (✉) · P. Das
Department of Economics, Vidyasagar University, Midnapore, West Bengal, India
e-mail: akashdandapatn5@gmail.com

P. Das
e-mail: pdasvu@mail.vidyasagar.ac.in

© The Author(s), under exclusive license to Springer Nature Singapore Pte Ltd. 2022
R. C. Das (ed.), *Microfinance to Combat Global Recession and Social Exclusion*, https://doi.org/10.1007/978-981-16-4329-3_9

predominant for the generation of employment, income enhancement, increasing purchasing power and creation of entrepreneurial spirit. In addition, financial institutions play a vital role in firms' growth and productivity. To combat the recessionary situation all the national governments including India increase their fiscal spending to revive growth. In this situation, continuous financial support to entrepreneurs is also required for a quick recovery. In India, unorganized manufacturing enterprises (UMEs) are hub of employment for millions of people. But this sector faces difficulty to get loan from formal financial institutions. The availability of microfinance can bridge the gap between small unorganized entrepreneurs and big formal financial sources. It can reduce the dependence of small entrepreneurs on informal sources. Microfinance is of low-cost available capital for functioning of these UMEs. It is very small amount of loan provided by microfinance institutions, self-help groups and various banks.

In their study, Bhavani and Bhanumurthy (2014) analysed availability of loan from formal or official sources and proportion of productive or fruitful investment which was not financed by formal resources in unorganized manufacturing sector of India. According to them, lending to unorganized enterprises associated with higher production and behavioural risk. Reducing risk and transaction costs is the solution of the problem of limited financial access. Structural transformation indicates upgradation of manufacturing units from small traditional family-owned informal firms (PHEs) to medium (MHEs) and large (LHEs) firms which employ non-family labourers' too. RBI should focus on availability of adequate corpus funds through the term lending institutions such as Small Industries Development Bank of India (SIDBI) to lend these PHEs and make easier transformation for PHEs by borrowing collateral free loans from institutional sources (Raj & Sen, 2015). Kunt and Levine (2008) showed that access to finance plays an important role not only in the development process of an economy but also have an influence particularly to equalize opportunities and reduce inequalities. World Bank Report on Financial Access 2010 revealed that only half of the total households in the world had deposit account in any formal financial institution. In case of South Asia, it was less than 25%. But non-standard financing mechanism or informal financing can never be an effective substitute of formal financing channels in promoting growth of small businesses. A study of formal versus informal finance based on Chinese financial system showed that the performance of private firm is positively associated with the use of formal financing channels. China is the largest growing economy still China had an underdeveloped financial system and institutions which is comparable to other developing economy (Ayyagari et al., 2010). Institutional underdevelopment influenced cross country variations in the types of obstacles firms faced in financing (Beck et al., 2004). Some specific financial tools like leasing and factoring could facilitate larger access to finance in small & medium enterprises even in the underdeveloped institutional structure (Beck & Kunt, 2006). Enterprises may prefer informal financing due to predatory regulatory environment or frequent problem of bribes (Safavian & Wimpey, 2007). Perhaps MSMEs borrowers often don't have any financial track records as well as they were not able to provide reliable information, which become a likewise constraint in access to bank loan. In maximum of the cases, formal financial institutions lack the appropriate instruments for managing risk and know-how to reach the MSME market. Hence, it is essential to ensure that, MSME should not be penalizing in terms of loan constraint to avoid risk pooling (World Bank Report, 2010).

Although microfinance is considered as a risky venture in the sense of banker's perception but it also has a positive side. In the state of Punjab, more than 60% bankers reported above 90% rate of repayment. Previous studies also identified that less awareness among potential beneficiaries (less than 5% among total) about microfinance programs works as another major constraint here (Arora & Meenu, 2012). Debt level varies with firm size. Larger manufacturing firm had relatively greater debt than the smaller ones (both were below 10 years from their incorporation), but ratio of debt to assets considerably falls for small firms while it was stable for large firms (Love & Peria, 2005). Carpenter and Petersen (2001) discussed about the theory of internal finance in small firms. Their research result suggests that the growth rates of firm facing internal financing constraint is approximately independent of firms' size because case flow (scaled by assets) was approximately independent of size. Again, variance of rate of growth may decline with size because the variance of internal finance may decline with firms' size. Microfinance also acts as an instrument of poverty eradication. Government should help MSMEs for capacity building initiatives and credibility enhancing and ensure transparency through disclosure (Gupta, 2011). Bank credit goes to mainly large and medium size manufacturing units which indicate a structural retrogression of credit to MSME (Bhattacharya, 2013). Therefore, consequences needed better co-ordination between small scale industries and financial institutions and planning & control of working capital (Kumar & Gugloth, 2012). Currently, among 32 existing major national level economic development funds in India, only 13 funds were related to the Small Manufacturing Enterprise sector, non-farm unorganized sector or Micro Enterprise sector. Many of these funds were maintained by NABARD and SIDBI (NCEUS, 2007).

The role of microfinance for promoting the growth of UMEs in not adequately analysed in the existing literature. The study is also limited to analyse the accessibility of loan by UMEs. This analysis is crucial as the role of microfinance is gradually increasing in India. Thus this study is innovative as it analyses the accessibility of microfinance and its role to promote growth of UMEs at the enterprise level. The present study sets two-fold objectives:

1. To examine the influence of microfinance on the performance of UMEs in India.
2. To analyse the factors that affect the financial access of UMEs in India.

The remaining part of the study is sequenced as follows: Sect. 9.2 presents the methodology used to fulfil the above-mentioned objectives. Section 9.3 deals with the results and discusses it. Section 9.4 concludes.

Empirical Methods and Database

Database

National Sample Survey Organisation (NSSO) conducts a dedicated quinquennial sample survey on unorganized manufacturing enterprises. We have used the unit level data of the 67th (2010–11) and 73rd (2015–16) rounds to explore the above-mentioned objectives. We have matched the data of two rounds at unit level based on NIC 2008 and removed the outliers from the dataset. Again, the newest round of the survey captured data on electricity power generation in manufacturing category. But we have excluded this item from our analysis as it is not listed in earlier survey. The unit level study shows that this category has very negligible share. Moreover, we have excluded non-market enterprises as those enterprises do not sell their output at market determining prices.

Micro Financial Sector (Development & Regulation) Bill 2007 has mentioned loan up to Rs. 50,000/- as microcredit. According to Reserve Bank of India (RBI) guideline of 2019, loan amount up to Rs. 125,000/- to a household with annual income not more than Rs. 200,000/- can be considered as microfinance. It is evident that more than 60% of the UMEs received the loan amount less than Rs. 50,000 in a year in both 2010–11 and 2015–16. The number of UMEs in this slab increased by around 2% during 2010–11 to 2015–16. Around 30% UMEs received loans between Rs. 50,000 to below Rs. 500,000 in a year but the share has unfortunately reduced during 2010–11 to 2015–16. The other slabs have very negligible shares. It can be thus seen that around 80% UMEs have received loan up to Rs. 125,000. This means that the lions' share of loan of UMEs is microcredit or microfinance type. Thus, we have compared the performance of those UMEs who received microfinance with those UMEs who didn't receive microfinance. We have further excluded those UMEs who have received the loan amount above Rs. 125,000.

m-logit *Model to Analyse the Status of Growth*

The status of growth (STGR) of UMEs is classified under three categories viz., expanding, stagnating and contracting. NSSO has defined the types of status of growth of enterprises on the basis of their performance during last three years. We have assigned values 0 for expanding nature of enterprises, 1 for stagnating nature of enterprises and 2 for stagnating nature of enterprises. It is hypothesized that the firm level characteristics like loan accessibility, ownership of enterprise, partnership, perennial & seasonal nature of operation, nature of enterprise, regular maintenance of account, registration of the firm, firm size and profitability are significantly influence the STGR of UMEs. A multinomial logit regression (m-logit) model is called for to analyse the impact of these characteristics of UTEs on their STGR. UTEs it is specified as follows:

$$STGR_i = \beta_0 + \beta_1 LOAN_i + \beta_2 OWN_i + \beta_3 PARTNER_i \\ + \beta_4 NOPN_i + \beta_5 NSOPN_i + \beta_6 EST_i + \beta_7 ACOUNT_i \\ + \beta_8 REGS_i + \beta_9 SZFRM_i + \beta_{10} PROFT_i + \mu_i$$

Here the dependent variable STGR is multinomial in nature. It is hypothesized that availability of loan or microfinance (LOAN) improves the growth status of the enterprises. In our regression equation LOAN is a dummy variables which takes 1 if the enterprise has accessed loan and 0 otherwise. It is assumed that proprietary male ownership of enterprises has experienced expanding nature of growth. We have assigned 1 for proprietary male ownership (OWN) and o otherwise. We have also hypothesized that partnership (PARTNER) enhances the status of growth of an enterprise. As regards the duration of functioning of UMEs the nature of enterprises are three types, namely perennial, seasonal and casual. We have assigned two dummy variables for nature of enterprises: NOPN for perennial and NSOPN for seasonal. It is hypothesized that establishment type enterprises are more likely to be expanding compared to OAEs. EST is a dummy variable and it takes 1 for establishment enterprises and 0 for OAEs. It is also hypothesized that the enterprises that maintain account (ACOUNT) on a regular basis are more likely to be expanding. ACOUNT is specified as a dummy variable (takes 1 for enterprises that maintain account and 0 otherwise). Registered enterprises are more likely to be expanding. Registration (REGS) is a dummy variable where 1 value is assigned for registered enterprises and 0 otherwise. The volume of fixed assets is crucial for the growth of UTEs and size of the firm (SZFRM) is specified by it. Besides SZFRM, the profitability also plays an important role for the UTEs. We have measured the profitability by the ratio of net profit to total number of labour in the enterprise. μ_i is an error term.

Heckman Selection Model (Two Step) to Analyse the Financial Access of UMEs

Heckman selection (two step) model (1979) is used to analyse the factors that affect the financial access of UMEs in India. The model is appropriate here as it helps us to analyse whether the UMEs accessed microfinance or not and the extent of finance that they received. Let us consider a model that has two variables m_i and p_i which linearly depend on apparent explanatory variables z_i and x_i respectively.

$$m_i = z_i \gamma + \upsilon_i$$

$$p_i = x_i \beta + \varepsilon_i$$

The error terms υ_i and ε_i are independently (across observations) and jointly normally distributed with covariance $\rho \delta_\varepsilon$.

In the present case m_i shows whether i-th enterprise has financial access or not and p_i shows the extent of loan of the i-th enterprise. We observe m_i when the latent variable m_i^* is 1 when the enterprise has received loan and 0 otherwise. Similarly, the value of the variable $p_i = p_i^*$ is only observed if m is 1. That is,

$$m_i = 1 \text{ if the enterprise has received loan}$$
$$= 0 \text{ otherwise}$$
$$p_i = p_i^* \text{ if } m_i = 1$$
$$\text{n.a. otherwise.}$$

Heckman's (1979) two-step procedure contains the estimation of a standard probit and linear regression model.

Step 1 is the estimation of γ by ML using the full set of observation in the standard probit model

$$m_i^* = z_i \gamma + v_i \text{ (First Equation)}$$
$$m_i^* = 1 \text{ if } i\text{-th enterprise is received loan, 0 otherwise.}$$

Heckman (1979) suggested for the estimation of the **Inverse Mills Ratio** (λ_i) for all observations.

Step 2 is the estimation of the regression equation with the (λ_i) as an additional variable

$$p_i^* = x_i \beta + \beta_\lambda \lambda_i + u_i \text{ (Second Equation)}$$

For the sub-sample of full observations.

Here b_i^* is the extent of loan (i.e. amount of loan) of the i-th enterprise. The OLS regression yields $\beta, \beta_\lambda, \beta_\varepsilon$ and thus the correlation $\rho = \beta_\lambda / \delta_\varepsilon$.

There is no selectivity bias if the coefficient of Inverse Mills Ratio (λ) is statistically not significant.

It is hypothesized that the financial access by UTEs also affected by firm level characteristics like nature of ownership (PROP), partnership (PARTNER), nature of operation (NPON), type of enterprise (EST), account maintenance (ACOUNT), registration (REGS) and size of the firm (SZFRM).

Results and Discussions
Status of Microfinance of UMEs

There is a wide market for microfinance in UMEs, because very few UMEs in India receive any type of finance or loan. In 2010–11, there were 17,231,937 UMEs existed out of which only 6% UMEs received any type of loan whereas in 2015–16, the number of UMEs increased to 8% only. There are mainly two types of sources of loan of UMEs namely formal and informal sources as presented in Table 9.1. They grant loan to small businessman or UMEs sometimes without security. Inadequacy of formal sources increases the presence of this informal finance market. Shroff Committee 1954 noted that around 90% of financial market is captured by informal bankers (Singh, 1954). Still now the situation has not changed. RBI many times tried to drag these informal lenders into formal process but it never happened. The problem of informal financial market is that they charge high interest rate on loan. As the amount of fixed assets, profitability and productivity of unorganized part in UMEs are quite low in comparison with big enterprises so the formal bankers are not interested to grant loan to these enterprises. Among the formal sources, 30% of the loan is received from commercial banks and microfinance institutions itself whereas in case of informal source, 50% of the loan is received from money lenders, friends and relatives. Further, it can be noted that, the share of loans from formal source has reduced in all cases except microfinance institutions and other institutions agencies during 2010–11 to 2015–16 which implies the reduced importance of government and formal financial institutions.

NSSO has classified all unorganized manufacturing enterprises into twenty-five activities based on NIC 2008. These activities include 01632 and 10–33 two-digit level industries. The study reveals that only ten activities have more than 80% share in total loan outstanding and the other enterprises have very negligible share in both the study periods. These top ten activities are Manufacture of Food Products, Manufacture of Wearing Apparel, Manufacture of Textiles, Manufacture of Fabricated Metal Products, Manufacture of Furniture, Manufacture of Tobacco Products, Manufacture of Wood Products, Other Manufacturing, Manufacture of other non-metallic Mineral Products, Manufacture of Machinery and Equipment. Among all the activities, Food product activity had the maximum share of loan that was 19.7% followed by Manufacture of

Table 9.1 Amount and sources of loan and performance of UMEs in relation to microfinance in India, 2010–11 and 2015–16

	2010–11		2015–16	
	Number	% share	Number	% share
(A) Loan amount (in Rs.)				
0–50,000	589,902	60.23	978,572	62.18
50,001 to 125,000	173,126	17.67	265,631	16.87
125,001 to 500,000	148,735	15.18	199,590	12.68
Above 500,000	67,662	6.9	130,095	8.2
Total	979,425	100	1,573,888	100
(B) Sources of loan				
Central and state level term lending institutions	11,188	1.07	4755	0.28
Government bodies	36,401	3.49	36,768	2.14
Commercial banks	205,386	19.67	292,079	16.97
Co-operative banks	116,273	11.13	108,383	6.3
Microfinance institutions	51,809	4.96	196,991	11.44
Other institutional agencies	23,098	2.21	64,721	3.76
Other informal sources	600,269	57.47	1,017,912	59.13
(C) Performance of UMEs in relation to microfinance				

Indicators per enterprise	2010–11			2015–16		
	Received loan	No loan	Difference	Received loan	No loan	Difference
Employment	4.23	1.89	2.34*	3.34	1.7	1.64*
Gross value added	340,021	81,434	258,587*	371,852	102,354	269,498*
Fixed assets	817,972	209,516	608,456*	668,537	169,795	498,742*

Notes (1) Total number of UMEs will not be equal to 100% here because an enterprise may take loan from multiple sources; (2) The statistical test of differences are one-tailed tests where *t-test is statistically significant at 1% level
Source Authors' calculation based on NSSO data of 67th (2010–11) and 73rd (2015–16) rounds

Wearing Apparel (19.6%), Manufacture of Textiles (14.4%), Manufacture of Fabricated Metal Products (6.3%), Manufacture of Furniture (6.1%), Manufacture of Tobacco Products (6%), Manufacture of Wood Products (5.9%), Other Manufacturing (4.9%), Manufacture of other non-metallic Mineral Products (4.2%) and Manufacture of Machinery and Equipment(2.5%) in 2015–16. But in 2010–11, Manufacture of Textiles activity had largest share that was 18.8% which slightly reduced to 14.4%

in 2015–16. The share loan in Manufacture of Food Products, Manufacture of Wearing Apparel, Manufacture of Furniture, Manufacture of Tobacco Products, Other Manufacturing, Manufacture of Machinery and Equipment activities increased during the study period. The availability of adequate financial support may increase the performance of bottom fifteen activities. We can mention five activities that can grow faster with proper financial assistance. These are Manufacture of Beverages; Manufacture of Electrical Equipment; Manufacture of Motor Vehicles, Trailers and Semi-Trailers; Manufacture of Computer, Electronic and Optical Products; Manufacture of Pharmaceuticals and Medicinal Chemical and Botanical Products. These activities have a direct positive linkage with the growth of Indian economy. If economy as a whole grows then the demand for computer products will definitely increase. Similarly, other four activities can grow with the growth of Indian economy. All together these enterprises can generate huge additional employment opportunity and output. But the main hindrance of it is lack of financial access.

The access of microfinance widely varied across characteristics of UMEs. In India, 8% of the UMEs had access to microfinance in 2015–16 which was 5.7% in 2010–11. Across location, it can be observed that the access of microfinance by UMEs was higher in the urban areas than rural areas as the share was 8.5% and 7.7%, respectively, in 2015–16. Based on the nature of operation, the microfinance was mostly accessed by the seasonal enterprises but the share has reduced from 11.8% in 2010–11 to 8.7% in 2015–16. The UMEs which maintained account had comparatively higher access to microfinance as compared to those who didn't maintained account and the share has eventually increased. Similarly, the registered UMEs also had comparatively higher access to microfinance than the unregistered UMEs. Based on ownership, access to microfinance was much higher if the owners belong to different households followed by those belonging to the same households, male owner and female owner. The share has gradually increased in case of all types of owners except those belonging to different households during 2010–11 to 2015–16. Further, the share of establishment type enterprises was significantly higher than the own account type enterprises who had access to microfinance which eventually increased.

Performance of UMEs in Relation to Microfinance

Per enterprise employment as observed from Table 10.1 was found to be comparatively higher among those UMEs who received finance as compared to those who didn't receive loans which holds true in both 2010–11 and 2015–16. Per enterprise employment of those UMEs who received loans has reduced from 4.23 in 2010–11 to 3.34 in 2015–16. But there has been upsurge in the employment growth rate by 5.35% during 2010–11 to 2015–16. Per enterprise gross value added (GVA in Rs.) which is the ratio of GVA and the number of enterprises has increased from Rs. 340,021 to Rs. 371,852 for those UMEs who received loans. The growth rate of GVA was almost double for those UMEs who received loans than those who didn't receive loans. Per enterprise fixed assets has reduced considerably during 2010–11 to 2015–16. The growth rate of fixed capital was 6.27% who received loan but those who didn't receive loan observed negative growth in fixed capital which was by 1.93%.

Status of Growth of UMEs in Relation to Microfinance

The results of two multinomial logit regressions, one for the year 2015–16 and other for the year 2010–11, are presented in Table 9.2. The result shows that those enterprises who have access to loan (LOAN) are more likely to be expanding than stagnating and contracting in 2010–11 as well as in 2015–16. Besides, those enterprises maintain account (ACOUNT) regularly and registered (REGS) are also more likely to be expanding than stagnating and contracting. ESTs are more likely to be expanding than stagnating and contracting in 2010–11 as well as in 2015–16. Perennial (NOPN) and Seasonal (NSOPN) enterprises are also more likely to be expanding than stagnating and contracting. Moreover, higher profit (PROFT) making enterprises too are more likely to be expanding than stagnating.

Analysis of the Status of Financial Access of UMEs

The empirical results of Heckman two-step estimation are presented in Table 9.3. The lower panel shows the results of probit estimation of access of loan (LOAN) and the upper panel is the OLS estimation of the extent (i.e. amount) of loan received by UMEs. Here the Inverse Mills

Table 9.2 Multinomial logistic regression of status of growth of UMEs

2010–11	2015–16
Number of obs = 83,728 LR $\chi^2(20)$ = 3471.13 Prob > χ^2 = 0.0000 Log likelihood = −78,630.72 Pseudo R^2 = 0.0216 Base outcome: Expanding = 0	Number of obs = 69,472 LR $\chi^2(20)$ = 2124.57 Prob > χ^2 = 0.0000 Log likelihood = −67,323.675 Pseudo R^2 = 0.0155 Base outcome: Expanding = 0

		Coef.	z	P > z	Coef.	z	P > z
Stagnating = 1	LOAN	−0.147	−5.26	0.00	−0.105	−3.88	0.00
	OWN	0.814	3.24	0.00	−0.291	−0.59	0.56
	PARTNER	0.761	2.98	0.00	−0.382	−0.76	0.45
	NOPN	−0.952	−6.46	0.00	−1.184	−6.09	0.00
	NSOPN	−0.805	−5.13	0.00	−0.805	−3.92	0.00
	EST	−0.533	−30.16	0.00	−0.492	−25.63	0.00
	ACOUNT	−0.233	−8.07	0.00	−0.090	−3.34	0.00
	REGS	−0.101	−5.22	0.00	−0.119	−5.84	0.00
	SZFRM	−0.00080	−2.13	0.03	−0.00013	−0.22	0.83
	PROFT	−0.00005	−19.32	0.00	−0.00002	−13.18	0.00
	_cons	0.768	2.65	0.01	2.022	3.78	0.00
Contracting = 2	LOAN	−0.017	−0.37	0.71	−0.098	−2.56	0.01
	OWN	0.587	1.6	0.11	0.254	0.31	0.76
	PARTNER	0.669	1.79	0.07	0.227	0.28	0.78
	NOPN	−1.452	−8.59	0.00	−1.361	−6.17	0.00
	NSOPN	−0.916	−4.97	0.00	−0.490	−2.1	0.04
	EST	−0.687	−23.2	0.00	−0.525	−18.49	0.00
	ACOUNT	−0.127	−2.62	0.01	−0.052	1.29	0.20
	REGS	0.050	1.57	0.12	−0.008	−0.27	0.79
	SZFRM	−0.0009	−1.42	0.16	0.001	−1.45	0.15
	PROFT	−0.0001	−23.8	0.00	−0.0001	−19.61	0.00
	_cons	0.203	0.5	0.62	0.612	0.72	0.47

Note STGR = Status of Growth is categorized as 1 if expanding, 2 if stagnating, 3 if contracting; LOAN = Whether the enterprise has access of loan or not (Yes = 1, No = 0); OWN = Nature of Proprietary Ownership: Whether the enterprise is proprietary male ownership or not (Yes = 1, No = 0); PARTNER = Nature of Partnership Ownership: Whether the enterprise is partnership male ownership or not (Yes = 1, No = 0); NPOPN = Nature of perennial operation: Whether the enterprise is perennial or not (Yes = 1, No = 0); NSOPN = Nature of seasonal operation: Whether the enterprise is perennial or not (Yes = 1, No = 0); EST = Nature of enterprises: Whether the enterprise is establishment or not (Yes = 1, No = 0); ACOUNT = Account Maintain: Whether the enterprise maintain accountant or not (Yes = 1, No = 0); REG = Registration: Whether the enterprise registered under act or not (Yes = 1, No = 0); SZFRM = Size of the firm is calculated by the volume of fixed asset (in Rs. crore); PROFT = Profitability of UMEs is measured by the ratio of net profit to total number of labour of an enterprise
Source As in Table 10.1

9 ROLE OF MICROFINANCE TO PROMOTE THE GROWTH ... 143

Table 9.3 Heckman selection model—two-step estimates

2011–12					2015–16		
Number of obs = 99,282					Number of obs = 82,754		
Censored obs = 90,477					Censored obs = 72,881		
Uncensored obs = 8805					Uncensored obs = 9873		
Wald $\chi^2(7)$ = 49.03					Wald $\chi^2(7)$ = 89.63		
Prob > χ^2 = 0.0000					Prob > χ^2 = 0.0000		

		Coef.	z	P > z	Coef.	z	P > z
OLS estimation	PROP	−15,020.54	−1.14	0.26	−387,790.9	−1.1	0.27
	PARTNER	23,639.1	2.00	0.05	895,695.2	3.29	0.00
	NOPN	−16,378.6	−2.39	0.02	−714,083.5	−2.57	0.01
	EST	40,247.4	2.73	0.01	1,303,673.0	2.48	0.01
	ACOUNT	25,464.2	3.56	0.00	96,092.1	0.41	0.68
	REGS	31,728.8	2.76	0.01	836,057.4	2.21	0.03
	SZFRM	9.8	4.56	0.00	0.5	0.03	0.97
	_cons	−164,965.4	−2.69	0.01	−6,330,521.0	−3.9	0.00
Probit estimation	PROP	−0.26	−2.17	0.03	−0.29	−6.44	0.00
	PARTNER	0.16	1.28	0.20	0.06	1.02	0.31
	NOPN	0.05	0.49	0.63	0.21	1.82	0.07
	EST	0.53	39.44	0.00	0.48	36.24	0.00
	ACOUNT	0.27	15.43	0.00	0.21	12.99	0.00
	REGS	0.42	30.88	0.00	0.35	25.92	0.00
	SZFRM	0.0001	4.17	0.00	0.0001	3.7	0.00
	_cons	−1.62	−10.43	0.00	−0.99	−7.95	0.00
	Mills lambda	88,283.89	0.67	0.61	−3,655,866	0.78	0.53
	Rho	1.00			−0.88811		
	Sigma	88,283.89			4,116,456.3		

Notes and Source As in Table 10.2

Ratio (λ) is found to be statistically not significant indicating that the estimation is free from selectivity bias. All the considered characteristics like PARTNER, EST, ACOUNT, REGS and SZFRM are found to be statistically significant for financial access as well as extent of loan for the years 2010–11 and 2015–16. All the variables except PROP and NPON are directly related with dependent variable in both the years. If an enterprise is found to operate with partnerships, then the probability of financial access of that enterprise increases, and the extent of loan received by them is slightly higher than the others categories. The ESTs have more chance to get loan and they have received higher amount of loan than OAMEs. Further, regular maintenance of account increases the scope of financial access. Registration of enterprises under act or authority too increases the access as well as the amount of loan received by the UMEs. The accessibility of microfinance is significantly high or larger size of firm.

Conclusions

In spite of being the hub of employment of millions of people, UMEs faces difficulties in getting loans from the formal financial institutions. Nearly 80% of the UMEs received loans up to Rs. 125,000 indicating that the lions' share of loan is microcredit or microfinance type. Among these UMEs around half of them received loans from money lenders and relatives and concerningly the share has increased over time. The share of loans from government bodies is negligible and the share of finance from the government institutions and co-operative banks has reduced over time. Across twenty-five activities, only three activities, namely Food Product, Manufacture of Wearing Apparel and Manufacture of Textiles activities captured almost 55% of total loan. Among bottom fifteen activities in terms of share of total loan, five activities specifically Manufacture of Beverages, Manufacture of Electrical Equipment, Manufacture of Motor Vehicles, Trailers and Semi-Trailers, Manufacture of Computer, Electronic and Optical Products, Manufacture of Pharmaceuticals and Medicinal Chemical and Botanical Products can grow faster with proper financial assistance as these have strong linkage with the growth of Indian economy.

Strikingly, only 8% of the UMEs have access to microfinance in 2015–16 which was lesser in 2010–11. Per enterprise employment was comparatively higher among the UMEs which received finance as compared to those which didn't receive loans. Further, the enterprises which have financial access maintain account regularly and registered are more likely to be expanding than stagnating in both 2010–11 and 2015–16. Together with that perennial and seasonal enterprises as well as establishment are also more likely to be expanding than stagnating and contracting. Financial accessibility is relatively high for the establishment and registered enterprises, enterprises which maintain accounts, have partnership, and have higher fixed assets. Microfinance has played a vital role in the growth of employment, GVA and fixed assets of UMEs. Thus, to promote the growth of UMEs in India, the facility of microfinance must be extended to them. Effective policies in this direction are inevitable for UMEs led equitable growth and development of the Indian economy.

REFERENCES

Arora, S., & Meenu. (2012). The banking sector intervention in the microfinance world: A study of bankers' perception and outreach to rural microfinance in India with special reference to the state of Punjab. *Development in Practice, 22*(7), 991–1005.

Ayyagari, M., Demirguc- Kunt, A., & Maksimovic, V. (2010). Formal versus informal finance: Evidence from China. *The Review of Financial Studies, 23*(8), 3048–3097. https://doi.org/10.1093/rfs/hhq030

Beck, T., & Kunt, A. (2006). Small and medium-size enterprises: Access to finance as a growth constraint. *Journal of Banking and Finance, 30*(11), 2931–2943. https://doi.org/10.1016/j.jbankfin.2006.05.009

Beck, T., Kunt, A., Laeven, L., & Maksimovic, V. (2004). *The determinants of financing obstacles* (Policy Research Working Paper 3204) (pp. 1–26). World Bank.

Bhattacharya, A. (2013). Credit retrogression in the micro and small enterprise sector. *Economic and Political Weekly, 48*(35), 105–114.

Bhavani, T., & Bhanumurthy, N. (2014). Financial access—Measurement and determinants: A case study of unorganised manufacturing enterprises in India. *Indian Economic Review, 49*(1), 85–108.

Carpenter, E. R., & Petersen, B. C. (2001). Is the growth of small firms constrained by internal finance? *The Review of Economics and Statistics, 84*(2), 298–309. https://doi.org/10.1162/003465302317411541

Gupta, G. (2011). Micro-finance as a poverty reduction tool-A critical aspect of India. *The Indian Journal of Political Science, 72*(1), 259–271.

Heckman, J. J. (1979). Sample selection bias as a specification error. *Econometrica, 47*(1), 153–161.

Kumar, N., & Gugloth, S. (2012). Financial management in MSMEs in India. *International Journal of Exclusive Management Research, 2*, 9.

Kunt, A., & Levine, R. (2008). *Finance, financial sector policies and long run growth* (Policy Research Paper WPS4469) (pp. 1–79). World Bank.

Love, I., & Peria, M. (2005). *Firm financing in India: Recent trends and patterns* (Policy Research Working Paper WPS3476). World Bank.

NCEUS. (2007). *Report on financing of enterprises for enterprises in the unorganised sector & creation of a national fund for the unorganised sector*. National Commission for Enterprises in Unorganised Sector, Government of India, New Delhi.

Raj, R., & Sen, K. (2015). Finance constraints and firm transition in the informal sector: Evidence from Indian manufacturing. *Oxford Development Studies*, *43*(1), 123–143. https://doi.org/10.1080/13600818.2014.972352

Safavian, M., & Wimpey, J. (2007). *When do enterprises prefer informal credit?* (Policy Research Working Paper 4435). World Bank.

Singh, K. B. (1954). The Shroff committee report—A review. *The Economic Weekly*, 855–857.

World Bank. (2010). *The state of financial inclusion through the crisis.*

CHAPTER 10

Assessing Microfinance Potentiality in India with Special Reference to Odisha: Combating Global Recession Through Local Intervention

Navin Kumar Rajpal and Sharmila Tamang

INTRODUCTION

Microfinance program doesn't need any introduction. Though the formal emergence of program was reported from Bangladesh in 1970 (through microfinance movement), its origin can also be traced during fifteenth century in form of community-oriented pawnshop in Italy and so on. The program has created revolution in twentieth century by facilitating extensive features of community participation, self-regulation and intervention.

N. K. Rajpal (✉)
Assistant Professor in Economics, Sidho-Kanho-Birsha University, Purulia, West Bengal, India
e-mail: rajpal300@gmail.com

S. Tamang
Department of Economics, Mizoram University, Aizawl, Mizoram, India

© The Author(s), under exclusive license to Springer Nature Singapore Pte Ltd. 2022
R. C. Das (ed.), *Microfinance to Combat Global Recession and Social Exclusion*, https://doi.org/10.1007/978-981-16-4329-3_10

The distinctive component of the program is extension of the financial and related support via formal institutions/agencies without any collateral and security. Being among the largest social development program, microfinance now covers 139.9 million borrowers worldwide including 80% women borrowers. The dominance of microfinance program is observed in South Asian region with India as the largest player covering 100.14 lakh SHGs and linking 1224 lakhs households. The mode of operation and service delivery mechanism is found be different in many countries; for example, in France, the microfinance is supported by state and executed by social workers while that in case of Latin America and Caribbean NGOs play dominant role. Further, limited outreach of the program is observed in 48 countries of sub-Saharan Africa holding only 2% of microfinance institutions and 12% of banking households.

Globally, microfinance provides a ray of hope for unbanked poor. The program is linked with the global financial systems and thus is also subject to several market risk and shocks. Financial crisis and global recessions as part of macroeconomy also severely affect the microfinance sector in terms of coverage, outreach, composition and performance. Before proceeding further for highlighting the impact of financial crisis and assessing potentiality of related sector, it becomes necessary to elaborate the definition and impact of such crisis on banking institutions and economy. The economic crisis is not anything unpredicted/new, but the problem is that people have not learnt from previous experiences. During last 100 years, the world had witnessed seven major financial crises as explained below.

Year	Crisis	Impact
1932	Great Depression	Nearly 30 million US $ were lost in a day. The Great Depression lasted from 1929 to 1939 and was worst economic turndown in history
1956	Suez Crisis	Created political tension between Israelis, Britishers and French troops and environment of nuclear war arises
1982	International Debt Crisis	Mexico and other Latin American countries default on its sovereign debt. A sharp decline in international reserves force to devaluate the peso leading of dominance of dollar. Fails also to repay international borrowing

(continued)

(continued)

Year	Crisis	Impact
1992–1997	Russian Economic Crisis	On August 13, 1998, the Russian bond, stock and currency market collapsed as a result of devaluation and default on domestic debt. This results in contraction of economy by 5.3% and GDP per capita reaches to lowest level since formation of Russian federation
1994–2002	Latin American Debt Crisis	The effect of the crisis is also termed as "Tequila effect/shocks". In December 1994, Mexico peso was devalued causing global currency crisis and resulting bailout package $ 50 billion from IMF. Both domestic political and international factors were responsible for this crisis
1997–2001	East Asian Economic Crisis	Also known as Asian economic crisis. This currency crisis began in Thailand and extend in other neighboring countries when Bangkok unpegged the Thai Baht from US dollar. This leads to drop in capital inflows of more than 100 billion dollars during first year of crisis and subsequently extended to global crisis covering Russian and Brazilian economy
2007–2009	Global Economic Recession	Also known as global financial crisis created due to excessive risk taken by banks. It was also followed by European debt crisis in 2009

Source Compiled by the authors

The financial crisis origin is considered from collapse of credit market caused by losses in certain important sectors/premises of economy, but its effect is not limited to financial market (Firtescu, 2012). The banking and financial crises are an essential part of modern economic history, and due to globalization, its effects were observed beyond boundaries. Since Great Depression, the world has witnessed more than 112 systematic banking crises since 1970 including common characteristics, i.e., lax regulatory regime and mismatch between risk and capacity bearing. The financial crisis transforms into economic turndown due to freezing of credit market, fall in aggregate demand, diminishing community purchasing capacity, continuing pay and labor cuts and production collapsed (Kumar & Vashisht, 2009).

The impact of global economic crisis effects the poor and marginalized in more harsh way as compared to upper sections of community. Debroy (2009) considered three major impacts of slowdown, i.e., on macroeconomic variables, poverty and welfare schemes and lastly upon fiscal measures. Further, rural marketing association in their study in 2008 concluded no evidence of slowdown on agriculture sector while marginal impact on trade and commerce. Further, Mahajan V. (2009) also found little or no impact of slowdown on sectors catering lower end of domestic demand, i.e., food, clothing and shelter and even no danger of job loss in agriculture sector. Further, the investment in food processing industry in India also not affected by slowdown due to engagement of industries on regular use items.

The microfinance program had proven potentiality in generating rural employment and directly influencing the consumption level, saving and investment pattern and decision at individual, household and community level. Rajpal (2014) found divergence of microfinance loans on other economic activities such as leased and owned farming (area expansion and coverage) has helped other members of households/community in generating gainful employment and income. Easy credit availability creates crowding out effect at local levels, and with microfinance target-oriented approach, positive attitude related to transparency and bargaining power is observed.

Literature Review

Review of earlier literature done by Debroy (2009) categorized effects of the slowdown on growth of three sectors, i.e., external inflows and out flows, poverty reductions and government revenue. He asserted that people who are more integrated and connected with organized market suffer a lot, and therefore, the rural population who are engaged in agricultural production suffer less due to less dependency on financial institutions and markets. Further, according to Ghosh (2006), volatility in output prices poses serious threat to farmers in addition of infrastructural crisis, weather uncertainties and reduced assistance (after 1991). Datta and Sahu supported empirical facts for positive economic impact among sample respondents during pre-loan and post-loan situation. Priyadarshee

(2016) linked the microfinance program with social protection through incorporating participation in various welfare schemes and suggested for effective continuation of such program along with microfinance for boosting rural demand and financial environment.

Reddy (2013) made study about the deepening problems of rural labor market and concentration of labor on agriculture production. He asserted that with increasing demographic pressure and dependency on agriculture in rural areas, credit linkage extension should focus on development of non-farm sector and employment. The risk associated with agricultural production should be counterattack with simultaneous participation in non-farm employment activities.

Methodology and Sample Selection

This study tried to support the title through taking into consideration 240 WSHG members from two district of Odisha, i.e., Balasore and Mayurbhanj. The two districts being considered based upon human development reports identified as developed and underdeveloped. The Balasore is categorized as industrial endorsed district while Mayurbhanj as tribal dominant district. The study was executed in six blocks of each selected district covering 12 panchayats and 120 households (10 households from each panchayat).

Period of Study and Brief Description of Selected Area

The study was carried out in both the selected district in between the months of January and June 2013. Both districts pose different geographical characteristics and infrastructural availability. The Balasore district is well connected through road and railways with Bhubaneswar and Kolkata, while Mayurbhanj is a tribal-dominated district having biosphere reserves and roadways are major public transport.

Analysis and Interpretation

Economic insecurity, unemployment and social backwardness were always in top priority to be addressed by emerging countries. Further, the economic recession breaks the backbone of economy and severely affects the existing socioeconomic environment. The crisis connotes a repercussive situation where different negative effects and experiences are observed on different disciplines, sections, sectors and professions (Ahiafor, 2019). According to the reports of CGAP on financial crisis, impact on MFIs observed harder to access funding and sinking portfolios while that of their client's severe economic contraction, high food prices and prioritizing consumption expenditure makes harder for repayment. Borrowers engaged in petty businesses, trading and manufacturing are most affected by the crisis. The observed reasons of various crisis are monetary mismanagement, consumption and related demand crisis, sectoral stagnation, system failure, regulatory absence or mismanagement/failures and unpredictable human behavior. Majority of the microfinance entrepreneurs in India are engaged in primary/production-based activities followed by distribution or reselling of agricultural-based minor processed products. Very rare cases of joint activities in large scale related to manufacturing are observed via literature review and other sources.

The objectives of the microfinance program are to facilitate affordable credit to the poorest, vulnerable and deprived sections of society at continuous and transparent manner and promoting livelihood. Further, the creation of sustainable shock proof employment opportunities with benefits of government subsidy and support was among major themes of the program. Our study therefore tries to highlight the engagement of WSHG respondents on livelihood promotion activities exploring income sources and its sustainability, activity-wise classification and financial stability in the study area.

Financial Linkage and Loan Portfolios

The microfinance-based women entrepreneurs in both selected districts have undertaken individual multiple businesses, thereby mitigating the possible effects of losses. Their engagements were observed in two types of economic activities classified as main occupation and SHG-based occupation (Table 10.1).

The selected 68% respondents of Mayurbhanj pose less than 1 acre of land while that in case of Balasore district is 82%. The study observed an average association of 7 years with the program by the WSHG respondents of Mayurbhanj. Further, 80% of respondents are from BPL households and are mostly illiterate (41%) and attended primary education (22%). Within a span of 7 years, the respondents have availed on an

Table 10.1 Socioeconomic and employment details

Components	Mayurbhanj	Balasore
Avg. duration of existence (yrs.)	7	5
BPL composition (in %)	80	84
Illiterate members (in %)	41	22
Before joining group		
Total employment (man-days)	13	13
Total income (INR)	464	1420
After joining group		
Average loan per member (INR)	7692	16,578
No. of loans	1.4	2.4
Total employment (man-days)	17	23
SHG-based employment	8	12
Total income (INR)	1176	2495
SHG-based income (INR)	679	1322

Source Primary data

average 1 loan (basically targeting subsidized loan) with an average loan amount of Rs. 7692. The respondents have engaged on an average by 17 days per month after joining the group (combined main and group occupation) with an average income per month of Rs. 1176 with share of group business of 58%. While that in case of Balasore district the average duration of existence is 5 years with 84% representatives from BPL category. The composition of illiterate members is low (22%) as compared to Mayurbhanj district (41%). The average days of employment per month before joining group were 13 man-days which has increased to 23 man-days after joining the program. Further, the amount of loan availed by each respondent is more than double (Rs. 16,578) as compared to WSHG respondents of Mayurbhanj (Rs. 7692). The number of loans availed also found to be higher in Balasore district as compared to Mayurbhanj and meanwhile employment and income from group as well as other sources (total).

As observed after joining the program, the employment and income of the respondents have increased via various sources of their engagements and therefore to predict the impact of economic crisis, the classification of engagements is reflected in Table 10.2. The main occupation is broadly classified into four categories, mainly no work, daily labor, farmers and others. In Balasore, 78% of respondents are engaged in farming activities (leased and owned) and only 10% are working as daily labor, while that

Table 10.2 Activity-wise employment details

Main occupation	Freq. (%)	Avg. emp	Avg. income
Balasore			
No work	4	0	0
Daily labor	10	10	1133
Farmers	78	11	1210
Others	8	11	1337
Mayurbhanj			
No work	6	0	0
Daily labor	10	7	440
Farmers	66	8	475
Others	18	13	1286

Activities	Percentage	Avg. emp	Avg. income
SHG financed occupation (Balasore)			
Animal husbandry	27	9	1031
Vegetable farming	12	13	1500
Rice business	4	14	1760
Puffed rice	8	12	1500
Leaf plate stitching	14	11	1211
Bari and papad	8	13	1480
Fishery	10	12	1475
Shop	9	7	714
Others	8	10	1133
SHG financed occupation (Mayurbhanj)			
Animal husbandry	44	9	559
Sabai grass business	6	7	477
Vegetable farming	4	10	723
Shop	6	8	500
Rice business	12	7	393
Leaf plate stitching	10	6	250
Bamboo work	8	9	485
Others	10	8	474

Others includes artisans, servant, shop, asha workers, etc.
Source Primary data

in case of Mayurbhanj 66% WSHG respondents are engaged in farming activities followed by 10% daily labor.

The employment and income from main occupation are higher among respondents of Balasore due to large size of productive land holding and infrastructural support. Majority of the respondents are engaged in traditional agriculture and related activities such as animal husbandry, leaf stitching, vegetable farming and fisheries. Further, the employment from the group activities ranges from 7 to 14 man-days and income Rs. 714 to 1760 per month.

In Mayurbhanj, higher percentage of respondents are engaged in animal husbandry business followed by kendua leaf plates, sabai grass rope making and bamboo work. The availability of natural resources of Simlipal national forest and grazing land provides round the year employment and livelihood opportunities to poor and marginalized tribal population. Majority of WSHG respondents are dependent upon common property resources available in district and thus contributing proportionate share in livelihood. The average man-days employment via group financed activities varies from 7 to 10 days with income ranging between Rs. 250 and 559 per month. The other section includes poultry, pottery, tailoring, masala grinding and packaging, and ground nut production, etc.

Saving and Expenditure Composition

The program seeks to promote saving habits among poor with formal financial institutions keeping in view the rendering cost of services. Thus, regular individual member savings are accumulated and deposits in group corpus fund. Though at micro-level the amount seems to be low but as per reports of NABARD till March 2020, the SHGs have accumulated a saving of more than Rs. 26,152 crores with average saving per SHG of Rs. 25,551.

Table 10.3 shows the average saving accumulated by WSHG respondents after joining SHG program. The average contribution per members ranges between Rs. 50 and 100 in Balasore, while that in case of Mayurbhanj is Rs. 20 and 100. The average amount of saving made by each WSHG members since inception is Rs. 2985 in Balasore, while that in Mayurbhanj is Rs. 4137. Therefore, the average loan availed by WSHG respondents of Mayurbhanj is 1.85 times multiple of saving, while that in case of Balasore is 5.55 times of saving. Further, the monthly rate of return (RoR) compared to investment/loan is found to be higher

Table 10.3 Saving and expenditure composition (INR)

Saving composition	Balasore	Mayurbhanj
Saving range	50–100	20–100
Accumulated saving	600–3600	480–9600
Average saving	2985	4137

Monthly average family expenditure (INR)

Composition	Balasore	Mayurbhanj
Food	1618	1640
Clothing	75	141
Health	81	179
Recreation	153	105
Social occasions	160	244
Transportation	89	147
Others	422	179
Total	2598	2635
Total exp. before joining program	2035	1280
% change	28	105

Source Primary data

with WSHG respondents of Mayurbhanj district (8.8%) as compared to respondents of Balasore (7.9%).

Table 10.3 further shows higher expenditure by WSHG respondents of Mayurbhanj as compared to Balasore. The respondents of Balasore are actively engaged in agriculture and allied activities and thus fulfilling their fooding expenditure side by side. The comparison between income of women respondents and total family expenditure found higher contributing share of WSHG respondents of Balasore (96%), while that of Mayurbhanj is 45%. Further, fooding expenditure constitutes a significant share of total expenditure among respondents of both selected districts. Further, after joining program due to increase income of the respondents, significant increase in total family expenditure is observed in both selected districts (with higher increase among tribal respondents).

Conclusion

The objectives of the several welfare programs are to boost rural economic environment through increasing employment and participation in economic growth process. The facilitation of low-cost banking services to rural poor through microfinance has provided an opportunity to increase employment, income, becoming self-reliant and improving economic conditions. As similar to the findings of Swain R. (2006), our study also found significant improvement in macroeconomic variables through spillover effects of investments and rotational savings. Majority of beneficiaries are either marginal or small farmers, and thus, focus of microfinance program should be at developing non-farm activities for diversification of risk and mitigation. The diversification of investments on multiple activities and continuation of main occupation (traditional farming/daily labor) result in better man power and activities management. Since the microfinance works under local economy catering the requirements of daily investment needs often resultant lower demand as well as return. But with sizeable amount of investment in both farm and non-farm sectors possible (with increasing loan amount) further growth in economic variables and development in socioeconomic environment may be anticipated.

References

Ahiafor, A. (2019). *Strategies for mitigating the effects of crisis in microfinancing institutions in Ghana*. Walden University. https://scholarworks.waldenu.edu/cgi/viewcontent.cgi?article=8638&context=dissertations

Debroy, B. (2009). Growth downturn and its effects. In *Global financial crisis: Impact on India's poor some initial perspectives*. UNDP, India.

Firtescu, B. (2012). Causes and effects of crises on financial system stability in emerging countries. *Procedia Economics and Finance, 3*, 489–495.

Ghosh, J. (2006). Global crisis and the Indian economy. In *Global financial crisis: Impact on India's poor some initial perspectives*. UNDP, India.

Impact of the financial crisis on microfinance institutions and their clients. (2009). Brief CGAP. https://www.cgap.org/sites/default/files/CGAP-Brief-The-Impact-of-the-Financial-Crisis-on-Microfinance-Institutions-and-Their-Clients-May-2009.pdf

Kumar, R., & Vashisht, P. (2009). *The global economic crisis: Impact on India and policy responses* (ADBI Working Paper 164). Asian Development Bank

Institute, Tokyo. http://www.adbi.org/working-paper/2009/11/12/3367.global.economic.crisis.india/

Mahajan, V. (2009). Impact of economic downturn on non-farm sector workers. In *Global financial crisis: Impact on India's poor some initial perspectives*. UNDP, India. https://www.undp.org/content/dam/india/docs/impact_of_the_financial_crisis_on_the_poor_in_india_some_initial_perspectives.pdf

Microfinance Barometer. (2018). *Microfinance and Profitabilities* (9th ed.). https://www.convergences.org/wp-content/uploads/2018/09/BMF_2018_EN_VFINALE.pdf

Mitra, A., & Das, D. (2018). Inclusive growth: Economics as if people mattered. *Global Business Review. 19*(3), 756–770.

Priyadarshee, A. (2016). Microfinance and poverty reduction. *Journal of Development Policy and Practice, 1*(1), 35–52.

Rajpal, N. K. (2014). *Microfinance and women empowerment—A case study of Mayurbhanj district in Odisha* (Ph.D Thesis, Mizoram University).

Reddy, N. (2013). Formal credit and rural occupational diversification: Recent experience in India. *Journal of Land and Rural Studies, 1*(1), 1–24.

Swain, R. (2006). Microfinance: A catalyst for development at macroeconomic level? *Finance and Bien Commun*, pg. 83–87. https://www.cairn.info/revue-finance-et-bien-commun-2006-2-page-83.htm

PART II

Role of Microfinance in Reducing Social Exclusion of the Countries and Regions

CHAPTER 11

Financial Inclusion Through Microfinance: Is It Possible?

Arti Yadav, Vani Kanojia, and Megha Jain

OVERVIEW

For any nation, whether a developing or developed, credit penetration is a fundamental condition to ensure economic progress. The simultaneity of inclusion of marginalized sections along with credit deepening is the key to unlock unrealized potential of any nation. The same cannot be made possible until these financially excluded (poor and vulnerable) strata have sufficient opportunity to access various banking services at the desired time of requirement. Timely addressal of the above condition could be

---

A. Yadav (✉)
Department of Management Studies, Ramanujan College, University of Delhi, Delhi, India
e-mail: artiyadavdse@gmail.com

V. Kanojia
School of Management, Gautam Buddha University, Greater Noida, India

M. Jain
Department of Commerce, Daulat Ram College, New Delhi, India

the only way forward to contain social paradoxes such as poverty, unemployment, and social disintegration. In this context, the main objectives of this chapter are as follows:

- To explain the notion of microfinance and financial inclusion.
- To explain the role and significance of microfinance and financial inclusion.
- To examine whether it is possible to achieve financial inclusion through microfinance.
- To find out the issues faced in the role of microfinance institutions toward financial inclusion and suggest measures for the sustainability of both.

In light of the above objectives, it is essential to understand first microfinance and financial inclusion unambiguously.

Microfinance: According to the Reserve Bank of India (2011), "Microfinance consists of the provision of credit also with services like insurance, counseling, money transfers, savings, etc. The key objective of Microfinance is to make a way out of poverty for the poor and lead to economic development". In other words, microfinance is a provision of financial services (deposit, credit, repayment, insurance, and savings) to the deprived section (those who are poor and can't offer collateral) to access the conventional financial services (Littlefield et al., 2003; Robinson, 2001). Reduction in the level of poverty and increased socioeconomic development through easy availability and accessibility of the credit market are the ideas behind the introduction of microfinance (Samer et al., 2015).

Also, the survey by the World Bank and NCAER in 2003 purported that almost 79% of rural households do not have the opportunity to avail credit from formal sources; therefore, microfinance has a long way to sail toward greater financial inclusion (Basu & Srivastava, 2005).

Financial Inclusion: According to the Reserve Bank of India (2016), "Financial Inclusion is the process of making accessible to the vulnerable groups such as weaker sections and in general to all the sections of society, the appropriate financial products and services in a fair and transparent manner by mainstream institutional players at an affordable cost". In other words, with the help of financial inclusion, financial products and services such as payments, credit, transactions, insurance, and savings are made available at an affordable price and in a sustainable manner (World Bank, 2018). Additionally, the Center for Financial Inclusion defines financial inclusion as "A state in which everyone who can use them has access to a full suite of quality financial services, provided at affordable prices, in a convenient manner, with respect and dignity. Financial services are delivered by a range of providers, in a stable, competitive market to financially capable clients".

Earlier Scenario: Since the inception of independence, credit lending has been mainly via informal channels like informal moneylenders, non-institutional sources, etc., where banks' share in the total credit requirements used to be negligible. This scenario continued till 1971, after that formal source of credit share started increasing steadily. Therefore, the key challenge remained to extend the financial services to each section of the society by the banks. Accessibility and affordability were the prime concerns for wider reach.

Current Scenario: It is only in the year 2006 that RBI structured the entire roadmap of financial inclusion via a systematic focused approach, taking both the demand and supply sides. Since then, microfinance has started gaining relevance even more. Its potential is reported in Bharat Microfinance Report 2019 where microfinance institutions now operate in 29 states, 5 UTs, and 570 districts in India. As India's 70% population inhabited in villages, Regional Rural Banks and Cooperative Banks act as a catalyst to meet the total micro-financial needs to pave the road ahead for financial inclusion. The need for financial inclusion with the advent of technology in the banking system could facilitate efficient experience to the end-users with greater accessibility of finance, specifically to financially excluded population. Facilities like digital onboarding could play a vital role in achieving the broader objective of financial inclusion. Further, the huge growing working population (financially excluded) wants to shift to the middle-class category with the help of institutional support using available means like emergency loans, consumption loans, business loans, working capital loans, housing, etc.

Therefore, the last hope of the poor is to take loans irrespective of their requirements as new entrepreneurs or laborers. Unfortunately, the opportunities of credit availability for the laborers (with skills and creativity) remain grim. Further, if these skilled laborers could be provided the required microfinance credit, they too have the potential of becoming future successful entrepreneurs.

The basic objective of financial inclusion is to provide financial and banking services to individuals irrespective of their income and savings. Providing financial education in terms of making the best use of the money by the deprived section of the society is also one of the aims of financial inclusion (Atkinson & Messy, 2013). Further development in technologies in the form of digital transactions is trying to make financial inclusion an achievable concept (Arun & Kamath, 2015).

Microfinance can be beneficial to society in many ways (Fig. 11.1). It can empower the poor or vulnerable section to become part of the conventional banking system. Various studies have suggested that microfinance is capable of having a significant impact on the well-being of society at various levels such as women's empowerment, food security, asset acquisition, health, social cohesion, and educational level (Armendariz & Morduch, 2010; Roodman & Morduch 2009; Samer et.al., 2015).

Financial inclusion can help in building among the poor the concept of savings which will lead to the strengthening of the economic resources and ultimately bring inclusive growth along with sustainable economic development (Omar & Inaba, 2020). So, both financial inclusion and microfinance are part of the sustainable economic growth of an economy, as financial inclusion provides access to useful financial tools, while the use

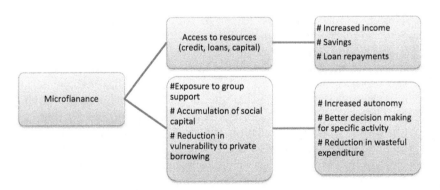

Fig. 11.1 Advantages of microfinance (*Source* Sketched by the authors)

of those tools leads to positive benefits for those living in poverty through microfinance (Ozili, 2018).

The remaining chapter is organized as follows. Section two entails the existing literature review. Section three specifies the overview of financial inclusion through microfinance, followed by a discussion on key concerns related to the role of microfinance in promoting financial inclusion. Last but certainly not least, the current chapter concludes the study with key policy remarks.

Review of Existing Studies

There are several studies that have investigated the role of microfinance via financial inclusion. But there is a paucity of literature that has considered the recent Global Findex database 2017 to examine the above. A study by Pitt and Khandker (1998) proposes that microfinance enables the well-being of poor households with extended positive holistic impacts in case the credit availability opportunities are provided to women like an increase in household income, production, employment, etc. The study by Littlefield et.al. (2003) and Simanowitz (2004) has discussed the emerging role of microfinance toward the achievement of MDGs. These studies have indicated that microfinance plays a pivotal role in shaping the global financial system that caters to the requirements of marginalized sections of society. Another study conducted by Gurses (2009) in Turkey found that financial inclusion through microfinance could prove to be an effective instrument to reduce poverty.

Guerin et al. (2009) said microfinance is a double-edged sword through reducing the financial vulnerability of households and worked as a significant poverty alleviation strategy or even a means of incorporating excluding potential borrowers into the institutional finance system. The definition of social performance is extended by Gutierrez-Nieto et.al. (2009). They add an indicator, the number of women borrowers, and an indicator that measures the degree to which microfinance institutions' activities can support the poorest to measure social performance.

A study by Ibrahim (2010) has made an attempt to evaluate the consolidated performance of RRBs in India for the period 2005–2006 using secondary data analysis. The paper concludes with a key finding that, despite the reduction in the total number of RRBs over the period 2001–2009, the overall branch network of RRBs has expanded. The paper confirms the penetration of microfinance via financial inclusion. Sriram

(2010) has also pointed toward a different aspect of transformation to "get rich quickly" capitalism, used in the past decade in India via microfinance inclusion. This study also examines in detail the "transformation" of four prominent MFIs in India (SKS Microfinance Ltd, Share Microfin Ltd, Asmitha, and Spandana). In some cases, the study has notified that even the private promoters could be enriched using various means.

Furthermore, according to Ali and Alam (2010), microfinance is an effective tool for increasing the availability of loans and other basic facilities and has a positive impact on people's lives, raising living standards in areas such as health, education, food, and other social benefits, as well as alleviating poverty. Another study by Paramanandam and Packirisamy (2012) compares NABARD in India along with its counterparts such as Grameen Banks in Bangladesh. This study highlights that microfinance via self-help groups (SHGs) successfully established the linkage between SHGs and banks that enabled a reduction in poverty. Additionally, a study by Bruhn and Love (2014) proposes that the advent of financial inclusion leads to assess to finance on poverty using labor market channel as well as access to finance that has the potential to reduce poverty and increase employment and income in low-income regions. Therefore, via financial inclusion, socioeconomic growth can be achieved. In a study by Jain (2019), it has been found that financial inclusion has become a focus area for various types of organizations such as financial technology organizations, banks and non-banking financial companies. Further, the author highlighted the significance of technology in terms of enhancement of the end user experience.

Research Methodology

The present study adopts a descriptive methodology based on various secondary sources of data such as the Global Findex database, World Bank database, various research papers, and reports. The time frame for data inclusion is till 2017 from the Global Findex database due to the non-availability of the data, while from other sources it is till 2019. The scope of the present study covers the microfinance and financial inclusion scenario mostly from the perspective of the major regions of the world.

Financial Inclusion Through Microfinance

The sustainable development goals of the United Nations have prioritized the elimination of poverty by 2030 as the key goal. For this, a target of universal financial access was set up by World Bank and International Finance Corporation (The World Bank, 2018). To achieve financial inclusion, the first step consists of having access to a transaction account that will help in various activities, for instance, send and receive payments and keeping money. It also provides opportunities to access other financial services like to start or expand businesses, health or educational investment, insurance, and credit facilities. However, according to a report, 50% of transaction accounts in developing countries are dormant (Global Findex, 2017).

An increase in the number of poor active accountholders (approximately 500 million) does not signify that most of the low-income group people came under the financial system, as it is just a fraction of the total potential market of 3 billion poor people (Helms, 2006; Omar & Inaba, 2020). The lack of basic financial services for the poor gave rise to many issues for them, for instance, how to pay for children's school, for family needs, and for work requirements (Bage, 2008). These financial services which are the need for poor or low-income people are mostly tried to be satisfied with the help of microfinance (Helms, 2006). Microfinance might offer a solution to these problems. For the financial inclusion of the unprivileged section, activities under microfinance play a significant role, mainly in the form of a bridge that leads to last-mile connectivity (Gupta, 2020). The main aim of microfinance is to move the focus from the supply side to the demand side, i.e., to shift from institutions to individuals (Duvendack & Mader, 2019).

Table 11.1 shows the financial inclusion around the world; over the years, an improvement has been witnessed in terms of various account holders including the poorest, young adults, older adults, low-income groups, rural, and female. Among developed countries, France is at the top with the adults over the age of 15 years, around 94% are having a bank account, whereas this average is less than 63% in developing countries. The reason behind such increase in the number of accountholders is partly attributed to digital payments system development by the policymakers and increased use of the digital platform due to easy access to availability of the Internet and mobile phones (Demirguc-Kunt et.al., 2018). Beneficial to the financiers, development, and alleviation of poverty are some

Table 11.1 World's financial inclusion of adults (% 15+)

	2011	2014	2017
Account (% age 15+)	51	62	69
Account, male (% age 15+)	55	66	72
Account, in labor force (% age 15+)	56	69	74
Account, out of labor force (% age 15+)	38	49	59
Account, female (% age 15+)	47	58	65
Account, young adults (% ages 15–24)	37	47	56
Account, older adults (% ages 25+)	54	66	72
Account, primary education or less (% ages 15+)	37	48	56
Account, secondary education or more (% ages 15+)	66	73	79
Account, income, poorest 40% (% ages 15+)	41	55	61
Account, income, richest 60% (% ages 15+)	57	67	74
Account, rural (% age 15+)	44	58	66

Source Compiled by the authors from the Global Findex database

of the main objectives of microfinance and financial inclusion, both are kind of overlapping practices (Mader, 2017). The scope of microfinance expanded because of financial inclusion as the latter leads to financing the needy not only through microfinance institutions but also tries to incorporate corporations like credit card companies, large banks, and mobile networks (Barajas et. al., 2020). However, various studies in the past questioned the ability of microfinance institutions to alleviate poverty as cases where more harm has been caused by these institutions in the areas like overindebtedness (ability to repay load by borrowing) and funds oversupply (Roodman, 2012; Schicks, 2013). There is enormous potential related to the role of microfinance in financial inclusion and so are the challenges associated with it.

Table 11.2 presents the regional scenario of the financial institutions' participation based on the number of account holders in general who are above 15 years, poorest 40%, and richest 60% for the years 2011, 2014, and 2017. According to the Global Findex database, the rate of growth of account holders in some regions has surged at a much higher rate, while it is much slower in other regions due to the prevalence of various disparities like gender issues and income inequality.

Some of the issues concerning the role of microfinance in financial inclusion are as follows:

Table 11.2 Regional participation scenario of financial institutions

Region	Year	Financial institution account (% age 15+)	Financial institution account, income, poorest 40% (% age 15+)	Financial institution account, income, richest 60% (% age 15+)
East Asia & Pacific	2011	60%	46	69
	2014	72%	65	76
	2017	73	63	80
Europe & Central Asia	2011	69	68	70
	2014	78	74	80
	2017	81	76	85
Middle East & North Africa	2011	38	31	42
	2017	47	39	52
South Asia	2011	32	24	38
	2014	46	37	51
	2017	68	65	71
Sub-Saharan Africa	2011	23	13	29
	2014	29	19	36
	2017	33	23	39

Source Compiled by the authors from the Global Findex database

According to Damodaran (2013) in the process of financial inclusion, the issues faced by regions for instance, in Asian and African region, consist of lack of money creating financial distress; due to high level of illiteracy, both economic development and social development get affected; too expensive banking services or are not easily assessable; religious and cultural issues and prevalence of institutional regulations. It has also been found that formal financial institutions often ignore the weaker section of the society affecting the financial service accessibility and therefore, reducing their chance to come out of poverty (Deep Knowledge Analytics & Future FinTech, 2018). Microfinance has also been criticized around the world because of issues like debt traps, land grabbing (found in Cambodia), the association of loan sharks with microlenders (in India), selling of organs through labor agreements (in Bangladesh), and overstuffed informal sectors (Handley, 2019; Karim, 2011). It has also been found that in various aspects the microfinance programs are based on weak theories as they are not very plausible; for instance, financial transactions are expected to help poor people's money management at the micro-level, and at the macro-level, they are expected to be drivers of growth (Khanvilkar, 2016; Wondirad, 2020).

On the policy front, it has been found that instead of funding public goods and infrastructure, financial institutions are funded by the concerned governments leading to a misdirection of funding toward private financial development (Chakraborty et al., 2016). The main aim of microfinance is to provide loans at an affordable cost; however, on average the interest rate is around 25%, which is significantly high in comparison with the traditional loan system rates. High service cost is one of the reasons for the high loan rates (Shankar, 2013; Microfinance Barometer, 2018). In addition to that, there are ethical challenges associated with microfinance in the form of "responsible microfinance" and "social performance management" which is mostly voluntary forms and their results are vague. Along with that, entry of global organizations in the space of financial inclusion has given rise to various issues related to ethics and regulations (Kleynjans & Hudon, 2016; The World Bank, 2013). The role of microfinance has been extended recently beyond the contemporary model as both banking and non-banking institutions are participating and even attracting foreign capital investment; therefore, the goal of such institutions has emerged from just being social welfare to commercial gains (Mermod, 2013). So, the objective of the authorities should be to develop a system which should make the institutions socially responsible. Further, it should be made clear that both microfinance and financial inclusion help each other to sustain as according to a study, in developing economies the poor have high propensity to save which ultimately leads to financial deepening (Conroy, 2008; The World Bank, 2018).

The Way Forward and Conclusion

Even in the twenty-first century, there is a long road ahead before reaching the goal of financial inclusion; however, microfinance can help to cover this distance if applied and monitored in the true sense of its vision. The era of digitalization through the growth of mobile phones and the Internet has led to data explosion in various sectors of the economies around the world. This has opened lots of opportunities for the low-income customers who can also participate using the Internet on e-commerce platforms, and this has led to the generation of informal and formal databases for microfinance institutions. In addition to that, innovation in the form of machine learning and artificial intelligence is also providing greater application areas for lending firms and institutions in order to enhance the accessibility of financial services. To achieve universal financial inclusion, synergistic efforts from various participants (microfinance institutions, banks, non-banking financial institutions, etc.) are the need of the hour. Not only public institutions but also private and social sectors are needed for the sustainability of the efforts in terms of models that are innovative enough to motivate more toward financial inclusion at an affordable cost and quality services. Also from the perspective of the targeted group, the microfinance institutions should try to build up their trust level not only in letters but also in spirit by working in a transparent and effective environment through following the code of conduct and code of responsible lending.

Further, enhancement of digital literacy is highly recommended in order to minimize the negative impact of digital technology in terms of online frauds, cybersecurity, data threats, etc. A key role in any economy is played by the policies of the regulatory authority and the government of the concerned economy, so, through providing incentives to the microfinance institutions, the government can persuade them to increase their outreach to the rural areas and low-income groups. A regular check on the fraudulent practices, interest rates, excess interference, and undercapitalization can also be put on by the government in order to make the outcome more qualitative. In addition to that in various developed and developing economies to achieve financial inclusion, there is a need for well-developed legal and institutional infrastructure depending on the culture of the concerned economy. Also to encourage the spread of the efforts of microfinance institutions evenly toward financial inclusion, incentive packages based on the target areas can be provided.

Therefore, the present study emphasized the link between microfinance and financial inclusion by giving an overview of the individual concept and highlighting the need and issues with the practical approach. It is solely based on the secondary database and captures mostly the macro-aspect of microfinance and financial inclusion. Therefore, further research can be based on primary data, individual sector, or specific economy, or scenario of one group of economies can be compared with the other one.

References

Ali, A., & Alam, M. A. (2010). *Role and performance of microcredit in Pakistan* (Independent thesis). Department of Economic and IT. University West. Retrieved from https://www.diva-portal.org/smash/record.jsf?pid=diva2%3A323460&dswid=-1969

Armendariz, B., & Morduch, J. (2005). *The economics of microfinance*. MIT Press.

Arun, T., & Kamath, R. (2015). Financial inclusion: Policies and practices. *IIMB Management Review, 27*(4), 267–287. https://doi.org/10.1016/j.iimb.2015.09.004

Atkinson, A. & Messy, F. (2013). *Promoting financial inclusion through financial education: OECD/INFE evidence, policies and practice* (OECD Working Papers on Finance, Insurance and Private Pensions, No. 34). OECD. Retrieved from https://doi.org/10.1787/5k3xz6m88smp-en

Bage, L. (2008). Microfinance: A lifeline for poor rural people. *Uluslararasi Ekonomik Sorunlar. Turkish Ministry of Foreign Affairs*. Retrieved from https://www.ifad.org/en/web/latest/speech/asset/39031205

Barajas, A. Beck, T., Belhaj, M. & Naceur, S. B. (2020). *Financial inclusion: What have we learned so far? What do we have to learn?* (IMF Working Paper, WP/20/157). Retrieved from file:///C:/Users/dell/AppData/Local/Temp/wpiea2020157-print-pdf.pdf

Basu, P., & Srivastava, P. (2005). *Scaling-up microfinance for India's rural poor* (Policy Research Working Paper; No. 3646). World Bank, Washington

Bruhn, M., & Love, I. (2014). The real impact of improved access to finance: Evidence from Mexico. *The Journal of Finance, 69*(3), 1347–1376.

Centre for Financial Inclusion. (2013). Microfinance vs. Financial inclusion: What's the difference? *Blog Post*. Retrieved from https://www.centerforfinancialinclusion.org/microfinance-vs-financial-inclusion-whats-the-difference

Chakraborty, P., Chakraborty, L. & Mukherjee, A. (2016). *Social sector in a decentralized economy: India in the era of globalization*. Cambridge University Press. Retrieved from https://openknowledge.worldbank.org/bitstream/handle/10986/23937/SocialSectorinaDecentralizedEconomy.pdf?sequence=1

Conroy, J. D. (2008). *Financial inclusion: A new microfinance initiative for APEC*. The Foundation for Development Cooperation. Retrieved from https://www.findevgateway.org/sites/default/files/publications/files/mfg-en-case-study-financial-inclusion-a-new-microfinance-initiative-for-apec-jan-2008.pdfor

Damodaran, A. (2013). Financial inclusion: Issues and challenges. *AKGEC International Journal of Technology, 4*(2). Retrieved from https://www.researchgate.net/publication/309194840_Financial_Inclusion_Issues_and_Challenges

Deep Knowledge Analytics and Future FinTech. (2018). *Financial inclusion developing world landscape overview*. Retrieved from http://analytics.dkv.glo bal/data/pdf/Financial-Inclusion-Developing-World.pdf

Demirguc-Kunt, A., Klapper, L., Singer, D., Ansar, S. & Hess, J. (2018). *Global findex database 2017: Measuring financial inclusion and the Fintech revolution*. World Bank. Retrieved from https://openknowledgeworldbank.org/handle/10986/29510.

D'Espallier, B., Guérin, I., & Mersland, R. (2009). *Women and repayment in microfinance* (RUME-Working Paper Series [Rural Microfinance and Employment]), 2(4).

Duvendack, M. & Mader, P. (2019). Impact of financial inclusion in low- and middle-income countries: A systematic review of reviews. *Campbell Systematic Reviews*. Wiley. https://doi.org/10.4073/csr.2019.2

Global Findex. (2017). *The global findex database 2017: Overview*. The World Bank. Retrieved from https://globalfindex.worldbank.org/basic-page-overview

Gopalaswamy, A. K., Babu, M. S., & Dash, U. (2015). *Systematic review of quantitative evidence on the impact of microfinance on the poor in South Asia Protocol*. EPPICentre, Social Science Research Unit, Institute of Education, University College London.

Guerin, I., Morvant-Roux, S., & Servet, J-M. (2009). *Understanding the diversity and complexity of demand for microfinance services: Lessons from informal finance* (RUME Working Paper Series, No. 7). Retrieved from https://www.rumerural-microfinance.org

Gupta, S. (2020). *Nothing too small about it: The role of MFIs in financial inclusion*. Nagarro. Retrieved from https://www.nagarro.com/en/blog/role-mic rofinance-financial-inclusion

Gurses, D. (2009). Microfinance and poverty reduction in Turkey. *Perspectives on Global Development and Technology, 8*(1), 90–110.

Gutiérrez-Nieto, B., Serrano-Cinca, C., & Mar Molinero, C. (2009). Social efficiency in microfinance institutions. *Journal of the Operational Research Society, 60*(1), 104–119.

Handley, E. (2019). *Australia called to reassess ties to Cambodian microfinance amid reports of child labour, debt bondage*. ABC News. https://www.abc.net.au/news/2019-08-11/microfinance-loans-land-loss-rights-abuses-cambodia-report/11386962

Helms, B. (2006). *Access to all building inclusive financial systems*. The World Bank, 35031. Retrieved from http://documents1.worldbank.org/curated/ru/526891468138594047/pdf/350310REV0Access0for0All01OFFICIAL0USE1.pdf

Ibrahim, M. S. (2010). Performance evaluation of regional rural banks in India. *International Business Research, 3*(4), 203.

Jain, M. K. (2019). *Microfinance as the next wave of financial inclusion*. Speech, RBI Bulletin. Retrieved from https://rbidocs.rbi.org.in/rdocs/Bulletin/PDFs/04SP11122019531953DE392D482B9D036C79C35912E1.PDF

Karim, L. (2011). *Microfinance and its discontents women in debt in Bangladesh*. University of Minnesota Press.Retrieved from https://www.upress.umn.edu/book-division/books/microfinance-and-its-discontents

Khanvilkar, A.S. (2016).Challenges faced by Microfinance Institutions. nelito. Retrieved from https://www.nelito.com/blog/challenges-faced-microfinance-institutions.html

Kleynjans, L., & Hudon, M. (2016). A study of codes of ethics for Mexican microfinance institutions. *Journal of Business Ethics, 134*, 397–412. https://doi.org/10.1007/s10551-014-2434-y

Littlefield, E., Jonathan, M., & Syed, H. (2003). Is microfinance an effective strategy to reach the millennium development goals? *Focus Note*, 24. CGAP. Retrieved from https://www.cgap.org/sites/default/files/CGAP-Focus-Note-Is-Microfinance-an-Effective-Strategy-to-Reach-the-Millennium-Development-Goals-Jan-2003.pdf

Mader, P. (2017). *How microfinance and financial inclusion impinge on human rights*. Committee for Abolition of illegitimate Debt. Retrieved from https://www.cadtm.org/How-microfinance-and-financial

Mermod A.Y. (2013) Microfinance. In S. O. Idowu, N. Capaldi, L. Zu , & A. D. Gupta (Eds.), *Encyclopedia of corporate social responsibility*. Springer. Retrieved from https://doi.org/10.1007/978-3-642-28036-8_85

Microfinance Barometer. (2018). *Microfinance and profitabilities*. Convergences. Retrieved from https://www.convergences.org/wp-content/uploads/2018/09/BMF_2018_EN_VFINALE.pdf

Omar, M. A., & Inaba, K. (2020). Does financial inclusion reduce poverty and income inequality in developing countries? A panel data analysis. *Economic Structures, 37* (9). Retrieved from https://doi.org/10.1186/s40008-020-00214-4

Ozili, P. K. (2018). Impact of digital finance on financial inclusion and stability. *Borsa Istanbul Review, 18*(4), 329–340.

Paramanandam, D. A., & Packirisamy, P. (2012). A comparative study on the performance of the India's NABARD with the Bangladesh's Grameen Banks. *The International Journal's Research Journal of Social Science and Management, 2*(1), 20–23.

Pitt, M. M., & Khandker, S. R. (1998). The impact of group-based credit programs on poor households in Bangladesh: Does the gender of participants matter? *Journal of Political Economy, 106*(5), 958–996.

Reserve Bank of India. (2011). *Report of the sub-committee of the Central Board of Directors of Reserve Bank of India to study issues and concerns in the*

MFI sector. Retrieved from https://www.rbi.org.in/Scripts/PublicationRepo rtDetails.aspx?ID=608#L4

Reserve Bank of India. (2016). *Financial inclusion in India—The journey so far and the way ahead*. Retrieved from https://www.rbi.org.in/SCRIPTS/BSS peechesView.aspx%3FId%3D1024

Robinson, M. (2001). *The microfinance revolution sustainable finance for the poor*. World Bank.

Roodman, D. (2012). *Due diligence: An impertinent inquiry into microfinance*. Center for Global Development.

Roodman, D., & Jonathan, M. (2009). *Impact of microcredit on the poor in Bangladesh: Revisiting the Evidence*.

Samer, S., Majid, I., Rizal, S., Muhamad, M. R., Halim, S., & Rashid, N. (2015). The impact of microfinance on poverty reduction: Empirical evidence from Malaysian perspective. *Procedia—Social and Behavioral Sciences, 195*, 721–728.

Schicks, J. (2013). Microfinance over-indebtedness: Understanding its drivers and challenging the common myths. *Oxford Development Studies, 41*, 95–117. https://doi.org/10.1080/13600818.2013.778237

Shankar, S. (2013). Financial inclusion in India: Do microfinance institutions address access barriers? *ACRN Journal of Entrepreneurship Perspectives, 2*(1), 60–74.

Simanowitz, A. (2004). *Issues in designing effective microfinance impact assessment systems* (No. 1765-2016-141588).

Sriram, M. S. (2010). Commercialization of microfinance in India: a discussion of the emperor's apparel. *Economic and Political Weekly* (pp. 65–73).

The World Bank. (2013). *The new microfinance handbook: A financial market system perspective*. Retrieved from https://openknowledge.worldbank.org/bit stream/handle/10986/12272/9780821389270.pdf

The World Bank. (2018). *Financial inclusion*. Retrieved from https://www.wor ldbank.org/en/topic/financialinclusion/overview

Wondirad, H. (2020). Competition and microfinance institutions' performance: Evidence from India. *International Journal of Corporate Social Responsibility, 5*, 6. Retrieved from https://doi.org/10.1186/s40991-020-00047-1

World Bank. (2018). *The World Bank annual report 2018*. The World Bank.

CHAPTER 12

Political Economy of Microfinance from the Gender and Politics Point of View: Enhancing Social Inclusion of Women to the Workforce

Egemen Sertyesilisik

INTRODUCTION

There is need for poverty elimination strategy due to the considerable amount of poverty in the world. According to the WB (World Bank) (2000), 1.2 billion people lived on less than $1 per day (WB, 2000 as cited in Robinson, 2001). Low-income people need capital to be encouraged to establish their own businesses. As poor people cannot get the simple financial services, providing them with bank facilities is important to help reduce poverty (Helms, 2006, p. 1). As it is difficult for poor people to get loan from formal banks as small amount of loans and deposit is not profitable for the banks, they have to go to informal

E. Sertyesilisik (✉)
Marine Industries, Izmir, Turkey
e-mail: egemens@alumni.bilkent.edu.tr

© The Author(s), under exclusive license to Springer Nature Singapore Pte Ltd. 2022
R. C. Das (ed.), *Microfinance to Combat Global Recession and Social Exclusion*, https://doi.org/10.1007/978-981-16-4329-3_13

commercial money lenders suffering very high cost (Robinson, 2001, p. 9). Poor people's difficulties in having access to financial services lead them searching for new funding opportunities.

Microcredit aims to enhance welfare of the poor people. Microfinance is a finance tool created for the poor people, who cannot have the possibility to have access to formal banks and their services (Demir, 2016, p. 59). The failure of the efforts of the traditional banks to support the poor people caused the rapid growth in microfinance industry (Allen et al., 2011; Chikalipah, 2018). Microcredit is a tool to alleviate the poverty problem and to integrate poor people into the labour market enabling them to become productive and to enhance their economic and social statuses (Altay, 2007 as cited in Ören et al., 2012). Microcredit is about providing poor people opportunity to get involved in income-providing activities with the help of small start-up capital (Akbıyık & Şahin, 2010). In the Microcredit Summit in 1997, microcredit concept has been defined as a small-scale credit programme to create income for poor people to care their family and themselves (Ceyhan, 2010, p. 1; Erdoğan, 2004, p. 13). The UN Secretary-General Kofi Annan defines microcredit as a "weapon against poverty and hunger" (Njiraini, 2015).

Microcredit has become the hope for poor people. MFIs (microfinance institutions) have their origins in Bangladesh and Bolivia (Gutiérrez-Nieto & Serrano-Cinca, 2019, p. 183). Acknowledging that the traditional banking system fails in meeting the needs of illiterate, poor people and women, Prof. Dr. Muhammad Yunus started his activities to help to these people whose talent and productivity he believed in (Adaman & Bulut, 2007, p. 27: Ceyhan, 2010, p. 6). Microcredit started with $27 loan allocated to 42 poor people by Prof. Dr. Muhammad Yunus (Ören et al., 2012, pp. 320–321). Prof. Dr. Muhammad Yunus developed a banking system in Bangladesh to prevent the poverty with the aim of creating a new type of entrepreneurship and capitalism called as "social working" which is dedicated to solve the social, economic and environmental issues on humanity (Yunus & Weber, 2012 as cited in Demir, 2016, p. 61). Microfinance sector assumes that the poor people have the ability to generate and increase their income in case they have the opportunity to access adequate credit and insurance (Dutta & Banerjee, 2018). In case opportunities are provided to the poor to unleash their hidden entrepreneurship, they can become entrepreneurs (Dutta & Banerjee, 2018; Fernando, 2004). Microcredit can support welfare of the people and encourage women to participate in the workforce which is vital for sustainable development and for reducing the gender gap in the workforce. Increase in female employment level can support productivity growth (WB, 2012; Klasen & Pieters, 2015, p. 3), whereas increase in gender gaps can reduce average income. For example, "... gender gaps cause an average income loss of 15% in the OECD" (Cuberes & Teignier, 2016 as cited in Datta & Kotikula, n.d., p. 8). As microcredit is an important tool for reducing poverty and enhancing welfare, it is a tool for political economy. Adam Smith and David Hume (Smith [1776] 1961) described political economy as a tool for enhancing people's welfare (Nurmi, 2017, p. 1 as cited in Sertyesilisik, 2018, p. 171). Based on an in-depth literature review, this chapter aims to investigate political economy of microfinance from the gender and politics point of view. This chapter particularly focuses on microfinance's role in empowerment of women and in social inclusion of women to the workforce.

Widespread of Microcredit and Microfinance

Microcredit summits acted as important pillars for the widespread of microcredit and microfinance all around the world. "In the first microcredit summit in 1997, the participants (e.g., Citibank, WB) declared their special fund for microcredit" (Muhammad, 2009, p. 37). Furthermore, Citibank opened "Citi Microfinance" in 2005 which was called by the UN as the "International Year of Microcredit" (Muhammad, 2009, p. 37). The campaign report of the 2nd international microcredit summit emphasized that 100 million people benefitted from the $2.5 bn credits provided by 3.000 MFIs (Harford, 2008 as cited in Muhammad, 2009, p. 38). Annually, approximately over one hundred million people can have access to microfinance (Cull & Morduch, 2017; Gutiérrez-Nieto & Serrano-Cinca, 2019, p. 183). Furthermore, the agricultural micro-insurance market grew more than 400% in the five-year period between 2010 and 2015 (Kuwekita et al., 2015 as cited in Chikalipah, 2018, p. 38).

Microfinance has started to be used as a tool to reduce poverty in many countries. Microfinance is an investment tool, especially for developing regions and international institutions (e.g. European Union, UN, WB) (Miled & Rejeb, 2015, pp. 705–706). For example, one-third of households in Bolivia, Indonesia and Bangladesh are clients of MFIs (Credit and Development Forum, 1999; Robinson, 2001, p. 55). The average microloan in Bangladesh is between $75 and 100 (Hashemi et al., 1996,

p. 636 as cited in Isserles, 2003, p. 39). China allowed microfinance in 2005 (Njiraini, 2015). After experimenting microfinance as a tool for reducing poverty, the microfinance industry has grown rapidly in China after 2005 (Njiraini, 2015). Furthermore, the microfinance grew 10% per year in sub-Saharan Africa during the last 20 years (Chikalipah, 2017, 2018). Country experiences reveal that the Grameen Bank model can be widespread in and accepted by different countries having different government forms and socio-economic priorities (Muhammad, 2009, p. 38; Todd, 1996).

Relationship Among Microcredit and Microfinance, Political Economy and Sustainable Development

Microcredit and microfinance can support sustainability and contribute to the sustainable development of the countries. Microenterprises can contribute to the environment and protection of the nature. As Robinson (2001, p. 12) emphasizes, microenterprises can support recycling and repairing of goods so that they are not wasted. Furthermore, microcredit and microfinance can contribute to the economy and they can provide benefits to all their stakeholders. The poor people are the main stakeholder benefitting from them. Microcredit can support poor people to establish their business-enhancing community's social recovery (Altay, 2007; Demir, 2016). Furthermore, the benefits of the Grameen Bank model microcredit system include (Islam et al., 2012, p. 78): approximately 97% repayment rates; higher income; successful group savings; benefitted landless and marginal landowners; contribution to poverty alleviation and economic improvement at the national level. A questionnaire survey applied to the ones who benefitted from the microcredit in Malatya in Turkey revealed that the income of the borrowers increased by 25% and that increased their self-confidence and savings, established their own business, employed other workers and contributed employment rate in their city (Akbıyık & Şahin, 2010, p. 1744).

As microcredit and microfinance can support countries to enhance welfare of their people, MFIs can enable the countries to reduce their poverty head count ratio. Cross-country data (e.g. inflation rate, GDP or gross loan per capita) show that countries with higher MFIs' loans tend to have lower poverty levels (Miled & Rejeb, 2015, pp. 705–706).

Microenterprises play an important role in increasing employment rate and providing new job opportunities. Microenterprises can increase employment (Robinson, 2001, p. 12). 500 million people are running micro- and small enterprises (Women's World Banking, 1995) thanks to the microfinance practitioners and similar donors (Ledgerwood, 1999, p. 1).

As microcredit can reduce the unemployment rate of the countries, countries' unemployment wage payment can be reduced. In this way, countries and their politicians can make more investment to other fields (e.g. education, sustainability, infrastructure) which are vital for well-being and welfare of their people as well as for sustainable development of their countries. These policies can support politicians in the elections.

Microcredit and microfinance can contribute to the children's education which can have impact especially on sustainability and sustainable development. According to Wydick (1999), based on a research made in Guatemala, using microfinance credits can reduce the possibility for the children to be withdrawn from school (Wydick, 1999 as cited in Beck, 2015, p. 21). Furthermore, according to researches of two MFIs and Grameen Bank revealed that microcredit had small but effective favourable impact on the house expenditures, assets and children education (Beck, 2015, p. 20; Pitt & Khandker, 1998).

Successful microcredit cases can support community's social development. Microcredit and microfinance can enable poor people to have hope for their future. Although microfinance cannot solve all poverty issues, it can help poor people to make their daily decisions and plan their way to go out of poverty (Helms, 2006, p. 1). Furthermore, microenterprises can support poor people providing them cheap food, clothing and transportation (Robinson, 2001, p. 12). Microcredit and microfinance can support gender equality in the workforce. They are keys for increasing women participation in the employment and in establishing their own companies.

Social Inclusion and Empowerment of Women Through Microcredit and Microfinance

Grameen Bank, as the first microcredit institute, gave credit to men and women equally with low interest rate and without any profit purpose (Ören et al., 2012, p. 320). Afterwards, the percentage of women, who used microcredit, increased (Armendariz & Morduch, 2005, p. 17; Ören et al., 2012, p. 320). In 1997, 2.23 million borrowers were women

(Isserles, 2003, p. 46; Rahman, 1998, p. 94). About 190 million people, among them approximately 128 million were women, used microcredit by the end of the year 2009 (Reed, 2011, p. 3 as cited in Ören et al., 2012, p. 321). Not only banks but also municipalities have started to also provide microfinance. For example, Sariyer Municipality in Istanbul has microcredit centre to support women participation for doing business. According to the declaration made by the Sariyer municipality due to the teachers' day, women in Sariyer enjoyed selling their product in fair activity (Sariyer Municipality, n.d.). The main target in microcredit is to support women with small credit loans instead of granting (Demir, 2016, p. 58). Microcredit programmes are tools for mitigating the poverty and empowering women (Balkız, 2015, p. 542). These programmes use feminist language and suggest that in case the economic and political power of women increases, community becomes more competitive, equitable and fair (Balkız, 2015, p. 542).

According to Mahmud (2003, pp. 580–581), empowerment of women can be defined as increase in their welfare, literate and education levels, their participation into the workforce as well as improvement in their health and nutrition condition (Mahmud, 2003, pp. 580–581 as cited in Balkız, 2015, p. 550). Microcredit helps women to have better living condition by providing them opportunities to have access to training and education (Schuler et al., 1997; Isserles, 2003, p. 40). Furthermore, other factors related to empowerment of women include: gender equality in the family and in the control of family affairs (Mahmud, 2003, pp. 580–581 as cited in Balkız, 2015, p. 550).

As Malaysia acknowledged women's important role in their country's development, many programmes were introduced by the Ministry of Women, Family and Community Development to attract women to economic activities (Othman, 2015, p. 1047). Furthermore, a research made in Bangladesh revealed that women who borrowed microcredit and their family were happier and their welfare level was higher than women who did not get microcredit (Ceyhan, 2010, p.10; Ruhul et al., 1998, pp. 221–226).

Women's economic exclusion, due to social discrimination, hinders their control over financial and household issues (Serrano-Cinca & Gutiérrez-Nieto, 2014; Drori et al., 2018). Even if in developing countries women tend to deal with most of the household activities (Berniell & Sánchez-Páramo, 2011; WB, 2012 as cited in Tanaka & Muzones, 2016, p. 2), allocating their talent efficiently to the workforce, they could be productive workers (Tanaka & Muzones, 2016). In this way, they can support household income. According to the TSPI (Tulay sa Pag-unlad, Inc., 2004), the rate of the women who managed the household income in the Philippines increased from 33 to 51% (Ceyhan, 2010, p. 61).

Achieving gender equality can support countries' economy and sustainable development. Elimination of gender inequality in education, labour and household can increase per capita and aggregate income by 30.6% and 6.6%, respectively, over a generation in an Asian economy (Kim et al., 2016; Tanaka & Muzones, 2016).

UN draft proposal on the roles of microfinance in the solution of poverty issues indicates that women are the main customer target segment of these programmes and that women get benefit from the microfinance as they employ themselves and participate in basic economic and political process of the community (Balkız, 2015, p. 542; Keating, et al., 2010, p. 6). Furthermore, women can contribute to the success of the microcredit programmes. According to D'espallier et al. (2011), women have higher credibility than men (Gutiérrez-Nieto & Serrano-Cinca, 2019, p. 191). Lassoued (2017)'s research revealed that loans provided to women reduced MFIs' credit risk in 87 countries (Chikalipah, 2018, p. 39).

Women, who acknowledge their talent and are successful in their life and whose social status is improved, can become politically effective as well. Success in microcredit can support the successful people first can require fulfilment of their primary needs and later their secondary needs in compliance with the Maslow's hierarchy of needs. If they are successful, they can enhance their microbusinesses and can become socially more active. Furthermore, women who are successful in their microcredit supported works can gain self-confidence, and if they have a goal to be active in politics, they can be more willing to actively take part in politics. For this reason, women, who get benefit from the microcredit, can become economically and politically more active.

Recommendations for the Success of Microcredits and Microfinance to Enhance Women Empowerment

Enhancing success of microcredits and microfinance can support social inclusion and empowerment of women. Success in the microcredit and microfinance cases can support widespread of this system and encourage women to participate more in this system. Enhancing success of microcredits and microfinance relies on effective risk management considering all critical success factors and unique characteristics of this system.

The microcredit and microfinance system works differently compared to commercial banks. For example, while commercial banks require mortgage, guarantee and guarantor, microcredit does not require such guarantees (Akbıyık & Şahin, 2010, p. 1740). Furthermore, in microfinance, officials refund money by visiting villages weekly, whereas commercial bank borrower should go to bank for regular payment (Akbıyık & Şahin, 2010, p. 1740). Additionally, there is no legal institution between lender and borrower in the microcredit system (Ceyhan, 2010, p. 24). Confidence is essential in microcredit as there is no bond, guarantee or bill, and microcredit is based on the belief that credit is a human right (Akbıyık & Şahin, 2010, p. 1737; TİSVA, 2009).

Microentrepreneurs can encounter risk of cash shortage or difficulty in payment. According to the theorists (e.g. Drucker, 2012; Knight, 2005), entrepreneurship is related to taking innovation-related risk (Dutta & Banerjee, 2018, p. 72). There is credit risk in microfinance (Chikalipah, 2018, p. 38). Furthermore, the climate and geography of the country can affect risk, success and failure of microcredit and microfinance. Microfinance is vulnerable to adverse shocks (e.g. natural disasters) which may occur in large geographic areas affecting borrowers adversely causing illiquidity, insolvency and losses in the MFI's loan portfolio (Klomp, 2018). On the other hand, increase in geographic diversification can cause higher loan loss and as remote operations create difficulties in monitoring clients, geographic diversification is not beneficial to MFIs (Zamore et al., 2019). Geographic diversification is, however, in compliance with the portfolio theory. Geographic diversification of MFIs can reduce potential risks of credit, liquidity and insolvency (Liang & Rhoades, 1988; Zamore et al., 2019, p. 2). As risk emerges for MFIs if a disaster occurs in one region and causes farming crisis in a specific geographic area, or if some natural events adversely affect borrowers' works in cities, geographic diversification limits the risk into the affected region and reduces the loss of MFI (Liang & Rhoades, 1988; Zamore et al., 2019, p. 2).

Geography, development level and political situation of the countries can affect the success of microcredit. Economic stability and expected growth of a country are understood by its annual GDP growth which provides indication of potential opportunities for donors and microentrepreneurs as well as MFI's funding requirements (Ledgerwood, 1999,

p. 27). The economic condition and political situation of a country affect the success of the microcredit system in mitigating poverty (Ramezanali & Assadi, 2018, p. 64). The less educated people should be trained in financial education and entrepreneurship techniques so that they can get the loans (Ramezanali & Assadi, 2018, p. 64). Government policies (e.g. excessive regulation, high taxation, laxity about black market) as well as harassment of public officials) can affect microfinance enterprises (Ledgerwood, 1999, p.29). Economic policies, affecting the inflation, economic growth rate and market freedom, can have impact on the credit interest rate, entrepreneurs' success and effectiveness of MFIs' financial services (Ledgerwood, 1999, p. 26). In case a country, with high microcredit loan per capita, can control the factors such as credit amount in GDP, international openness and inflation rate that can reduce poverty can be achieved to reduce the poverty headcount ratio (Miled & Rejeb, 2015).

Feasible business branch needs to be determined accurately so that microcredit risk can be reduced. Preliminary studies need to be done in order not to waste the microcredits. In their decision whether or not to provide financial services to microentrepreneurs, public and private microfinance providers must analyse the market, providers and the degree at which market needs being met as well as competitors and their impacts on the market (Ledgerwood, 1999, p. 14). Furthermore, importance of risk assessment in dealing with microcredit risks has been noticed by Prof. Dr. Muhammad Yunus. Prof. Dr. Muhammad Yunus, the founder of the Grameen Bank, lent 42 people and he expanded microfinance to new borrowers upon which they repaid their loans (Islam et al., 2012). In that case, however, as some of the borrowers did not repay their loan, he decided to approve and supervise the loans as well as select trustworthy clients and monitor them (Islam et al., 2012). Based on his experience on repaid and unpaid loans, he started to approve and supervise the loans as well as select trustworthy clients and monitor them. Furthermore, micro-insurance (Helms, 2006; Latortue, 2003) can be one of the tools for managing these risks. Regular monitoring and group lending can contribute to reduce risk and increase success of microcredit (Chikalipah, 2018, p. 38; Emekter et al., 2015).

As Adam Smith and David Hume (Smith [1776] 1961) indicated the main aim of political economy as to enhance people's welfare, political economy is a tool for politicians to enhance people's wealth (Nurmi, 2017, p. 1 as cited in Sertyesilisik, 2018, p. 171). In compliance with the aim of political economy, microcredit and microfinance have the same aim and they can support achievement of this aim. Microcredit can enable low-income people to launch and expand their businesses creating employment and contributing to the country's economy. Politicians should pay attention to microcredit as spreading the usage of microcredit can enable them to support solution of the poverty issue. Microcredit and microfinance supporting policies need to be integrated with other policies aiming to enhance welfare of the people and to solve poverty issue. Additionally, people willing to participate in microcredit can be guided, trained and mentored so that they can gain at least management-related basic knowledge and skills. These guidance, training and mentorships can have potential to increasing the success in the microcredit. Furthermore, as success in the microcredit and microfinance system can reduce unemployment rate reducing people's need for unemployment wages, country's budget can be allocated more to other fields to support sustainable development.

In compliance with the political economy principles, policies need to focus on finding ways for enhancing success of microcredits and microfinance and for widespread usage of this system. These policies can further support empowerment of women and countries' sustainable development. Furthermore, these policies can have potential to support politicians' success in the elections as these policies can act as tools for increasing employment rate, solving poverty problem and increasing welfare of the people.

Policies aiming to support sustainable development need to consider ways for enhancing effectiveness and success of the microcredit and microfinance as an enabler for empowering women and sustainable development. Women can contribute more effectively to the sustainable development in case they are empowered. Furthermore, they can act as change agents for empowering other women. Their success can influence and encourage other women. This can act as a multiplier effect in the widespread of the microcredit and microfinance. Political economy of microcredit and microfinance supports empowerment of women and sustainable development which is further supported by the empowered women (Fig. 12.1). Figure 12.1 shows relationship among political economy of microcredit and microfinance, sustainable development and empowerment of women. Sustainable development supported by enhanced welfare based on empowered women and gender equality in the business and workforce can support countries' future to be socially, economically and environmentally strong. Impacts of the success in

Fig. 12.1 Relationship among political economy of microcredit and microfinance, empowerment of women and sustainable development (*Source* Sketched by the author)

microcredit and microfinance on sustainable development reveal their butterfly effect as even a very small and micro-amount of credit can change people's life in a positive way. For this reason, microcredit-related topics need to be addressed and covered in the sustainable development plans of the countries strategically.

Conclusion and Recommendations

Based on an in-depth literature review, this chapter focused on the political economy of microfinance from the gender and politics point of view and emphasized microfinance's role in social inclusion of women to the workforce and empowerment of women. Following microcredit's first launch in Bangladesh by Prof Dr. Muhammad Yunus, it spread rapidly all around the world supporting poor people, their hopes, well-being and welfare everywhere. Microcredit enables poor people to launch their business, to actively take part in the labour force and to contribute to their countries' economy and sustainable development. Microcredit plays important role in gender equality. Microcredit is an important tool to empower women and to enable women to participate in the workforce. Microcredit can provide women opportunity to become financially more powerful enabling them to create employment and support increase in the employment rate.

Microcredit and microfinance can make a butterfly effect in the empowerment of women, in reducing poverty and in achieving sustainable development. Even a micro-amount of credit can be a big step and enable a great change in people's life. Women play important role in their countries' sustainable development. Microcredits can help them to launch their microbusiness. If they can successfully use and get benefit from microcredits, they can generate income and support their families. They can support their children's education and influence next generation's education level. From this aspect, microcredit can support improvement in education, income and social level of the countries. Women who get microcredits and improve their financial level can start providing more jobs to other people. By setting examples and being change agents, empowered women can encourage and inspire other women to be empowered. Their success can influence other women and their willingness to participate in the microcredit and microfinance programmes. This reveals the multiplier effect of microcredit and microfinance on sustainable development. Women who launch their own businesses with their own efforts can gain self-confidence. If they want to become politically more active, they can trust themselves in achieving their life goals with the help of their own confidence. This is in compliance with the Maslow hierarchy of needs pyramid which suggests that people can achieve their life goals and reach to the upper levels in the Maslow hierarchy of needs.

Spreading the usage of microcredit can be an important way of increasing the welfare of the society and empower the women's role in society. Increase in the success stories and cases of microcredits can encourage women to take part in the microcredit financed works. Furthermore, these success stories can encourage MFIs to widespread and increase microcredit for further resulting in more people to get benefit from the microcredit. Additionally, success in microcredit can support sustainable development of countries and social welfare and well-being. For this reason, considering the political economy aspect of microcredits emphasizes importance of microcredits supporting policies on gender equality, sustainability and sustainability development. Future researches are recommended to analyse country, culture and industry-specific cases of microcredit and microfinance practices. This chapter will be beneficial to all stakeholders of microcredit and microfinance including political scientists, politicians and economists.

References

Adaman, F., & Bulut, T. (2007). *Diyarbakır'dan İstanbul'a 500 Milyonluk Umut Hikayeleri Mikrokredi Maceraları*, İletişim Yayınları, Istanbul.

Akbıyık, N., & Şahin, L. (2010, April 15–16). *Mikro Kredi Uygulaması Ve Ekonomik Kriz*. Turgut Özal Uluslar arası Ekonomi ve Siyaset Kongresi-I, Malatya http://ozal.congress.inonu.edu.tr/pdf/102.pdf

Allen, F., Otchere, I., & Senbet, L. W. (2011). African financial systems: A review. *Review of Development Finance, 1*(2), 79–113.

Altay, A. (2007). Küreselleşen Yoksulluk Olgusunun Önlenmesinde Mikrofinansman Yaklaşımı. *Finansal Politik Ve Ekonomik Yorumlar Dergisi, 44*(510), 57–67.

Armendariz, B., & Morduch, J. (2005). *The economics of microfinance*. MIT Press.

Balkız, Ö. (2015). Mikro Kredi ve Toplumsal Cinsiyet: Eleştirel Bir Değerlendirme. *Gaziantep University Journal of Social Sciences, 14*(3), 535–557.

Beck, T. (2015). *Microfinance—A critical literature survey* (IEG Working Paper 2015/4). Independent Evaluation Group, The World Bank Group, Washington, D.C.

Berniell, M., & Sánchez-Páramo, C. (2011). *Overview of time use data used for the analysis of gender differences in time use patterns*. Background paper for the World Development Report 2012.

Ceyhan, H. (2010). *Yerel İktisadi Kalkınma Bağlamında Mikro Kredi Uygulamalrının İstihdama Etkisi Ve Karaman İlinde Bir Uygulama*. Yüksek Lisans Tezi, Karamanoğlu Mehmetbey Üniversitesi İktisadi Ve İdari Bilimler Fakültesi Kamu Yönetimi Bölümü.

Chikalipah, S. (2017). Financial sustainability of microfinance institutions in sub-Saharan Africa: Evidence from GMM estimates. *Enterprise Development & Microfinance, 28*(3), 182–199.

Chikalipah, S. (2018). Credit risk in microfinance industry: Evidence from sub-Saharan Africa. *Review of Development Finance, 8*, 38–48.

Cuberes, D. & Teignier, M. (2016). Aggregate effects of gender gaps in the labor market: A quantitative estimate. *Journal of Human Capital, 10*(1) (Spring). University of Chicago Press.

Credit & Development Forum. (1999). *Various issues*. CDF Statistics (published semiannually).

Cull, R., & Morduch, J. (2017). *Microfinance and economic development. Manuscript submitted for publication Handbook of finance and development*. Edward Elgar.

Datta, N., & Kotikula, A. (n.d.). *Fostering quality of employment for women, not just more, but better—Fostering quality of employment for women working paper* (Jobs Working Paper Issue No. 1). World Bank Group Jobs, Washington, DC. https://openknowledge.worldbank.org/bitstream/handle/10986/26274/113175-REVISED-Not-Just-More-but-Better-Fostering-Quality-of-Employment-for-Women.pdf?sequence=1&isAllowed=y

Demir, Ö. (2016). İstihdam Yaratmada Mikrokredi Uygulamalarının Etkinliği. *İş Ve Hayat, 2*(3), 57–75.

D'espallier, B., Guérin, I., & Mersland, R. (2011). Women and repayment in microfinance: A global analysis. *World Development, 39*(5), 758–772.

Drori, I., Manos, R., Santacreu-Vasut, E., Shenkar, O., & Shoham, A. (2018). Language and market inclusivity for women entrepreneurship: The case of microfinance. *Journal of Business Venturing, 33*, 395–415.

Drucker, P. (2012). *Managing in the next society*. Routledge.

Dutta, A., & Banerjee, S. (2018). Does microfinance impede sustainable entrepreneurial initiatives among women borrowers? Evidence from rural Bangladesh. *Journal of Rural Studies, 60*, 70–81.

Emekter, R., Tu, Y., Jirasakuldech, B., & Lu, M. (2015). Evaluating credit risk and loan performance in online Peer-to-Peer (P2P) lending. *Applied Economics., 47*(1), 54–70.

Erdoğan, N. (2004). *Yoksullukla Mücadelede Etkili Bir Enstrüman Mikro Kredi*. Finansal Forum Özel Eki.

Fernando, J. L. (Ed.). (2004). *Microfinance: Perils and prospects*. Routledge.

Gutiérrez-Nieto, B., & Serrano-Cinca, C. (2019). 20 years of research in microfinance: An information management approach. *International Journal of Information Management, 47*, 183–197.

Harford, T. (2008, December 6). *The battle for the soul of microfinance*. The Financial Times Limited. https://www.ft.com/content/8080c698-c0d2-11dd-b0a8-000077b07658

Hashemi, S. M., Schuler, S. R., & Riley, A. P. (1996). Rural credit programs and women's empowerment in Bangladesh. *World Development, 24*(4), 635–653.

Helms, B. (2006). *Access for all: Building inclusive financial systems*. The International Bank for Reconstruction and Development/The World Bank

Islam, J. N., Mohajan, H. K., & Datta, R. (2012). Aspects of microfinance system of Grameen Bank of Bangladesh. *International Journal of Economics and Research, 3*(4), 76–96.

Isserles, R. G. (2003). Microcredit: The rhetoric of empowerment, the reality of "development as usual". *Women's Studies Quarterly, 31*(3/4), Women and Development: Rethinking Policy and Reconceptualizing Practice (Fall–Winter, 2003), 38–57.

Keating, C., Rasmussen, C., & Pooja, R. (2010). The rationality of empowerment: Microcredit, accumulation by dispossession, and gendered economy. *Signs, 36*(1), 153–176.

Klasen, S., & Pieters, J. (2015, March). *What explains the stagnation of female labor force participation in Urban India?* (Policy Research Working Paper 7222). http://documents1.worldbank.org/curated/en/539141468186871615/pdf/WPS7222.pdf

Kim, J., Lee J. W., & Shin, K. (2016). *A model of gender inequality and economic growth* (Economics Working Paper Series No. 475). Manila: Asian Development Bank (ADB).

Kuwekita, J. M., Gosset, C., Guillaume, M., Semutsari, M. P. B., Kabongo, E. T., Bruyere, O., & Reginster, J. Y. (2015). Combining microcredit, microinsurance, and the provision of health care can improve access to quality care in urban areas of Africa: Results of an experiment in the Bandalungwa health zone in Kinshasa, the Congo. *Medecine Et Sante Tropicales, 25*(4), 381–385.

Lassoued, N. (2017). What drives credit risk of microfinance institutions? International evidence. *International Journal of Managerial Finance, 13*(5), 541–559.

Latortue, A. (2003, July). *Microinsurance: A risk management strategy* (CGAP Donor Brief No. 16). Washington, DC: CGAP

Ledgerwood, J. (1999). *Sustainable banking with the poor, microfinance handbook: An institutional and financial perspective.* Washington, DC: The International Bank for Reconstruction and Development/The World Bank.

Liang, N., & Rhoades, S. A. (1988). Geographic diversification and risk in banking. *Journal of Economics and Business, 40*(4), 271–284.

Klomp, J. (2018). Do natural catastrophes shake microfinance institutions? *Using a New Measure of MFI Risk, International Journal of Disaster Risk Reduction, 27*, 380–390.

Knight, F. H. (2005). *Risk, uncertainty and profit.* Cosimo Classics.

Mahmud, S. (2003). Actually how empowering is microcredit? *Development and Change, 34*(4), 577–605.

Miled, K. B. H., & Rejeb, J. E. B. (2015). Microfinance and poverty reduction: A review and synthesis of empirical evidence. *Procedia—Social and Behavioral Sciences, 195*, 705–712.

Muhammad, A. (2009, August 29–September 4). Grameen and microcredit: A tale of corporate success. *Economic and Political Weekly, 44*(35), 35–42.

Njiraini, J. (2015). *Microfinance: Good for the poor?* Africa Renewal https://www.un.org/afrcarenewal/magazne/august-2015/mcrofnance-good-poor

Nurmi, H. (2017). *Models of political economy.* Routledge.

Othman, M. B. (2015). Role of women in achieving shared prosperity: An impact study of Islamic microfinance in Malaysia. *Procedia-Social and Behavioral Sciences, 211*, 1043–1048.

Ören, K., Negiz, N. & Akman, E. (2012). Kadınların Yoksullukla Mücadele Aracı Mikro Kredi: Deneyimler Üzerinden Bir İnceleme. *Atatürk Üniversitesi İktisadi Ve İdari Bilimler Dergisi, 26*(2).

Pitt, M. M., & Khandker, S. R. (1998). The impact of group-based credit programs on poor households in Bangladesh: Does the gender of participants matter? *Journal of Political Economy, 106*(5), 958–996.

Rahman, A. (1998). *Rhetoric and realities of micro-credit for women in rural Bangladesh: A village study of Grameen Bank lending* (Ph.D. dissertation). University of Manitoba, Canada.

Ramezanali, M., & Assadi, D. (April 2018). Does microfinance reduce poverty? The case of Brazil. *International Journal of Trade, Economics and Finance, 9*(2), 60–65.

Reed, L. R. (2011). *State of the microcredit summit campaign report 2011.* Microcredit Summit Campaign.

Robinson, M. S. (2001). *The micro finance revolution, sustainable finance for the poor.* The International Bank for Reconstruction and Development/The World Bank.

Ruhul, A., Becker, S., & Bayes, A. (1998). NGO-promoted microcredit programs and women's empowerment in rural Bangladesh: Quantitative and qualitative evidence. *The Journal of Developing Areas, 32*(2), 221–236.

Sariyer Municipality (n.d.). https://sariyer.bel.tr/Haber/kadinlarin-hayati-mikrokredi-ile-degisiyor/2164

Schuler, S. R., Hashemi, S., & Riley, A. P. (1997). The Influence of Women's Changing Roles and Status in Bangladesh's Fertility Transition; Evidence from a Study of Credit Programs and Contraceptive Use. *World Development, 25*(4), 563–575.

Serrano-Cinca, C., & Gutiérrez-Nieto, B. (2014). Microfinance, the long tail and mission drift. *International Business Review, 23*(1), 181–194.

Sertyesilisik, E. (2018, June 27–28). *Political economy of global climate change.* Full Paper Proceeding, International Conference on Empirical Economics and Social Sciences (ICEESS'18) (pp. 170–180). Bandırma–Turkey.

Smith, A. ([1776] 1961). *The wealth of nations.* J.M. Dent

Tanaka, S., & Muzones M. (2016, October). *Female labor force participation In Asia: Key trends, constraints, and opportunities.* ADB Briefs Series. https://www.adb.org/sites/publiations/female-labor-force-participation-asia

Todd, H. (1996). *Cloning Grameen Bank.* Practical Action Publishing.

TİSVA, Türkiye İsrafı Önleme Vakfı. (2009). *Türkiye Grameen Mikrokredi Projesi Bilgi Notu.* http://www.israf.org/pdf/TURKIYEGRAMEENMIKROKREDIPROJESIBILGINOTU.Pdf

TSPI (Tulay sa Pag-unlad, Inc). (2004). http://www.tspi.org

World Bank. (2000). *World development report 1999/2000: Entering the 21st century.* Oxford University Press.

World Bank. (2012). *World development report 2012: Gender equality and development.* World Bank. https://openknowledge.worldbank.org/handle/10986/4391 License: CC BY 3.0 IGO

Women's World Banking. (1995, April). *The missing links: Financial systems that work for the majority.* Global Policy Forum Women's

World Banking. http://documents1.worldbank.org/curated/en/330221468762298007/pdf/multi-page.pdf

Wydick, B. (1999). The impact of credit access on the use of child labor in household enterprises: Evidence from Guatemala. *Economic Development and Cultural Change, 47*, 853–869.

Yunus, M., & Weber K. (2012). *Sosyal İşletme Kurmak* (Trans., A Nebil İmre). Doğan Kitap.

Zamore, S., Beisland, L. A., & Mersland, R. (2019). Geographic diversification and credit risk in microfinance. *Journal of Banking and Finance, 109*, 105665.

CHAPTER 13

Assessing the Impact of Microfinance on Inequality: A Study of Major SAARC Nations Using Panel Causality Analysis

Amit Chatterjee and Kshitij Patil

INTRODUCTION

The origin of the term 'Microfinance' dates back to the 1970s when organizations like the Grameen Bank of Bangladesh defined a new facet of finance. Microfinance is particularly aimed at reducing global poverty and inequality by extending the access of credit to the poor. Microfinance is said to have a significant equalizing effect, which implies that it lowers inequality by increasing the income of poor and decreasing the income of rich. Hence, microfinance can be used as an effective redistribution tool which will prove to be an effective solution to the twin problem of poverty and inequality (Ahlin & Jiang, 2008; Kai, 2009). On the other hand, the link between microfinance, poverty and inequality is also highly influenced by the targeting strategies followed by the MFIs;

A. Chatterjee (✉) · K. Patil
School of Economics, MIT-WPU, Pune, India
e-mail: chatvitamit@gmail.com

hence, the link is country-specific (Bangoura et al., 2016). Even in presence of the literature on cross-country analysis of effects of microfinance, the results are mixed. Although the roots of microfinance are said to be in South Asia, surprisingly, no South Asian country, barring a few, was able to reduce its inequality in the years 1980–2015. Keeping these factors in mind, it is important to understand the efficacy of microfinance in a specific cluster of countries, in dealing with inequality, and to examine if the MFIs evidently contribute to the reduction in inequality.

The researchers observe that no region-specific study to evaluate impacts of microfinance has been conducted yet. The studies conducted till date consider only the economic similarities between the countries and hence consider groups like 'developing countries' for study purpose. Regional and other similarities based on problems faced by the countries are very seldom considered. There is no study done on the South Asian region as a whole, which leaves an open avenue for the researchers to explore the impact of microfinance in South Asia. The countries chosen from South Asia are similar in various aspects like the increasing inequality problems they have been facing for more than a decade; similar HDI, low health expenditure as a percentage of GDP and being a part of SAARC, these countries also share common macroeconomic interests.

This paper provides a detailed empirical cross-country analysis of 5 SAARC countries (viz. Sri Lanka, India, Pakistan, Bangladesh and Nepal) for the period 2000–2018. These nations portray a lot of commonalities in terms of both advantages and problems faced. All of these nations are struggling with problems of poverty, inequality and other macro-problems like inadequately developed infrastructure and corruption. India and Nepal have the highest rate of informal labour followed by Pakistan, Sri Lanka and Bangladesh. The increasing Quintile share ratios for all these countries over the last decade show that share of income of top 20% of population has been rising as compared to the bottom 20%.

The research objectives of this chapter are as follows:

> First, to analyse the impact of microfinance and other macroeconomic variables on inequality for the group of 5 SAARC countries. This gives a clear picture of the effectivity of microfinance in these SAARC countries and also explores additional factors that significantly affect inequality in these countries.

Second, to use panel data analysis for the selected countries and to discuss the persistent inequality problems in the South Asian region. This is a significant improvement over most of the studies using cross-sectional or time series data. Also, the existing literature on panel data includes large number of countries and region-specific problems and solutions are merely discussed.

Third, to explore a causality analysis between microfinance, other control variables and inequality, using the Granger Causality Analysis. This analysis not only serves the purpose of checking the causal relationship between microfinance and inequality, but also indicates other variables which have significant causal relationships with inequality. Such variables should be considered along with microfinance and should be used as a combined tool to eradicate the problem of inequality.

Fourth, to provide policy recommendations to reduce inequality primarily through the microfinance channel and also through other macroeconomic channels, specific to the 5 SAARC countries. The policymakers can use this information in microfinance targeting strategies to reduce the rising inequality in these countries.

The main hypothesis of this study is that microfinance doesn't significantly impact inequality, and there exists no causal relationship between them. The econometric estimation is conducted with utmost precision, and necessary steps are taken to avoid any kind of biases. All variables are converted into the natural logarithms, and cross-section SUR weights are used to tackle possible issues in regression analysis.

The rest of the paper is organized as follows: sect. "Literature Review" deals with the literature part of the study and the research gap, sect. "Data and Methodology" deals with the data analysis and econometric methodology, sect. "Results and Discussion" discusses the results, and sect. "Conclusion and Recommendations" concludes the findings and includes recommendations.

Literature Review

Microfinance acts as an effective tool and a viable substitute to curb poverty and inequality. Various studies conducted on microfinance show that it has been successful in combating poverty as well as inequality.

Bangoura et al. (2016) in their study of 52 developing countries explore a significant negative relationship between microfinance intensities and poverty as well as inequality measures. This study portrays the effectivity of microfinance for the developing countries. One of the important points derived from the study is that the effectivity of microfinance is country-specific which opens avenues for contrary results. The effects of microfinance can also be seen on primary level as beneficiaries of microfinance are found to be better-off than their counterparts.

Studies of Khandker (2005) and Razzaqu (2010) empirically prove how microfinance raises per capita consumption for participants in microfinance programmes for multiple households surveyed in Bangladesh, which in turn raises the chances of participants to get out of poverty. Microfinance not only benefits the participants of microfinance programmes but also the non-participants as they have increased income levels. The studies also provide a robustness check as both are conducted for different time periods and for different villages, yet the similar results were found. Khandker (2005) finds that even small MFIs are successful in poverty eradication. This is a clear indication of how microfinance eradicates poverty and inequality, and the effect is well spread.

Microfinance contributes to the reduction of inequality through multiple ways, one of them being the equalizing effect. According to Kai (2009), microfinance has a significant equalizing effect, which implies that it increases the income of the poor and redistributes the income from the rich to the poor. Hence, microfinance can be a viable alternative to traditional finance channels to decrease inequality and poverty. The following is the additional literature presented in a tabular format in Table 13.1.

It is observed that microfinance has vast impact on poverty as well as inequality which is evident from the significant relationships found in different kinds of studies conducted. Microfinance decreases inequality through various modes and acts as an effective redistribution tool to tackle the inequality problem. The impact of microfinance is country-specific, and hence, different regions may yield different results, based on which the microfinance policies need to be adjusted.

Data and Methodology

The hypothesis to be tested is as follows: -

Table 13.1 Review of literature

Authors	Dataset	Techniques	Variables	Results
Giuseppina Malerba and Marta Spreafico (2014)	25 Countries Time Period-1995–2010	GLS (Generalized Least Squares) Regression	Gini Index, decile ratios, GDP p.c. growth, public expenditure, housing loan, education level, (im)mobility, labour freedom	Inequality can be attacked through social public spending and the impact is greater when the extremes of the income distribution are involved
Eric S. Lin and Hamid E. Ali (2009)	58 Countries Time Period-1987–1999	Panel Unit Root tests and Granger Causality Test	Bpme, Lbpme, Sbpme, Lspme, Theil, EHII, ΔTheil, ΔEHII, etc. (all available inequality indices)	There is no Granger Causality in any direction between military spending and changes in economic inequality
S Mohapatra and Bimal Sahoo (2009)	Country—India 240 households, Year-2009	Binomial Probit Model, OLS Regression	Participation dummy, average household income per month, land owned, value of livestock, highest education level, dependency ratio, dummy variables for occupation, location	Mean household income is higher among the participants. Probability of participation in the microfinance programme increases with the rise in land holding
Syed Kalim Hyder, Qazi Masood Ahmed, and Haroon Jamal (2015)	Country—Pakistan Time Period-1979–2013	ARCH model, Wald Test, Log-Log Model	Poverty, GDP, Gini Index, per capita GDP, food prices, taxation, public investment, government spending, wage differential, terms of trade	Inflation, sectoral wage gap, and terms of trade in favour of manufacturing as the significant positive correlates of inequality

(continued)

Table 13.1 (continued)

Authors	Dataset	Techniques	Variables	Results
S. Saravanan and Devi Prasad Dash (2017)	Indian States Time Period-2007–2014	Instrumental Variable Method	Number of women SHGs, female population, female literacy and work force participation, bank loan, poverty rate, savings rate, agriculture growth rate and per capita income	MFIs have been quite successful in granting credit access to women. States with higher growth experience surge in number of women SHGs
Gérard Tchouassi (2011)	11 developing countries in Africa	Random Effects Model	GINI index, log (number of MFIs in the country), log (GDP per capita), square of the log of GDP per capita, inflation, poverty line	When the microfinance institutions in the country become dense, inequalities decrease
Ms. Sifat Adiya Chowdhury and Ms. Sarahat Salma Chowdhury (2011)	Country—Bangladesh Time Period-1991/1992 and 1998/1999	Fixed Effects Model	Outcome due to participation in programme, demand for credit for individual, village effects of the current and past obtained credit	Micro credit can only generate temporary empowerment effects on women in terms of income generation and asset accumulation

Source Authors' Compilation

H_0 = *Microfinance doesn't significantly impact inequality and there exists no causal relationship between them.*

The impact of microfinance is measured through 2 variables: weighted average number of active borrowers and weighted value of loans (Microfinance Intensities).

MF_1 = Average no. of active borrowers/total population of the country
MF_2 = Value of loans/GDP of the country (MF_1 and MF_2 are the major explanatory variables).

To assess the impact of microfinance on inequality, the following equation is analysed:

$$\log(\text{Gini}) = \beta_1 \log(MF_1) + \beta_2 \log(MF_2) + \beta_3 \log(Z) + \varepsilon \quad\quad (14.1)$$

The major or focus variables are BOR (weighted average number of active borrowers) and VOL (weighted value of loans). Z is a set of control variables, which are as follows: AGVA (agricultural value added, in percentage of GDP), ARLA (arable land, in percentage of land area), INF (inflation, GDP deflator), YOU (youth population ages 0–14, (% of total)), OPN (openness, trade to GDP ratio), EDEXP (government expenditure on education (% of GDP)), HEXP (current health expenditure (% of GDP)), POL(Polity score), GDPPC (GDP per capita (current $)), UNEMP (% of labour force) and RPOP (rural population (% of total population)). The dependent variable is GINI (Gini Index ((measure of income inequality)). ε is the error term of the Eq. (14.1).

Data on Gini Index was found to have significant missing observations. The missing observations were filled using a growth rate approach, whereby growth rate between two periods n and n + m was calculated and it was assumed the growth is constant for 'm' periods. Data on Gini Index is collected from the World Bank (World Development Indicators: http://datatopics.worldbank.org/world-development-indicators/) and World Income Inequality Database (https://www.wider.unu.edu/database/wiid). Data on polity score is collected from Polity5 Project (https://www.systemicpeace.org). Data on all other control variables is taken from the World Bank (World Development Indicators) as well.

This Eq. (14.1) is estimated using the Panel EGLS model using cross-section SUR (seemingly unrelated regression) weights (which correct for heteroscedasticity and contemporaneous correlation) and standard errors. Further, a causality analysis is conducted between the microfinance variables (MF_1 and MF_2), the control variables and Gini Index. This analysis provides deeper understanding of how the microfinance variables and other variables are linked to inequality. For this purpose, the Granger Causality Analysis is conducted. Prior to causality analysis, all the variables are tested for unit root using the ADF-Fisher Chi-square test. The variables are further converted into stationary, and then, Granger Causality Test is conducted.

Results and Discussion

To estimate the relationship between microfinance intensities and inequality, panel data for 19 years (2000–2018) is considered. Prior to any estimation, all variables are converted to natural logarithm. Firstly, an Estimated Generalized Least Squares (EGLS) regression is run between the microfinance intensities, control variables and Gini Index. The results of this regression are presented in the following table.

Table 13.2 shows that there is clear and highly significant negative relationship between MF_1 (weighted average number of active borrowers) and Gini Index. This indicates that with the increase in the number of borrowers the inequality tends to decrease. However, a positive relationship is observed between MF_2 (weighted value of loans) and Gini Index. This implies that with the increase in the value of loans the inequality increases. This unexpected result can be attributed to a number of factors like the changing and rapidly growing banking structure in the countries. Private Banks have started invading the space of MFIs in search for new avenues for profits. As a result of which, MFIs have to either get merged into a Private Bank or Private Banks are forming their subsidiary MFIs. Conversion to other bank types has become common in order to lend to greater majority and higher rates. Another important reason of this positive relationship is that only a handful of disbursed loans are used for income-generating activities. Higher values of loans also lead to debt-traps for the poor, thereby leading to higher inequality. A significant and negative relationship is observed between borrowers and inequality. As the number of borrowers increases, more people have the adequate funds

Table 13.2 EGLS regression with cross-section SUR weights and standard errors

Dependent Variable—Gini Index					
Variable	Coefficient	t-Statistic	R^2	Adjusted R^2	F-Stat
Agri. Value Added	−0.21216*	−4.41385	0.88433	0.84577	22.934*
Arable Land	−0.126077*	−3.30417			
Education exp	0.121518*	5.30564			
GDP per capita	−0.061952**	−2.2607			
Health exp	−0.100588***	−1.92496			
Inflation	−0.025435*	−4.69963			
Borrowers	−0.029439*	−3.45122			
Openness	0.1774*	4.879449			
Polity	−0.004604	−0.28338			
Rural Population	−0.031061	−0.19211			
Unemployment	0.042527*	2.859445			
Value of Loans	0.022533*	3.808087			
Youth	0.301429***	1.739914			

Source Author's own computation of results. All variables are converted into natural logarithm. (*), (**) and (***) denote the 1, 5 and 10% levels of significance, respectively

to run their small businesses or ventures, which help them to keep generating a steady income source resulting in narrowing of the rich-poor gap; hence, inequality decreases as borrowers increase.

The results also show a significant negative relation between agricultural value added, arable land and Gini Index. This means that agricultural activities actually contribute in inequality reduction. A higher agricultural produce implies that one of the most economically affected sections of the society, 'farmers' are well off, as they can sell their produce in markets or add value and supply raw materials to industries. Greater the amount of arable land, greater are the production and expansion opportunities for any farmer. The countries considered for the study are developing and focussing on manufacturing and services. Hence, these countries shouldn't neglect the importance of agriculture in inequality reduction. An insignificant relationship is observed between polity, rural population and inequality. The results also show that unemployment has a significant positive relationship with Gini Index. This indicates that if unemployment decreases inequality also tends to decrease. It is logically quite deducible that an increase in unemployment will lead to a downward shift in income and thereby consumption of the unemployed individuals and also their families in case of economies with high dependency ratios. This creates a rift between the employed and unemployed and rises inequality. Hence, rise in unemployment leads to a rise in inequality and vice versa. Microfinance itself has an ulterior motive of promoting employment, by providing the necessary finance to small and emerging enterprises which would further reduce inequalities.

An interesting phenomenon is observed in case of education and health expenditure. While education expenditure has a negative relation with inequality, health expenditure has a positive relation with inequality. Education expenditure can actually increase inequality as the education expenditure is focussed only on external infrastructure of schooling or colleges. It's a commonly observed phenomenon in these nations that many people are not fit for jobs at all because the level and understanding are quite low. Thus, what education expenditure does is, just enables more students to be a part of the institutions, but the level of education is lacking. This just drives more and more unworthy candidates in the job markets, and when they fail to get a job, it adds to up to the unemployed population of the country, causing more inequality. Whereas, as health expenditure increases, the poor have higher chances of getting access to healthcare facilities, better health allows them to work more and hence earn more, driving the inequality downwards. Openness is seen to have a positive relationship with inequality. Ideally, as a measure of amount of total trade, openness would be expected to decrease inequality. But openness can also lead to higher regional disparities in the primary sector, i.e. agriculture. Since foreign trade to developed countries is governed by multiple regulations and quality checks, only well-equipped farmers are able to export their produce and get incentives to produce export-worthy crops. Another aspect is that import of machinery and new methods of production replace unskilled labour with machines and hence causes unemployment and thereby inequality.

Table 13.3 (a) shows the results of the ADF test which shows the level at which the variables are stationary. It is observed that except Youth and Gini Index, all variables are stationary at 1st Difference. For performing Granger Causality Analysis, all the variables are first converted into stationary. The Granger Causality Analysis is conducted to explore the causal relationships between different variables and Gini Index. This analysis is supplementary to the results obtained from the regression analysis, and similar results would further strongly validate the findings.

Table 13.3 ADF Fischer Unit Root Test and Granger Causality Analysis

3 (a) ADF Fischer Unit Root Test

Variable	1st Difference	2nd Difference
Agri. Value Added	20.4743*	–
Arable Land	41.2866*	–
Education exp.	35.5137*	–
GDP per capita	29.8353*	–
Health exp.	40.9208*	–
Inflation	40.0204*	–
Borrowers	56.0061*	–
Openness	36.0273*	–
Polity	27.9915*	–
Rural Population	37.825*	–
Unemployment	27.3745*	–
Value of Loans	47.5648*	–
Youth	–	35.6247*
Gini	–	64.3030*

3 (b) Granger Causality Analysis

Variables (X – Y)	X doesn't cause Y F-Stat	Y doesn't cause X
D(EDEXP) – D(GINI,2)	4.26111**	0.54593
D(GDPPC) – D(GINI,2)	0.24779	4.13722**
D(INF) – D(GINI,2)	5.72630*	4.29359**
D(BOR) – D(GINI,2)	4.35854**	5.91653*
D(VOL) – D(GINI,2)	8.22867*	0.54378

Source Author's own computation of results. All variables are converted into natural logarithm. (*), (**) and (***) denote the 1, 5 and 10% levels of significance, respectively

Table 13.3 (b) shows the results of the Granger Causality Test. The results show that the number of borrowers (weighted no. of active borrowers) has a bi-directional causal relationship with Gini Index. This validates the findings from the regression estimation and provides a robust evidence of the effectivity of increasing the number of borrowers in decreasing inequality. The second microfinance intensity measure and weighted value of loans have a unidirectional causal relationship with Gini Index; hence, it's not the appropriate microfinance intensity measure that should be used to reduce inequality.

It is seen that education expenditure Granger causes Gini Index. This also supports the positive and significant relationship between the two observed in the regression estimation. This implies that with the increase in government spending on education the inequality is increasing. It could be due to the persistent educational inequality, like unequal distribution of academic sources, books and technologies across these countries. A bi-directional relationship between inflation and Gini Index is also seen. The significant relationship between inflation and inequality seen from the regression estimation along with bi-directional causality indicates the major role played by inflation in causing inequality.

Conclusion and Recommendations

This paper explored the linkage between microfinance and inequality, through 2 microfinance intensity measures for 5 SAARC countries, for the period 2000–2018. This study was conducted to deduce the impact of microfinance on the selected countries, through Panel EGLS regression and Granger Causality Analysis. It is noticed that the number of borrowers has a bi-directional causal relationship with Gini Index and reduces inequality. This indicates that policymakers should focus on expanding the outreach of MFIs by expanding the number of existing borrowers. It was also noticed that value of loans doesn't contribute to the reduction in inequality due to various factors. Higher loan value seems to be a superficial method to measure outreach of microfinance as the amounts are not necessarily used for income-generating purposes, and higher loan amounts may also cause the poor to fall in a debt-trap. This indicates that the regulatory mechanism of the MFI in these countries has certain loopholes which should be addressed. The intervention of private banks is also causing trouble for the MFIs and forcing them to be profit-centric in order to sustain. A clear line regarding the activities and functionalities needs to be drawn between other types of banks and MFIs. Further, this paper also contributes to sustainable development goals by providing analysis and possible solutions for the 10th goal of reducing inequalities in the 5 countries. It is observed that government health expenditure significantly reduces inequality, but the 5 countries are seen to have low health expenditures, except Nepal which meets WHO's recommendation of health expenditure of 5% of the GDP. The results also show that unemployment increases inequality and only Sri Lanka has been able to substantially decrease unemployment rates.

The policymakers of these countries should understand the potential of microfinance and its combined impact in reducing inequality. Microfinance also helps to combat problems like unemployment and increase the purchasing power of poor people. The focus should be on sound and efficient policies for MFIs. Mechanisms similar to that of priority sector lending can be inculcated in MFIs, their priority sectors being small-scale industries and other small and upcoming enterprises. This paper somehow has certain limitations that need to be addressed in future studies. All SAARC countries couldn't be included due to lack of data. This paper doesn't include an inter-country analysis between the SAARC countries. Future research can be done for all SAARC countries using hierarchical clustering to analyse the characteristics of each country, taken into consideration their individual heterogeneity. The only obstacle is the difficulty of availability and compatibility of data.

REFERENCES

Ahlin, C., & Jiang, N. (2008). Can micro-credit bring development? *Journal of Development Economics, 86*(1), 1–21.

Bangoura, L., Mbow, M. K., Lessoua, A., & Diaw, D. (2016). Impact of microfinance on poverty and inequality a heterogeneous panel causality analysis. *Revue D'économie Politique, 126*(5), 789–818.

Chowdhury, S. S., & Chowdhury, S. A. (2011). Microfinance and women empowerment: A panel data analysis using evidence from rural Bangladesh. *International Journal of Economics and Finance, 3*(5), 86–96.

Hyder, S. K., Ahmed, Q. M., & Jamal, H. (2015). Simulating the impact of income distribution on poverty reduction. *The Pakistan Development Review, 54*(4), 931–944.

Kai, H. (2009). Microfinance and inequality. *Research in Applied Economics, 1*. https://doi.org/10.5296/rae.v1i1.304

Khandker, S. R. (2005). Microfinance and poverty: Evidence using panel data from Bangladesh. *The World Bank Economic Review, 19*(2), 263–286.

Lin, E. S., & Ali, H. E. (2009). Military spending and inequality: Panel Granger causality test. *Journal of Peace Research, 46*(5), 671–685.

Malerba, G., & Spreafico, M. (2014). Structural determinants of income inequality in The European Union: Evidence from a panel analysis. *Rivista Internazionale Di Scienze Sociali, 122*(1), 37–83.

Mohapatra, S., & Sahoo, B. K. (2009). *Impact of microfinance on rural poor: An empirical investigation from India*. Performance Evaluation and Enterprise Development, Allied Publishers Pvt.

Razzaque, M. A. (2010). Microfinance and poverty reduction: Evidence from a longitudinal household panel database. *The Bangladesh Development Studies, 33*(3), 47–68.

Saravanan, S., & Dash, D. P. (2017). Microfinance and women empowerment-empirical evidence from the Indian States. *Regional and Sectoral Economic Studies, 17*(2), 61–74.

Tchouassi, G. (2011). Microfinance, inequality and vulnerability: Empirical analysis from Central African countries. *Journal of Development and Agricultural Economics, 3*(4), 150–156.

CHAPTER 14

Sustainability of Indian Microfinance Institutions: Assessing the Impact of Andhra Crisis

Amar Nath Das and Arindam Laha

INTRODUCTION

Inspired by the success story of Grameen Bank in Bangladesh, Indian microfinance sector started its journey in 1990. In the context of financial liberalization policy, a semi-formal microfinance institution is expected to address the problem of inadequate 'poverty finance' in Indian economy. It was presumed that microfinance sector possesses a sort of transformational power and solidarity building capability through local community ownership and control (Bateman & Chang, 2012). In the process of development of microfinance sector, an intervention of NABARD through its

---

A. N. Das (✉)
Nabagram Hiralal Paul College, Hooghly, India
e-mail: amarnath.das.79@gmail.com

A. Laha
The University of Burdwan, Burdwan, India
e-mail: alaha@com.buruniv.ac.in

SHG-bank linkage programme is noticeable. Later on, the movement was supported by other Micro Finance Institutions (MFIs), Non-Government Organization (NGO), Non-Banking Financial Company (NBFC), credit unions and cooperatives. This transformation also leads to unsupervised and unsustainable growth of MFIs across the country.

However, MFIs was not allowed to raise deposit from their clients, rather they were largely depending on loan from financial institutions and donors fund from abroad. From 2005–2006, a trend of institutional transformation from not-for-profit to NBFC-for-profit sector attract private funding, and thereby practising commercialization at a large scale. As a result, the institutions were more specialized in designing credit delivery channels profitably. For the next couple of years, MFI industry grew multi-fold and witnessed several challenges like partial disclosure, over leverage, higher interest rate, lack of regulation, etc. (Mader, 2013). As a result, the average debt/equity ratio of Indian MFIs drops down from 11.05 in 2005 to 4.69 in 2009 and continues to decline to 2.41 by 2011–2012 (MFIN, 2012). Surprisingly, in 2009, Andhra Pradesh became the state which account for 30% of India's MFIs portfolio, despite only 7% of the population (Srinivasan, 2008). The state was outstretching its lending capacity and losing credit discipline also. Multiple borrowing, over-indebtedness of the borrowers and sanctioning loan without proper scrutiny by MFIs had become a common practice in Andhra Pradesh (Bateman & Chang, 2012).

In November 2010, Indian microfinance industry observed a serious repayment crisis in Andhra Pradesh. As an immediate effect, the state witnessed village suicide, coercive practice for collecting repayments, etc. (Haldar & Stiglitz, 2016). It attracted immediate Government intervention to stabilize the sector. Andhra Government introduced an Ordinance to protect borrowers from harassment by MFI agents and subsequent actions were taken to control the crisis. Thereafter, Reserve Bank of India constituted the Malegam Committee to study issues and concern of microfinance sector. The committee introduced specific regulations in the formation of a new category of NBFC, namely, NBFC-MFIs, in 2011. At present, Indian MFIs has an outreach in almost 600 districts across the country and credit supplied by multiple lenders (nearly 171) including Banks, Small Finance Banks, NBFC-MFIs and NBFCs (Purkayastha et al., 2020).

From the above discussion, crisis can be conceptualized by incidence of happening four situations sequentially. First, exceptional growth in microfinance sector coupled with oversupply of capital. Second, aggressive competitions among MFIs provided the necessary impetus for the inevitable 'microfinance bubble' which ultimately resulted in sub-prime style 'microfinance meltdowns' around the globe (Bateman & Chang, 2012). Third, over-indebtedness of borrowers, degradation in microfinance lending standard and unwillingness of mainstream banking sector in extending credit in small amounts aggravated the problem. Forth, a decline in credit growth coupled with rising in non-performing assets.

However, microcredit is regarded as a business serving high-risk borrowers with low returns on investment due to high transaction and information costs (Pollinger et al., 2007). A significant number of microfinance programmes depend on donors' fund from government or investors to meet this high cost of transactions. In this scenario, MFIs require to achieve borrower's loyalty resulting from spillover effect of efficient management system. This can be expected to have a far-reaching implication on the sustainability of MFIs.

Experience of Andhra crisis was observed to be a deep rooted connection on the sustainability of MFIs. The term sustainability of a financial institution was conceptualized in different dimensions in the existing literature. Some studies regarded sustainability as a means of financial stability in generating income from its operation to pay back all expenses and make a margin to keep up its growth (Ayayi & Sene, 2010; Chavan & Ramakumar, 2002; Meyer, 2002; Morduch, 2000; Pati, 2009), while others considered managerial efficiency coupled with satisfactory financial performance (Shetty, 2009; Srinivasan, 2008). Sustainability was also recognized as the ability to survive without donors' subsidy (Parida & Sinha, 2010) in the light of an inverse relationship between subsidies/grant and financial sustainability (Kereta, 2007; Peter, 2007). From the perspective of programme viability, a programme would be sustainable if it can recover the cost of lending and imprint a positive image in the mind of beneficiaries, which acts as an incentive for them to pay back their credit (Khandekar & Khalily, 1996). MFIs can sustain their operation if they achieve an acceptable financial and outreach performance (Bhanot & Bapat, 2015). In comprehensive term, sustainability implies an ability of MFIs to generate revenue which could recover the entire operating cost by way of delivering microfinance services to the poor clients in substantial numbers without external grant or donors' subsidy.

In line with the intrinsic objective of an MFI, sustainability of MFIs can be conceptualized from the perspective of financial and operating performance. Several studies considered this objective as a standard indicator to measure the sustainability of MFIs and identified a wide range of factors affecting the sustainability of MFIs. Some of them are number of borrowers, cost per borrower, yield to the portfolio, operational efficiency, quality of loan portfolio, size of capital assets, inflation, lending rate (Ayayi & Sene, 2010; Bogan, 2012; Hartarska & Nadolnyak, 2010; Kinde, 2012). In this respect, existing studies established a positive and significant relationship among a large number of borrowers and sustainability (Logotri, 2006), capital structure and sustainability (Iezza, 2012), asset size and sustainability (Bogan, 2012; Cull et al., 2007; Mersland & Storm, 2007), breadth of outreach and sustainability (Nyamsogoro, 2010; Quayes, 2012), staff productivity and sustainability (Crombrugghe et al., 2008). On the other hand, a negative relationship was observed in between ratio of gross outstanding loan portfolio to total assets and sustainability (Okumu, 2007). In the context of sustainability of Indian MFIs, Bhanot and Bapat (2015) observed a positive and significant relationship between large loan portfolio, staff productivity and return on assets with sustainability. On the other hand, portfolio at risk is inversely related to sustainability. In another study in India, revenue factor, cost-efficiency factor and growth factors were found to have positive impact over sustainability (Nadiya et al., 2012).

However, these studies did not consider any comprehensive approach towards measuring sustainability and the trend of sustainability before and after the crisis period. This study, therefore, objectively tries to address this research gap in the existing literature by developing a multidimensional sustainability index and to test the existence of structural break (caused by Andhra crisis) in the sustainability trend of Indian MFIs. This study also identifies how the crisis as a component together with other contributory factors can influence sustainability of Indian MFIs.

For convenience, this chapter is divided into four sections. The next section considers the data sources and methodological aspects relating to measure of sustainability and its determinants. In section. "Results and Discussion", empirical evidences on sustainability scores of MFIs and structural break during our study period are presented. Also, the effects of various factors in determining sustainability are identified. The concluding remarks are presented in the last section.

Data and Methods

In this study, we have compiled three individual indicators to construct a multidimensional index of sustainability. These three indicators are number of active borrowers, average loan balance per borrower and operational self-sufficiency ratio (following Bhanot & Bapat, 2015). After evaluating sustainability score of our sample MFIs, a panel regression analysis is employed to identify the factors affecting the sustainability of such MFIs.

Sample profile: The database of this study is exclusively secondary in nature. Data on MFIs is compiled from database of Microfinance Information Exchange (MIX), which covers exhaustive information on 109 MFIs operating in India. For the purpose of this study, we used panel data for 12 years right from 2005 to 2016. Depending on the availability of data on selected indictors during the entire time period of 12 years, ultimately sample size is reduced to only 25 MFIs in India. This yields a balanced panel dataset of 300 observations (i.e., a dataset of 25 MFIs for twelve respective years).

Measuring Sustainability of MFIs: This study considers a multidimensional aspect of sustainability, which is derived from three individual indicators. First, number of active borrowers (NAB) reflects a measure of breadth of outreach indicator. Second, average loan balance per borrower (ALPB) is considered as an indicator of depth of outreach and third, operational self-sufficiency ratio (OSS) represents financial performance indicator. 'OSS' is measured by using the following formula: OSS = [Financial Revenue /(Financial Expense + Net Impairment Loss + Operating Expense)]. We have transformed ALPB and NAB into natural logarithm as they are obtained in absolute terms.

Technique for Order Preference by Similarity to the Ideal Solution (TOPSIS) is generally used for solving Multiple Criteria Decision-Making (MCDM) problems (Roszkowska, 2013). We have applied TOPSIS method to compile individual indicators and thereby obtain comprehensive score as a measure of sustainability. This technique provides best alternative which should have the shortest Euclidian distance from the positive ideal solution (most preferable alternative) and the farthest from the negative ideal solution (least preferable alternative) (Benitez et al., 2007).

At first, we have developed a decision matrix. TOPSIS is used to rank P alternatives associated with N criteria, when the score of each alternative with respect to each criterion is available. In our model, $P = 25$ (total number of sample MFIs) and $N = 3$ (three criteria, i.e. NAB, ALPB, OSS).

At the second step, we normalized the dataset of each indicator by using the following normalization formula: $r_{ij} = \frac{x_{ij}}{\sqrt{\sum_{i=1}^{P}(x_{ij})^2}}$ where individual element in $P \times N$ matrix is represented by x_{ij}, $i \in P, j \in N$.

At the third step, we multiply each element of the normalized decision matrix (r_{ij}) by their respective weights (w_j) to enumerate the relative importance of the different selection criteria, i.e. $v_{ij} = w_j r_{ij}$. The objective weights[1] associated with the respective indicators are estimated by following Principal Component Analysis (OECD, 2008). The subjective choice to assign equal weights to the indicators is the simplest solution, but not 'neutral' or without critics (OECD, 2008). So, unlike in other studies (Bhanot & Bapat, 2015), this study utilizes objective approach in determining weights. In the statistical measurement, weights are calculated from the observed values of the variables, and therefore data driven in nature. In this approach, individual indicators are grouped with the highest factor loadings into intermediate composite indicators. In this study, two intermediate composites are aggregated by assigning a weight to each one of them equal to the proportion of the explained variance in the data set.

At the fourth step, the positive and negative ideal solutions are determined depending on whether a criterion is to be maximized or minimized. In this study, operational self-sufficiency and number of active borrowers are considered as positive ideal criteria which need to be maximised. On the other hand, average loan per borrower is taken as negative ideal criteria, which is required to be minimised. The positive ideal (A+) and the negative ideal (A−) solutions are defined according to

---

[1] The subjective choice to assign equal weights to the indicators is the simplest solution, but not 'neutral' or without critics (OECD, 2008). So, unlike in other studies (Bhanot & Bapat, 2015), this study utilizes objective approach in determining weights. In the statistical measurement, weights are calculated from the observed values of the variables, and therefore data driven in nature.

the weighted decision matrix.

$$A^+ = \{v_1^+, v_2^+, v_3^+\}, \text{ where}: v_j^+ = \{(\max(v_{ij}) \text{ iff } \in J); (\min v_{ij} \text{ if } j \in J')\}$$
$$A^- = \{v_1^-, v_2^-, v_3^-\}, \text{ where}: v_j^- = \{(\min(v_{ij}) \text{ iff } \in J); (\max v_{ij} \text{ if } j \in J')\}$$

where, J indicates beneficial attributes (OSS, NAB) and J' stands for non-beneficial attribute (ALPB).

In the step five, we measure Euclidian distance for each MFI from the positive ideal, (Si+) and that of from negative ideal solutions (Si−) as follows.

$$s_{i+} = \sqrt{\sum_{j=1}^{3}(v_{ij} - v_{j+})^2} \quad \text{for } i = 1, 2, 3 \ldots \ldots \ldots 106$$

$$s_{i-} = \sqrt{\sum_{j=1}^{3}(v_{ij} - v_{j-})^2} \quad \text{for } i = 1, 2, 3 \ldots \ldots \ldots 106$$

Finally, relative closeness of each MFI to the ideal solution (where ideal solution refers to nearest to the positive ideal and farthest from the negative ideal solution) is calculated as

$$C_{i+} = \frac{s_{i-}}{s_{i+} + s_{i-}}, 0 < C_{i+} < 1, \quad \text{for } i = 1, 2, 3 \ldots \ldots \ldots 106$$

The relative closeness of each MFI is calculated in such a way that the best alternative (which is nearest to the positive ideal and farthest from negative ideal solution) can be traced out. The values of C_{i+} (i.e., C_1 to C_{106}) indicate the sustainability score of each sample MFIs in our study. A higher value of C_{i+} indicates higher relative closeness to the ideal solution (i.e. C_{i+} approaches to 1), higher-ranking order and better performance than other alternatives. Therefore, TOPSIS helps us to get a relative sustainability score of sample MFIs across the country on the basis of distance from positive ideal and negative ideal solutions.

Determinants of Sustainability: After calculating sustainability score of the respective MFIs by using TOPSIS method, this study identified the determinants of the sustainability by regressing it against explanatory variables. We have compiled the following determining variables of the MFIs, for the same time frame 2005–2016, from MIX database: debt to equity ratio (DE), return on assets (ROA), return on equity (ROE), yield on gross portfolio (YGP), financial expenses to assets (FA), operating expenses to assets (OA), borrower per staff member (BSM), portfolio at risk (PR). In order to capture the effect of crisis took place in 2010, this study considers crisis (CR) as a dummy variable where 0 represents the period before crisis (i.e. 2005–2009) and 1 represents the period on and after crisis (i.e. 2010–2016).

The empirical model can be specified as:

$$\text{Sustainability Score}_{it} = \alpha + \beta_1 \text{CR}_{it} + \beta_2 \text{DE}_{it} + \beta_3 \text{ROA}_{it} \\ + \beta_4 \text{ROE} + \beta_5 \text{YGP} + \beta_6 \text{FA}_{it} + \beta_7 \text{OA}_{it} \\ + \beta_8 \text{BSM}_{it} + \beta_9 \text{PR}_{it} + u_{it} \dots \dots \dots \quad (14.1)$$

where $t = 1, 2, 3, \dots \dots T$ and $i = 1, 2, 3, \dots \dots n$

In model (14.1), sustainability score is the dependent variable, α is the intercept term, β are the $k \times 1$ vectors of parameters to be estimated, and u_{it} represents the error term.

In the panel data regression framework, three empirical models are available: Random Effects Model (REM), Fixed Effect Model (FEM) and Constant Coefficient Model (CCM). Although prior to the application of FEM or REM, it is imperative to know underlying regression framework: panel data regression or the pooled regression (i.e. CCM). Therefore, at first, Breusch-Pagan (BP) test is applied to ensure the application of FEM or REM instead of CCM. A significant χ^2 value (39.06) at 1% level of significance suggests that Panel regression framework is appropriate. Secondly, in a balanced panel dataset, Hausman test guides us in selecting an appropriate model (fixed effect panel regression, or random effect panel regression). In this study, random effect panel regression is ultimate selected by following Hausman test results.

Testing Structural Break: After examining the impact of crisis on sustainability score of the respective MFIs, this study examined the presence of structural break due to Andhra crisis in 2010. In the earlier regression analysis, we assume that the relationship has not changed much over the time period. In other words, the slope and intercept remain the same in this period. However, in the presence of structural break, the average regression function can be quite different from the true regression function (Stock & Watson, 2007). The existence of structural breaks and the impact of crisis on sustainability of MFIs were assessed by comparing the trend of sustainability score before and after the crisis period (2010). We considered the year of Andhra crisis (2010) as a single known break point. In the next stage, Chow Test was applied to test whether the series of sustainability score of MFIs has a significant break point in the year 2010. In fact, rejection of null hypothesis (i.e. no structural break) validates the structural change in the trend of sustainability score, which may be caused by the Andhra Crisis on the sustainability score.

Results and Discussion

Determinants of Sustainability

The regression result in Table 14.1 explains the determinants of sustainability scores obtained by using TOPSIS. It is evident from Panel regression analysis that crisis, return on assets, return on equity, yield on gross portfolio, financial expenses to assets, operating expenses to assets are crucial in explaining variation in sustainability score of MFIs.

ROA: The coefficient of ROA is observed to be positive in explaining sustainability of Indian MFIs and statistically significant (at 1% level). Return on assets is a measure of net income produces in relation to its total assets. It identifies how efficiently an MFI uses its assets to make surplus and continue to grow in the future. Sustainability requires ploughing back of profit into the business to increase portfolio size and reducing equity funding or external borrowing (Bhanot & Bapat, 2015). When an MFI make surplus, it can be reinvested in scaling up its business operation which improve its outreach capability and reduce dependency on donor's fund. It suggests that the practice of earning profit over assets helps MFIs to improve sustainability level. For the purpose of maintaining better return on asset, an MFI requires to achieve high staff productivity, higher loan portfolio, extension of outreach facility and above all good collection capability (Berger et al., 2006; Godquin, 2004).

ROE: ROE is another financial metric that can help to indicate the profitability of MFIs in utilizing investment financing to provide better return to the equity investors. ROE is seen to have a significant effect on sustainability of Indian MFIs with a positive coefficient at 1% level.

Table 14.1 The results of the determinants of sustainability of MFIs (Dependent variable: Sustainability Score)

Independent Variable	Description	Category	Coefficient (β)	t-stat
Debt to equity ratio	Total Liabilities/Total Equity	Financing Structure	0.000	0.165
Return on assets	(Net Operating Income-Taxes)/Average Total Assets	Financial Performance	0.994	0.000***
Return on equity	(Net Operating Income-Taxes)/Average Total Equity	Financial Performance	0.001	0.005***
Yield on gross portfolio	(Yield on Gross Portfolio (nominal)—Inflation Rate)/(1+Inflation Rate)	Financial Performance	0.367	0.002***
Financial expenses to assets	Financial Expense/Average Total Assets	Financial Performance	−1.106	0.000***
Operating expenses to assets	Operating Expense/verage Total Assets	Operating efficiency	−0.488	0.001***
Borrowers per staff member	Number of Active Borrowers/Number of Personnel	Productivity and Efficiency	0.000	0.333
Portfolio at risk > 30 days	Outstanding balance overdue 30 Days + renegotiated portfolio/Gross Loan Portfolio	Risk and Liquidity	0.008	0.786
Crisis	0 represents before crisis period, 1 represents on and after crisis period	Time indicator	0.089	0.000***
Constant			0.500	0.000***

Note***, and **indicate that the coefficient is significant at the 0.01 and 0.05 level of significance respectively
Source Author's own calculation

A rising ROE is a measure of MFIs capacity to generate income without reliance on external capital. It also suggests that an enterprise can grow (increase in outreach) with its internally generated profit or increase in equity without having borrowed capital. Eventually, it provides the ability to grow with its value and reinforce sustainability. Although, ROE should not be viewed in isolation, but higher ROE could also mean that MFI is operating with high debt and minimal equity. Higher debt-equity ratio with greater operating efficiency could lead to higher ROE and often associated with higher risk. It suggests that MFI is aggressive in debt financing and its potential growth is backed by external borrowings. In this respect, it is important to consider the industry debt-equity average. It would be a cause for concern if an MFI's debt-equity ratio is found to have above the industry average.

Yield on gross portfolio: It represents the earning performance of MFIs. In real term, it is calculated in cash accounting basis. It is a measure of financial revenue earned in the form of interest, fees, commission on loan portfolio with which financial and operating expenses are covered. Yield on gross portfolio have a significant positive effect on sustainability of MFIs. In fact, it is an indication of an MFI's efficiency in collecting loan repayments from its borrowers. It also provides an insight about portfolio quality as it is measured on cash basis. Earning revenue is an important step in becoming sustainable.

Return on Equity, Return on Assets and Portfolio Yield are the three indicators used to measure profitability. But for the purpose of understanding how an MFI earns its profits or losses, we need to know how well an MFI performs operationally. For this purpose, it requires to take into account other indicators like operating expenses to assets for measuring operational performance, financial expenses to assets and portfolio at risk for evaluating financial management and Borrowers per staff member for assessing productivity.

Financial expense to assets ratio: Financial expense means interest and fee expense on funding liabilities. A financial expense to assets is an indicator of financial management of MFIs. Financial management ensures that there is enough liquidity to meet institutional obligations after disbursement of loans to its borrowers. Decisions are taken in this domain can directly affect the bottom line of the MFI. It does have an impact on institution's profitability through the competent expertise with which liquid funds are invested. This indicator is found to have a significant effect on sustainability of MFIs with a negative coefficient at 1% level. As the result suggest, higher expenses on borrowed fund compared to asset base increases potential risk on liquidity. Adequate liquidity helps to withstand at all kinds of sudden shock waves that will be faced during future course of operation. It may cause institution's inability to meet its financial obligations when they come due. So, prudent practice of financial management could ensure sustainability of MFIs.

Operating expense to assets ratio: It indicates an overall efficiency of an organization. It measures the institutional cost of delivering loan services compared to average total assets. This ratio does not have any impact due to changes in the lending rate of MFIs. That's why it provides a better picture of an MFI's operational efficiency. This indicator is found to have a significant effect on sustainability of MFIs. A negative coefficient implies that the lower the operating expenses to assets ratio, the higher the efficiency. Moreover, a lower ratio is an indication of such level of assets base which is sufficient to cover its operational cost. Consistency in maintaining a decent operating expense to assets ratio over the time ensures long-term sustainability.

Crisis: In this empirical result, the coefficient of crisis is found to be a positive (significant at 1% level) and therefore signifies an impact of crisis on sustainability of MFIs. It implies that Andhra crisis does have some significant negative impact on the sustainability on Indian MFIs. Although crisis had developed a temporary tension in borrowers' mind, but several regulatory measures (undertaken by RBI) together with other state governments rendered an effective role in mitigating its far-reaching effect on the subsequent years.

A trend of sustainability score, as presented in appendix Fig. 14.1 also exhibited an increasing trend in sustainability of most of our selected MFIs after the Andhra crisis, 2010. However, the trend of sustainability in case of Spandana (a MFIs originating from Andhra Pradesh) revealed a sudden downward trend just after the experience of crisis in its originating state, but registered an upward trend after 2012. BSFL can be considered as an exception as a consistent declining trend of sustainability is evident even before the crisis period.

Structural Break

The trend of sample MFIs broadly suggests that Andhra crisis does not reflect any adverse impact on sustainability of Indian MFIs. For the purpose of fair understanding of the fact, this study examines the existence of structural break in sustainability of MFIs at a discrete time point (i.e. 2010) by using Chow test (Table 14.2). The outcomes of the Chow test revealed that out of 25 selected MFIs, structural break in their sustainability score was noticeable only for nine MFIs (Adhikar, Credit Access Grameen, GU Financial, Sanghamithra, Sarvodaya Nano, Mahashakti, RASS, Spandana, Village Financial) in the year 2010. As far as these nine

Table 14.2 The results of the Chow Test (F-statistics)

MFI	$F(2,8)$	P value	Originating State
Adhikar	4.44	0.05	Odisha
Asomi	0.63	0.55	Assam
Bharat Financial (SKS)	1.95	0.20	Telangana
BSFL	1.66	0.24	Bihar
BSS	1.81	0.22	Karnataka
BWDA	0.49	0.62	Tamil Nadu
Cashpor	0.63	0.55	Uttar Pradesh
CreditAccessGrameen	5.99	0.02	Karnataka
GramaVidiyal	1.60	0.26	Tamil Nadu
GU Financial	4.76	0.04	Odisha
Madura	1.15	0.36	Tamil Nadu
Mahasemam	2.68	0.12	Tamil Nadu
Mahashakti	3.00	0.10	Odisha
NEED Microfinance	0.51	0.61	Uttar Pradesh
RASS	3.59	0.07	Andhra Pradesh
RGVN	0.60	0.56	Assam
Sanghamithra	3.64	0.07	Karnataka
Sarvodaya Nano	3.23	0.09	Tamil Nadu
Satin	0.95	0.42	Delhi
SKDRDP	1.55	0.26	Karnataka
SMILE	1.54	0.27	Tamil Nadu
Sonata	1.00	0.40	Uttar Pradesh
Spandana	4.74	0.04	Andhra Pradesh
Ujjivan	1.29	0.32	West Bengal
Village Financial	15.24	0.00	West Bengal

Source Author's own calculation

MFIs are concerned five are originated from South Indian states (Andhra Pradesh, Karnataka, Tamil Nadu) and three are from Odisha. Only one MFI (Village Financial) was registered in West Bengal.

Conclusions

This study makes a holistic approach to measure sustainability of Indian MFIs in the parlance of self-sufficiency and outreach of microfinance services. A quantitative approach (TOPSIS) is followed in measuring sustainability of MFIs across the states in India. A comprehensive sample of 25 Indian MFIs is compiled from MIX database. Thereafter, the study made an attempt to capture the determinants of sustainability of MFIs in an integrated manner.

In regression analysis, crisis, return on assets, return on equity, yield on gross portfolio appeared as positive and significant determinants in explaining sustainability. Contrary to that, financial expenses to assets, operating expenses to assets emerged as negative and significant impact on sustainability. Crisis draws attention of policy makers to reorient their approach towards operation of microfinance in India. The legal status of MFIs was later on converted in Non-Banking Financial Company and subsequent implementation of Malegam Committee recommendations introduce a paradigm shift of this sector. It was a confidence building measure which helps to restore the believes in the mind of investors and clients also.

Return on assets measures how efficiently an MFI uses its assets to make surplus. When an MFI has surplus, the same can be ploughing back into the business to increase portfolio size, to reduce dependency on donor's fund. The result supports the claim of positive impact of ROA on sustainability of MFIs. ROE is a measure of MFIs capacity to generate income with existing capital base. It suggests that an enterprise can extend its outreach capacity with internally generated profit or by increase in equity without having borrowed capital. Eventually, it helps to grow its value and reinforce sustainability. Yield on gross portfolio is a measure of an MFI's efficiency in collecting loan repayments from its borrowers. It also indicates an insight about portfolio quality. Earning revenue helps MFIs to secure higher level of sustainability. The efficiency of MFIs in terms of operation management and financial management is reflected through operating expense to assets and financial expenses to assets. Both the indicators are inversely related with sustainability. It implies that the lower these ratios, higher the sustainability level. A lower operating ratio is an indication of such level of assets base which is sufficient to cover entire operational cost. On the other hand, financial expenses to assets ratio indicates desired level of liquidity to meet institutional obligations after disbursement of loans to its borrowers. Higher the ratio suggests increase in risk on liquidity. So, prudent practice in managing both the ratio could ensure sustainability of MFIs.

In addition, this study investigates the effect of 2010 Andhra crisis on the behaviour of sustainability of Indian MFIs. Although the crisis had a temporary effect on overall operation of MFIs in some specific region in India, but eventually retained a higher sustainability score in the post Andhra crisis. Out of 25 sample MFIs, nine MFIs (majority from South Indian states) experienced a structural break in the trend of sustainability in operation. A graphical presentation in this study also establishes an attainment of higher sustainability score of majority of our sample MFIs (including nine MFIs, which experienced a structural break in the sustainability trend) in the post Andhra crisis. Thus, empirical findings in this chapter negate the adverse effect of crisis on the sustainability of MFIs. A stringent government policy in regulating MFIs after Andhra crisis, in fact, facilitates an enabling environment, which is conducive for running microfinance business in a sustainable way.

Although, we have tried to generalize the results but this study is not exhaustive in nature. In addition to the limitation of small sample of MFIs, the MIX Market data does not allow us to consider other socio-economic factors in determining sustainability. There is further scope of study by considering social performance data set of MFIs to account for their effect on sustainability.

Appendix

See Fig. 14.1.

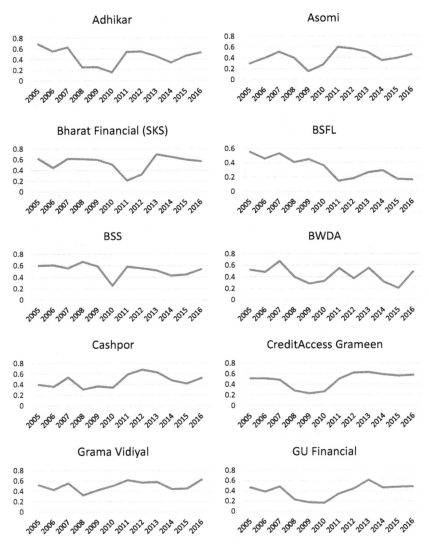

Fig. 14.1 Trend in sustainability scores of sample MFIs (*Source* Author's own presentation)

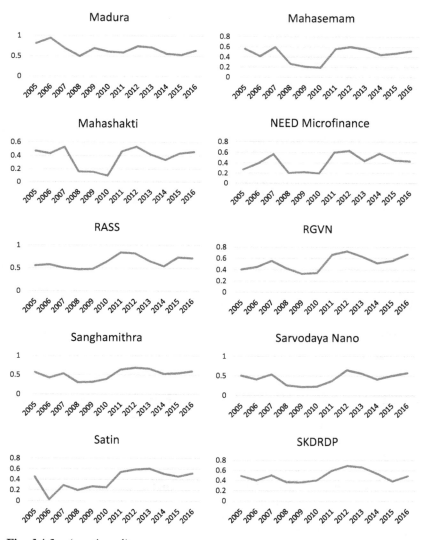

Fig. 14.1 (continued)

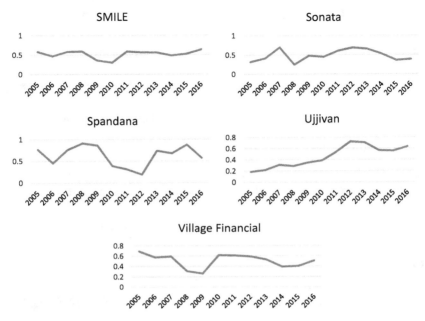

Fig. 14.1 (continued)

References

Ayayi, A. G., & Sene, M. (2010). What drives microfinance institution's financial sustainability. *The Journal of Developing Areas, 44*(1), 303–324.

Bateman, M., & Chang, H. (2012). Microfinance and the illusion of development: From Hubris to Nemesis in thirty years. *World Economic Review, 1*, 13–36.

Benitez, J., Martin, J., & Roman, C. (2007). Using fuzzy number for measuring quality of service in the hotel industry. *Tourism Manage, 28*(2), 544–555.

Berger, M., Otero, M., & Schore, G. (2006). Pioneers in the commercialization of microfinance: the significance and future of upgraded microfinance institutions. *Inside View of Latin American Microfinance* (pp. 37–77). Inter-American Development Bank.

Bhanot, D., & Bapat, V. (2015). Sustainability index of micro finance institutions (MFIs) and contributory factors. *International Journal of Social Economics, 42*(4), 387–403.

Bogan, V. L. (2012). Capital structure and sustainability: An empirical study of microfinance institutions. *Review of Economics and Statistics, 94*(4), 1045–1058.

Chavan, P., & Ramakumar, R. (2002). Micro-credit and rural poverty: An analysis of empirical evidence. *Economic and Political Weekly, 37*(10), 955–965.

Crombrugghe, A., Tenikue, M., & Sureda, J. (2008). Performance analysis for a sample of microfinance institutions in India. *Annals of Public and Cooperative Economics, 79*(2), 269–299.

Cull, R., Demirgüç-Kunt, A., & Morduch, J. (2007). Financial performance and outreach: A global analysis of leading microbanks. *The Economic Journal, 117*(517), F107–F133.

Godquin, M. (2004). Microfinance repayment performance in Bangladesh: How to improve the allocation of loans by MFIs. *World Development, 32*(11), 1909–1926.

Haldar, A., & Stiglitz, J. E. (2016). Group lending, joint liability, and social capital: Insights From the Indian microfinance crisis. *Politics and Society, 44*(4), 459–497. https://doi.org/10.1177/0032329216674001

Hartarska, V., & Nadolnyak, D. (2010). Do regulated microfinance institutions achieve better sustainability and outreach? Cross-country evidence. *Applied Economics, 39*(10), 1207–1222.

Iezza, P. (2012). *Financial sustainability of microfinance institutions: An empirical analysis* (Doctoral Dissertation, Department of Economics. Copenhagen Business School, Copenhagen).

Kereta, B. (2007). Outreach and financial performance analysis of microfinance institutions in Ethiopia. *African Economic Conference*, Addis Ababa, Ethiopia.

Khandker, S. R., & Khalily, B. (1996). *The Bangladesh rural advancement committee's credit programs* (World Bank Discussion Paper No. 324).

Kinde, B. (2012). Financial sustainability of microfinance institutions (MFIs) in Ethiopia. *European Journal of Business and Management, 15*, 1–11.

Logotri. (2006). *Building sustainable microfinance system: A growth of catalyst for the poor.* Local government training and research institute, society for development studies.

Mader, P. (2013). Rise and Fall of Microfinance in India: The Andhra Pradesh crisis in perspective. *Strategic Change, 22*(1–2), 47–66. https://doi.org/10.1002/jsc.1921

Mersland, R., & Strom, R. O. (2007). *Performance and corporate governance in microfinance institutions.* Agder University.

Meyer, R. L. (2002). *Track record of financial institutions in assisting the poor in Asia* (ADB Institute Research Paper No. 49, pp. 1–42). Asian Development Bank Institute, Tokyo.

MFIN. (2012). *The micro scape november 2012.* Microfinance Institutions Network, Gurgaon.

Morduch, J. (2000). The microfinance schism. *World Development, 28*(4), 617–629.

Nadiya, M., Polanco, F., & Ramanan, T. (2012). Dangers in mismanaging the factors affecting the operational self-sustainability (OSS) of Indian microfinance institutions (MFIs)—An exploration into Indian microfinance crisis. *Asian Economic and Financial Review, 2*(3), 448–462.

Nyamsogoro, G. D. (2010). *Financial sustainability of rural microfinance institutions in Tanzania* (Published Doctoral Thesis, University of Greenwich, London).

OECD. (2008). *Handbook on constructing composite indicators: Methodology and user guide*. OECD publishing.

Okumu, L. J. (2007). *The microfinance industry in Uganda: Sustainability, outreach and regulation* (Unpublished PhD Dissertation). University of Stellenbosch.

Parida, P., & Sinha, A. (2010). Performance and sustainability of self-help groups in India: A gender perspective. *Asian Development Review, 27*(1), 80–103.

Pati, A. (2009). Subsidy impact on sustainability of SHGs: An empirical analysis of micro lending through SGSY scheme. *Indian Journal of Agricultural Economics, 64*(2), 1–13.

Peter, C. (2007). *The success of microfinance: What really sustains this poverty relief effort*. School of Business, Nazarene University.

Pollinger, J. J., Outhwaite, J., & Guzmán, H. C. (2007). The question of sustainability for microfinance institutions. *Journal of Small Business Management, 45*(1), 23–41.

Purkayastha, D., Tripathy, T., & Das, B. (2020). Understanding the ecosystem of microfinance institutions in India. *Social Enterprise Journal, 16*(3), 243–261.https://doi.org/10.1108/SEJ-08-2019-0063

Quayes, S. (2012). Depth of outreach and financial sustainability of microfinance institutions. *Applied Economics, 44*, 3421–3433.

Roszkowska, W. (2013). Rank ordering criteria weighting methods-a comparative overview. *Optimum StudiaEkonomiczne NR, 5*(65).

Shetty, N. (2009). Index of microfinance group sustainability: Concepts, issues and empirical evidence from rural India. *The Microfinance Review, 1*(1), 131–152.

Srinivasan, N. (2008). *Sustainability of SHGs. In microfinance in India*. Sage.

Stock, J. H., & Watson, M. W. (2007). *Introduction to econometrics* (2nd ed.). Pearson Education Limited.

CHAPTER 15

Role of Microfinance Institutions in Social inclusion: A Study with Reference to India

Bappaditya Biswas and Rohan Prasad Gupta

BACKGROUND OF THE STUDY

The terminology 'social inclusion' is a technique which attempts to make certain same possibilities for all. It attempts to empower negative and marginalized human beings to avail the benefit of burgeoning international possibilities. Poverty is one of the predominant troubles of subject for enhancing the socio-financial popularity of the underprivileged and unprivileged human beings of growing international locations like India, Bangladesh, Nepal, Sri Lanka, etc. In this backdrop, Microfinance Institution is an agency that offers credit score and different monetary offerings to low-earnings institution of population. They create a direction through which they mobilize sources so that you can offer monetary, non-monetary offerings (like training, counselling etc.) and different guide offerings to the negative and mainly girls for feasible efficient earnings technology firms and permitting them to transport out in their poverty.

B. Biswas (✉) · R. P. Gupta
Department of Commerce, University of Calcutta, Kolkata, India
e-mail: aditya_2582@rediffmail.com

Apart from these, MFIs additionally presents capability constructing and enterprise training software that offers a possibility to end up self-reliant. The MFIs in India have grown swiftly for the reason that previous couple of years each in phrases of client's outreach and mortgage portfolio. At the identical time, the MFIs have end up a powerful device for poverty reduction, girls empowerment and social inclusion each in rural and concrete India. Now in India, MFIs presently function in 36 states and union territories and 563 districts. Currently, 168 MFIs (registered with Sa-Dhan) operates in India. As on 30 September 2020, NBFC-MFIs on an aggregated foundation have a community of 14,080 branches with 109,521 employees. This enterprise has a Gross Loan Portfolio (GLP) of INR 231,788 crores as on thirtieth September 2020, a growth of 14.90% YoY over INR 201,724 crores as on 30 September 2019. The Microfinance enterprise served 5.71 crore particular debtors with 10.50 crore mortgage account as on 30 September 2020. It has general mortgage portfolio of INR 231,788 crore for loans originated after February 2017, revelled microfinance establishments community in its thirty third problem of its micro metre file for January–march 2020 (Q2 F.Y. 2020–2021).

Review of Literature

The researchers have gone through several existing literatures in this area and few important of them are which are as follows:

Verma and Aggarwal (2014) of their studies paper emphasized at the idea of microfinance and microfinance institutions and its influences on economic inclusion with unique attention on poverty discount and women empowerment in India. MFIs play a vital function in economic inclusion and societal improvement.

Biswas and Sana (2015) observed that India has the most range of microfinance models, each current and indigenous. The fashions fluctuate from domestic spun sorts like SHGs and cooperatives to tailored fashions just like the Grameen Bank technique and for-income corporates. SHGs are the best micro creditors in India but majority of the MFIs in India follows the JLGs and person model. Aggarwal and Sinha (2010) objectives to examine the issues confronted through MFIs because of absence of devoted rules on paintings time and control of MFIs. Their paper indicates how MFIs are used as a device for the advent of latest authorities' rules and schemes to facilitate bad in higher way. Researchers observed that the maximum of the excellent appearing MFIs have followed diverse commercial enterprise fashions for its survival and sustainability.

Radhakrishna (2012) defined the importance increase in the enlargement of MFIs in India and the way there's an extrude in the working of MFIs which has become stimulating the enhancements in governance, accountable finance practices and regulatory capacity. The significance of SHGs in facilitating price range among bad and has decreased the load from MFIs and different banking sectors is likewise discussed. Shankar (2013) indicates that there are those who need to get entry to microfinance, however, aren't capable of achieve this because of diverse reasons.

De Crombrugghe et al. (2008) investigated 3 factors of sustainability for MFIs: outlay of coverage through revenue, compensation of loans and cost-control. Their findings advise that the undertaking of overlaying prices on small and partially unsecured loans can certainly be met, without always growing the scale of the loans or elevating the tracking fee. Further, they advise different methods to enhance the economic results, like a higher concentrated on of the hobby price coverage or growing the range of debtors according to discipline officer in particular in collective shipping fashions. Srinivasan (2011) evaluates the performances of the SHG and MFI fashions and discusses thematic troubles which includes social overall performance control and economic inclusion in detail. The document presents insights into maximum latest statistical facts regarding the sector's increase and enlargement throughout the chosen fashions. Raghunathan et al. (2011) amassed samples from borrowing corporations from a south Indian MFIs and analyzed the compensation performance of borrowing corporations and displays at the implications for agricultural microfinance loans. Their findings depicts that the common performance of the borrowing corporations analyzed turned into about 75% and that having a better per cent of agricultural loans accelerated borrowing institution performance while profits in performance additionally rose as the scale of the borrowing institution increases.

Mader (2013) presents an analytical attitude of the upward thrust and fall of Indian microfinance establishments and depicts that the disaster turned into now no longer a fabricated from wanton political machinations, however, turned into spawned through forces in the microfinance enterprise itself. Biswas and Sana (2017) tested the character of services and products availed through the customers in pick districts of West Bengal and the client's notion concerning the MFI's services.

They recommended that the MFIs have a large scope for development concerning health, education, economic literacy programme and coverage services.

Ho and Mallick (2017) analyzed the collusion choices confronted through the MFIs and their effect at the bank-linkage programme, which has been presented as a strategy to assist triumph over damaging choice and ethical danger issues withinside the credit score marketplace through harnessing nearby statistics thru MFIs. They in addition prolonged that financing possible initiatives could make micro-financing greater powerful in attaining inclusive economic improvement and thereby poverty discount in rural areas. Sharma (2018) said that microfinance applications are designed to assist bad rural humans to transform their capacity into effective venture. Researcher have observed that bad humans checked out microfinance establishments with the desire of having credit score in opposition to their social fame due to the fact they do now no longer have collateral to offer as a safety in opposition to credit score.

Mohd (2018) observed that MFI is powerful device for socio-monetary upliftment of bad and low-profits humans. It additionally performs a crucial function for poverty discount and socio-monetary improvement. MFIs availing mortgage from the banks in the course of the year 2013–2014 is growth through 28% over the year 2012–2013. Small sized of MFIs are rural centric. The mortgage incredible in opposition to MFIs accelerated all of the next years. It accelerated through 13.7% and 14.3% in 2015–2016 and 2016–2017.

Research Gap

Based on the extensive review of available literatures, the researchers witnessed that majority of research work has been done regarding the role of MFIs in providing financial inclusion in India but there is lack of any comprehensive study regarding the role of MFIs in providing social inclusion in India. Hence, the researchers identified the area as research gap and intends to bridge up the gap which is believed to be having significant socio-economic implications.

Objectives of the Study

Based on the research gap, the following research objectives have been identified:

1. To understand the role of MFIs in providing social inclusion in India.
2. To analyze the case studies of selected MFIs providing social inclusion in India.

Database and Research Methodology

This study is exploratory and descriptive in nature and is based on secondary data. Different working papers, case studies, journals, government reports, newspapers, magazines and websites are being consulted for this study. Under this study, the researchers intend to perform analysis of the role of MFIs in providing social inclusion in India. The analysis includes the study of the available data. Further, the researchers intensify their study in analyzing the case studies related to the selected MFIs in providing social inclusion in India.

MFIs in India—An Overview

'Micro Finance Institution' refers to a unit (irrespective of its organizational form), which delivers microfinance services in the form and manner as may be prescribed but does not include (i) a banking company; (ii) a cooperative society. 'Micro-finance services' refers to one or more of the ensuing financial services involving small amount to individuals or groups: (i) delivering micro credit; (ii) collection of thrift; (iii) remittance of funds; (iv) delivering pension or insurance services; (v) any other services as may be specified.

MFIs intend to develop a three-dimensional service podium which contains financial inclusion, sustainability of livelihood through network of MFIs and social inclusion to elevate and empower the marginalized and deprived parts of the society. Currently, a series of institutions in both the public and private sectors offer microfinance services in India. These institutions are roughly grouped into two categories, formal institutions and non-formal institutions. The formal class constitutes apex Development Financial Institutions, Commercial Banks, Regional Rural Banks and Cooperative Banks that deliver microfinance services in addition to their regular banking activities. The informal institutions, on the other hand, are referred to as the Microfinance Institutions (MFIs) and are mainly found in private sector.

Role of Indian MFIs in Social Inclusion

In Indian context, the role of MFIs has been expanded not only in terms of geographical outreach to the rural areas but also have their significant footfalls in providing social inclusion to the masses.

- MFIs aren't simplest running as a device for economic inclusion however additionally as device for social inclusion through enhancing the socio-financial situations of the clients.
- Significant contributions had been made through the MFIs in contributing price to the lives of the disadvantaged, marginalised and bad phase of the Indian sub-continent time-to-time via numerous insurance measures and interventions to decorate the general fine in their each day lifestyles and making them empowered each socially and financially.
- In recognition to offering social inclusion, MFIs in India are actively engaged in potential building, livelihood promotion, economic literacy, preventive healthcare, training and training, water and sanitation, etc. that is popularly termed as 'credit-plus' facilities, now-a-days.
- Traditionally, MFIs have centred around offering microcredit simplest. But with the speedy traits in socio-financial scenario, this quarter quickly began out to apprehend that the disadvantaged and bad wanted an extensive form of economic merchandise to enhance their lives, and consequently the idea of microcredit advanced into the idea of microfinance in India. Here, the time period microfinance consists of an extensive variety of economic offerings, which includes loans, savings, insurance and switch offerings, in addition to numerous remittances willing towards low-earnings clients.
- Conventionally, it become assumed that bad families are benefited from a mixture of those offerings supplied through the MFIs, instead of simply the supply of credit, and henceforth, a few MFIs initiated to increase their sports even further, which incorporates now no longer simplest offering economic offerings however additionally offering enterprise training, fitness care, and social offerings. These extra activities are called 'plus' activities, which renowned that although economic offerings are vital for offering microfinance; they may be essentially willing towards simplest one of the numerous troubles of the poor.

The different roles played by the Indian MFIs in social inclusion have been pointed out below.

Outreach to Special Segment of Borrowers (Women, SC/ST and Minorities)

World over the focus of microfinance has always been on serving women. In India as an alternate vehicle of credit, microfinance serves a large segment of people from Scheduled Castes, Scheduled Tribes and Minorities. Women clients constitute 96% of the total clients of MFIs. Similarly, SC/ST borrowers also constitute a substantial chunk (33%) of the clients (Table 15.1).

Focusing on microfinance services towards women, SC/ST and minorities, MFIs are contributing significantly to the wellbeing of the underprivileged, leading to a rise in their welfare and assisting with the financial inclusion agenda. Table 15.1 shows that the Indian MFIs are playing a very significant role in social inclusion by providing their services to the women, SC/ST, minorities and BPL cardholders.

Table 15.1 Category wise composition of borrowers

% to total borrowers

Year	Women borrowers (%)	SC/ST borrowers (%)	Minority borrowers (%)	Differently abled borrowers (%)	Borrowers having BPL card (%)
2011	94				
2012	95	20	23		
2013	96	21	23		
2014	97	19	14		
2015	97	28	18	0.05	
2016	97	30	27	4	
2017	96	20	10	0.12	
2018	96	33	17	2	65

Source Compiled by the authors from the Bharat Microfinance Report, 2018

Credit Plus Services

Different MFIs are offering a huge range of 'plus' offerings. The carrier stages from get right of entry to markets, commercial enterprise development, fitness provision and literacy schooling. Generally, the MFIs offer plus offerings which incorporates both Business Development Services (BDS) and social offerings. BDS ambitions to decorate competitiveness through better productiveness, progressed carrier delivery, higher product layout and stronger marketplace get right of entry to. The offerings furnished accommodates of a huge variety of non-economic offerings, which includes control or era get right of entry to; productiveness and product layout; accounting and criminal offerings; advertising and technical assistance; vocational competencies schooling and get right of entry to diverse statistics approximately standards, regulations or thoughts in an enterprise. On the alternative hand, social offerings, that is, offering social inclusion, integrates the credit score with fitness, education, and different such applications supposed to elevate fitness consciousness, fitness practices and the usage of formal healthcare, the various masses.

The Indian MFIs that commenced the adventure as an unmarried credit score product programme have now moved right into a distinctive realm with MFIs looking to recognize their client's economic desires in an extra significant manner and designing merchandise to healthy those desires with the scope of regulatory restrictions. The length 2005–2010 witnessed a severe increase on the price of innovation because it becomes less complicated to boom outreach with a popular product. The MFIs are actually offering credit score plus offerings i.e. they may be offering micro insurance, fitness offerings, cash remittance offerings, schooling and ability constructing offerings, etc. alongside formal credit score merchandise.

Micro Insurance

Micro insurance, commonly called as insurance for the poor, is referred as the provision of insurance services to low-income households, which serves as an important tool to reduce risks for the vulnerable population. Micro insurance in India has broadly developed as a sub sector of the insurance industry. India is among the few countries to draft and implement specific micro insurance regulations. The Rural and Social Sector Obligation (2002) and the Micro insurance Regulation (2005) have helped the growth of regulated micro insurance in India. There are around 52 items offered by all registered non-life insurance companies targeting low-income segment of the population which includes Cattle Micro Insurance, Kisan Agriculture Pumpset Micro Insurance Policy, Janata Personal Accident Sukshma Bima Policy, Silkworm Sukshma Bima Policy, Sheep and Goat Micro Insurance Policy, Sampoorna Griha Suraksha Policy, etc. Tables 15.2 and 15.3 listed out the MFIs that are providing life micro insurance and health micro insurance in India.

Table 15.2 MFIs involved in Micro Insurance—Life Insurance

S.N.	Name of the organization	State	No. of clients
1	Credit Access Grameen Ltd.	Karnataka	50,81,497
2	Svatantra Microfinance Pvt. Ltd.	Maharashtra	13,31,718
3	Midland Microfin Ltd.	Punjab	6,88,381
4	Sri Kshethra Dharmasthala Rural Development Project	Karnataka	3,35,066
5	Mahasemam Trust	Tamil Nadu	1,48,000
6	M Power Micro Finance Pvt. Ltd.	Maharashtra	1,34,924
7	Annapurna Mahila Cooperative Credit Society Ltd.	Maharashtra	65,449
8	Rashtriya Seva Samithi	Andhra Pradesh	53,917
9	Grameen Shakti Microfinance Services Pvt. Ltd.	West Bengal	24,407
10	BWDA Finance Ltd.	Tamil Nadu	24,116
11	Belghoria Janakalyan Samity	West Bengal	21,674
12	Self-Employment Voluntary Association	Manipur	10,960
13	Aparajita Mahila Sangh	Madhya Pradesh	4,857
14	Magalir Micro Finance Pvt. Ltd.	Tamil Nadu	4,800
15	Magilchi Foundation	Tamil Nadu	4,800
16	Anandita Micro Credit Services Foundation	Odisha	2,681
17	WeGrow Financial Services Pvt. Ltd.	West Bengal	2,581
18	Centre for Promoting Sustainable Livelihood	Bihar	1,160
19	Blaze Trust	Tamil Nadu	866

Source Compiled by the authors from the Bharat Microfinance Report, 2020

Table 15.3 MFIs involved in Micro Insurance—Health

S.N.	Name of the organization	State	No. of clients
1	Sri Kshethra Dharmasthala Rural Development Project	Karnataka	7,89,764
2	Svatantra Microfinance Pvt. Ltd.	Maharashtra	5,89,461
3	Annapurna Mahila Cooperative Credit Society Ltd.	Maharashtra	4,20,011
4	Muthoot Microfin Ltd.	Maharashtra	1,37,448
5	M Power Micro Finance Pvt. Ltd.	Maharashtra	1,02,907
6	S V Creditline Pvt. Ltd.	Haryana	63,522
7	South India Finvest	Tamil Nadu	35,301
8	BWDA Finance Ltd.	Tamil Nadu	22,559
9	Bullock-Cart Workers Development Association	Tamil Nadu	22,559
10	Welfare Services Ernakulam	Kerala	13,580
11	Sampada Entrepreneurship & Livelihoods Foundation	Maharashtra	12,966
12	KPB Fincare Pvt. Ltd.	Kerala	6,156
13	Credit Access Grameen Ltd.	Karnataka	1,059
14	Blaze Trust	Tamil Nadu	466

Source Compiled by the authors from The Bharat Microfinance Report, 2020

Micro Pension

Among the microfinance clients, the need for pensions is clearly felt and expressed. India Invest Micro Pension Services (IIMPS) has partnered with Nyaya Bhoomi for providing micro-pension to 85,000 rickshaw workers in Delhi. IIMPS has also partnered with BASIX and SEWA Bank for covering 7,00,000 working poor in 15 states of India. Sheperd India and Dhan Foundation are also implementing pension solutions for their customers. The large footprint pension schemes are UTI Micro pension scheme with over 1.25 lakh subscribers, promoted through BASIX, SHGs and other community based groups and the Society for Elimination of Rural Poverty (SERP)—Life Insurance Corporation partnered micro-pension scheme in which over 3.7 lakh women members of SHGs had subscribed as of April 2010. In West Bengal, Bandhan has started pension services through the New Pension Scheme (NPS) of Government of India. Arohan's micro-pension schemes are managed by UTI Retirement Benefit Pension Fund (RBPF) and Life Insurance Corporation of India (LICI) for investment sizes as small as Rs. 100 per month. The general development has been 26% in the period of March, 2020.

Other Development Services Which Lead to Social Inclusion

The Microfinance area (MFIs, SHPIs, SHG Federations and so on) along exclusive companions has been altogether contributing in giving miniature safety and miniature benefits. There are moreover numerous administrations which the MFIs and SHPIs give, for example, strengthening of the neighbourhood area (especially for the women), restrict building, instruction, financial education, wellness and sterilization, preparing, occupations uphold and so on. The developmental sports of MFIs consist of Capacity Building Initiatives and 30 MFIs are related to this, Education wherein 32 MFIs are associated, Financial Literacy wherein 37 are there, Water and Sanitation 32 of them are linked, Livelihood Promotion wherein forty one MFIs are associated, Preventive Healthcare for which forty MFIs are linked, Training Initiatives and different Initiatives 22 MFIs are there (The Bharat Microfinance Report, 2018).

Financial Literacy

Financial talent is pretty likely the principal intercession applications did through MFIs in India. It is essential for information the larger goal of financial consideration. A massive part of the negative has little data approximately formal financial exchanges as they depend essentially upon traditional coins moneylenders for all their financial requirements and regularly slip into the countless loop of debt-lure due to over-the-pinnacle tempo of hobby and degenerate practices. Information on wellsprings of money, financial exchanges, liabilities and risks related to taking credits, reasoning of reimbursement, reserve price range and frugality and so on allow the helpless debtors and assist them loose themselves from the grip of traditional coins mortgage professionals who've misused them for ages.

Some of the MFIs which are actively involved in financial literacy campaigns include Annapurna Mahila Cooperative Credit Society Ltd., Annapurna Microfinance Pvt. Ltd., Aparajita Mahila Sakh Sahakari Sanstha Maryadit, Bal Mahila Vikas Samiti, Balajee Sewa Sansthan, Bandhan Financial Services Ltd., Belghoria Jankalyan Samity, Grama Vidiyal Micro Finance Ltd., Grameen Koota Financial Services Pvt. Ltd., Growing Opportunity Finance (India) Pvt. Ltd., Hand in Hand India, Jagaran Microfin Pvt. Ltd., Mahashakti Foundation, Margdarshak Financial Services Ltd., Odisha, People Forum, Samhita Community Development Services, Sarala Women Welfare Society, Shri Mahila Sewa Sahakari Bank Ltd., etc. (The Bharat Microfinance Report, 2019).

Education

A decent number of MFIs in India are associated with training. These establishments' give essential schooling, professional instruction, grown-up and proceeding with training. Plus, MFIs too put together mindfulness crusades on different financial issues every once in a while. The Bharat Microfinance Report 2019 gives a demonstrative rundown of instructive administrations gave by the MFIs to help networks they serve. For instance, Belghoria Jankalyan Samity gives pre-tutoring programmes while Barasat Unnayan Prostuti runs schools for offspring of migrant labourers in block ovens. Mass Consideration Worldwide gives fundamental training to school drop women. Jeevankiran circulates free investigation materials, umbrellas and regalia and so on; Community for Advancing Practical Occupation gives instructive credits from nursery to designing.

Barasat Sampark assumes a significant part in creating instructive foundation. Also, a few MFIs are associated with instructing their recipient networks through different mindfulness crusades. Grameen Koota Monetary Administrations Pvt. Ltd. gives data on wellbeing, government plans and sustenance/food during its week after week gatherings while Suryoday Microfinance Pvt. Ltd. utilize its weekly meeting to sharpen the individuals on social prosperity. There are various other MFIs which are running instructive projects for their recipient networks and deliberate endeavours are basic in order to set up an extensive report on every such intercession.

Training

A few MFIs are associated with preparing of their customers. For instance, Grameen Development and Finance Pvt. Ltd. gives preparing on rice escalation and piggery while Kotalipara Improvement Society gives preparing in goat and duck raising (The Bharat Microfinance Report, 2015). Aparajita Mahila Sakh Sahkari Sanstha Maryadit runs preparing programmes on PCs, bookkeeping, banking and so forth (The Bharat Microfinance Report, 2015). MFIs can take up preparing more truly as a feature of their responsibilities to advance work. It is conceivable that the MFIs can team up with schools, modern preparing organizations, poly technique, universities and colleges in their area to offer some professional preparing most appropriate to their customers. Migrant labourers joining the hapless horde of easy-going specialists miss out on wages essentially because of absence of abilities and associative certificates.

Preventive Healthcare

MFIs are giving preventive medical care to their customers incredibly. As per the Bharat Microfinance Report 2015, Annapurna Mahila Agreeable Credit Society Ltd. has spearheaded preventive medical care by giving 24×7 Specialists Accessible as needs be. Community for Advancement of Reasonable Job offers 24×7 credits up to Rs. 5000 for treatment. Jeevankrian meets clinical costs of poor people. Balajee Sewa Sansthan gives health care coverage. Unnati Exchange and Fincon Pvt. Ltd. What's more, Saral Ladies Government assistance Society advance utilization of conventional medication among its customers offers free wellbeing registration. Wellbeing camps are coordinated by a great number of MFIs, for example, Annapurna Miniature Account Pvt. Ltd., Equitas Microfinance Pvt. Ltd., Organization of Rustic Credit and Business Improvement, ODISHA, Individuals Discussion, Prayas Miniature Credit, Samasta Microfinance Ltd., and so on.

A portion of the MFIs is giving preventive medical services preparing. MFIs leading such intercessions incorporate Bal Mahila Vikas Samiti—VAMA, Belghoria Jankalyan Samity, Blaze Trust, Inseparably India and Suryoday Microfinance Pvt. Ltd. In any case, considerably more is attractive on this front. MFIs have undiscovered chances of teaming up with essential wellbeing focuses, neighbourhood centres, private and state-run medical clinics to make mindfulness about solid living, yoga and so on among their customers. Furthermore, they can build up a pool of local area wellbeing labourers by giving far reaching preparing and functional openness during wellbeing camps. Such a move won't just make a second line of social protection in the event that of wellbeing crises among the less fortunate networks buts will likewise make work openings for such countless individuals in the deal.

CASE STUDY BASED ANALYSIS OF SOCIAL INCLUSION PROVIDED BY MFIs

In the following section few case studies related to social inclusion provided by the MFIs have been discussed.

Case Study 1: Community Development Initiatives—CASHPOR Micro Credit

The Wellbeing and Instruction administrations are the centre verticals of the Cashpor also are fundamental to guarantee that their BPL individuals can break the intergenerational chain of destitution. Cashpor understands that it is hard to rescue rustic helpless families once again from destitution without legitimate, viable and convenient mediation in their issues of wellbeing, which depletes great measure of their acquiring into treatment and their kids' schooling.

In this manner, on its central goal, the organization is giving wellbeing administrations to the families through 280 Mini Health Clinics (MHCs) and supporting quality Schooling to in excess of 30,000 kids through 1129 Children Education Centres (CECs). Out of which 167 are Junior CECs and 512 are Senior CECs, working at their 541 branches with monetary administrations under incorporated methodology with the goal that the BPL recipients and their family can remain solid and their school going youngsters push ahead through our supporting quality training. Under wellbeing administrations, Cashpor has made attention to wellbeing related consideration and fundamental wellbeing rehearses among 11,82,950 BPL recipients through 3,081 Local area Community Health Facilitators (CHFs) who are prepared by Recuperating Fields. In accordance with Swachh Bharat Mission, Cashpor has so far gave sterilization credits to 1,93,517 BPL recipients for development of latrines and plan to additionally grow its inclusion.

During this Coronavirus pandemic, each official of their work force was approached to settle on decisions to in any event. Individuals consistently make awareness programmes regarding Coronavirus infection, instruct them on preventive measures to make them completely mindful of the offices and help bundles reached out by State/local Government. Altogether, Rs. 71,34,196 were gathered and given alleviation measures to the BPL individuals and transient works in intense pain.

Case Study 2: Skill Development and Education—New Opportunity Consultancy Pvt. Ltd (NOCPL)

NOCPL gives locally appropriate and reasonable work abilities including essential specialized and systems administration abilities beside Bank credit to overcome any barrier. In relationship with its 100% auxiliary, Indian

Relationship for Investment funds and Credit, NOCPL is additionally endeavouring to add to the reason for improvement of deprived individuals from the general public by giving stage for wellbeing/natural mindfulness as likewise training for its borrowers and their relatives.

Ability Improvement: NOCPL encourages participants and their relatives to benefit from occupational abilities and other skill development programmes relating to polytechnics, Industrial Training Institutes (ITIs), other endorsed organizations and Bank supported Rural Self-Employment Training Institutes (RSETIs). On culmination of the course, individuals are given a proposal for position in a presumed association through network accomplices. Individuals are likewise roused to act naturally utilized, wherein they help them in profiting credit linkage through their accomplice banks. During 2019–2020, they have guided 314 such projects, with interest of 8264 members.

Training: Nukkad Pathshala: to support their individuals' kids, NOCPL has set up schooling focuses in different towns and towns of Tamil Nadu called 'Nukkad Pathshala'. These Pathshalas try to bring to each corner or 'nukkad' an unparalleled enthusiasm to learn. Nukkad Pathshala targets conveying fundamental English, Arithmetic and Science information to offspring of different age gatherings—going from five to fifteen, with the assistance of experienced teachers. The target of this activity is to ingrain certainty furthermore, enthusiasm for information in the youthful personalities. Presently, 40 Nukkad Pathshalas are operational across Tamil Nadu, with strength of 56 educators and 1350 understudies. Reception of an Ancestral Town: NOCPL had received a distant sloping ancestral town 'Pareli Pillur' arranged 80 km from Coimbatore with a populace of 75 locals living in 25 houses. NOCPL has conveyed out infrastructural improvement of the rudimentary government schools, by giving drinking water and transport facilities for students presently numbering 15, supported 2 young men for considering certificate courses in a Polytechnic School in Mettupalayam. The organization has likewise orchestrated for sun based lights and drinking water for the whole town.

Wellbeing: NPCPL banded together with recognized and reputed emergency clinics to do general health check-up, eye check-up, dental and paediatric check-ups of the their clients and their family members. 12 such offices were arranged during 2019–2020 profiting 960 individuals.

Case Study 3: Widows and Destitute Welfare- Bullock-Cart Workers Development Association & BWDA Finance Ltd.

Widows and destitute women have helpless social standing, are exceptionally trashed and regularly come up short on the help to support themselves. To make them self-practical, BWDA started a programme to enable widows and down and out ladies and to change them into small business units. BWDA gives minimal effort monetary access (18%) and offers job and limit advancement preparing to recipients. The programme additionally frames 'Pudhumai' bunch including 10 widows or dejected ladies there by making a help stage. They additionally offer promotion backing to individuals. BWDA likewise sorts out different mindfulness and inspirational projects which has profited more than 5000 widows. They have shaped 168 Pudhumai bunches with 1,863 individuals and has encouraged over Rs. 128.25 lakhs to these individuals. During the Coronavirus pandemics, BWDA gave help supplies to 3,191 widows to help them during the emergency.

Case Study 4: Promoting Women Entrepreneurship—Gramalaya Microfin Foundation (GMF)

Gramalaya Microfin Foundation (GMF) has set up Gramalaya Entrepreneurs Associates Tamil Nadu (GREAT) for giving skills training, technical supportand other market connected advancement exercises. Incredible is giving the accompanying expertise improvement trainings: Wire pack making, Masala powder planning, Saree stone work, Paper Gems and Earthenware gems, Kundan gems making, Millet esteem added items, Dairy cultivating and milk items, Poultry, Goat raising, Banana esteem added items, Jute items, Phenyl, dying powder making, Beekeeping, Nursery and Pickle making. The training programmes are of span up to 4 days. Extraordinary behaviours preparing with specialized help from different offices and having MoU with National Banana Research Foundation, Trichy for advancing banana value added items.

CONCLUSION AND RECOMMENDATIONS

The MFIs are serving more than 37 million poor across the nation. In the event that the public authority can channelize a portion of the government assistance through MFIs, it can doubtlessly have a gigantic effect. An incorporation of microfinance, social government assistance plans, food security and business assurance can increase the advantages accumulating to the poor in piecemeal way ahead. On the basis of above analysis and discussions that MFIs have covered along path in providing a sustainable social inclusion to the deprived sections of the Indian subcontinent. In this context, the critical analysis of the cases reveals that the role of SHGs is remarkable in significantly increasing the outreach to the marginalized and deprived section, specially, the women population and the youth.

The objective of financial inclusion can be successfully achieved only if the marginal farmers and landless labourers have easy reach to the monetary services like Savings, Credit, Micro insurance and payment facilities. Though there are various programmes existing managed by some SHGs and foundations, to alleviate poverty and empower rural folks, have performed significantly within the country, but more such programmes need to be organized. It is suggested that it is necessary to focus on instruments and institutions of MFIs which will promote financial inclusion to a larger extent, rather than only focusing on financial inclusion as a process of development.

The government should approach and give liberal monetary support to empower the MFIs expand their social improvement intercessions in wording of reach, quality, and generally sway on individuals who are living on the edges. Other than monetary support, generally adequate target measures and principles to survey social improvement intercessions are fundamental for taking forward the social plan of the MFIs what's more merge their situation as vital participant in social area.

The public authority needs to assume its part in social improvement also. What the helpless need the most is the business security. This can be accomplished by implementing the 'Make in India' programme into a functional platform on the grounds so that incredible open positions are made as unmistakable outcomes (Jha, 2015). To support the economy, the public authority can energize around improving the financial and biological system to expand utilization among the beneficiaries. MFIs can achieve the goal of holistic social inclusion with the help of government interventions.

Limitations and Future Research Scope

The present work is explorative and descriptive study. For future researches in this area more comprehensive and in-depth study can be done by conducting primary surveys along with the application of more sophisticated statistical tools for quantification of the scheme.

References

Agarwal, P., & Sinha, S. (2010). Financial performance of microfinance institutions of India. *Delhi Business Review, 11*(2), 37–46.

Biswas, B., & Sana, A. K. (2015). Microcredit delivery models in India. *The Management Accountant, 50*(7), 26–28.

Biswas, B., & Sana, A. K. (2017). Perception study of clients towards products and services delivered by MFIs—A study with reference to select districts of West Bengal. *Research Bulletin, 42*(4), 113–125.

De Crombrugghe, A., Tenikue, M., & Sureda, J. (2008). Performance analysis for a sample of microfinance institutions in India. *Annals of Public and Cooperative Economics, 79*(2), 269–299.

Ho, S. J., & Mallick, S. K. (2017). Does institutional linkage of bank MFI foster inclusive financial development even in the presence of MFI frauds? *Scottish Journal of Political Economy, 64*(3), 283–309.

Jha, S. (2015). Make in India: The road ahead. *FIIB Business Review, 4*(2), 3–8.

Jha, S., Mohapatra, A. K., & Lodha, S. S. (2019). Political economy of farm loan waivers in India. *FIIB Business Review, 8*(2), 88–93.

Mader, P. (2013). Rise and fall of microfinance in India: The Andhra Pradesh crisis in perspective. *Strategic Change, 22*(12), 47–66.

Mohapatra, A. K., & Jha, S. (2018). Bank recapitalization in India: A critique of public policy concerns. *FIIB Business Review, 7*(1), 10–15.

Mohd, S. (2018). A study on the performance of microfinance institutions in India. *International Academic Journal of Accounting and Financial Management, 5*(4), 116–128.

Raghunathan, U. K., Escalante, C. L., Dorfman, J. H., Ames, G. C., & Houston, J. E. (2011). The effect of agriculture on repayment efficiency: A look at MFI borrowing groups. *Agricultural Economics, 42*(4), 465–474.

Shankar, S. (2013). Financial inclusion in India: Do microfinance institutions address access barriers. *ACRN Journal of Entrepreneurship Perspectives, 2*(1), 60–74.

Sharma, S. (2018). Growth of micro finance in India: A descriptive study. *Global Institute for Research & Education, 7*(2), 20–31.

Srinivasan, N. (2011). *Microfinance India: State of the sector report, Microfinance in India (MFI)*. Sage India.

The Bharat Microfinance Report. (2015, 2019). http://www.sa-dhan.net/bharat-microfinance-report/
The Bharat Microfinance Report. (2018). https://www.firstpost.com/tag/bharat-microfinance-report-2018
Verma, S., & Aggarwal, K. (2014). Financial Inclusion through Microfinance Institutions in India. *International Journal of Innovate Research & Development, 3*(1), 178–183.

CHAPTER 16

Role of Microfinance in the Reduction of Rural Poverty in West Bengal

Kishor Naskar and Sourav Kumar Das

INTRODUCTION

Across the globe nearly each economic system has to stand the poverty. Poverty is the state of affairs wherein low-earnings human beings cannot meet the simple desires of lifestyles. This circumstance results in many fold problems like reduced fitness facilities, excessive illiteracy rate, reduced first-class of lifestyles and plenty of extra. Poverty discount is one of the maximum critical additives of Sustainable improvement goal (SDG) of United Nation (UN). Financing micro-marketers for task advent in addition to earnings producing sports indicates a few achievements in lots of growing international locations like India.

K. Naskar (✉)
Department of Economics, Budge Budge College, Kolkata, India
e-mail: naskark783@gmail.com

S. K. Das
Department of Economics, Lalbaba College, Howrah, India

© The Author(s), under exclusive license to Springer Nature Singapore Pte Ltd. 2022
R. C. Das (ed.), *Microfinance to Combat Global Recession and Social Exclusion*, https://doi.org/10.1007/978-981-16-4329-3_17

Again, extra than half of the globe's working-age adults (approximately 2.5 billion) nevertheless do now no longer have get admission to monetary offerings of regulated monetary institutions (Fouillet et al., 2013). Therefore, some of working-age adults round the sector rely upon casual moneylenders for loans to begin or hold a micro-organization. Globally, there are extra than 3100 microfinance institutions (MFIs) presenting loans to over one hundred million customers to boost them out of poverty (Cull et al., 2007; Epstein & Yuthas, 2011; Hartarska & Nadolnyak, 2007). Microcredit emphasizes the supply of credit score offerings to low-earnings customers, generally withinside the shape of small loans for micro-organization and earnings producing sports. Use of the term 'microcredit' is frequently related to an insufficient quantity of the cost of financial savings for the terrible. In maximum cases, the supply of financial savings offerings in 'microcredit' schemes sincerely includes the gathering of obligatory deposit quantities which are designed simplest to collateralize the ones loans. Additional voluntary financial savings might also additionally gather however the customers have constrained get admission to their enforced financial savings. These financial savings come to be the principal supply of capital withinside the monetary institutions. Microfinance is a key poverty discount method that has unfold unexpectedly and broadly over the past 20 years, presently working in extra than 60 international locations (Bateman, 2010). According to many researchers and coverage makers, microfinance encourages entrepreneurship, will increase earnings producing pastime for this reason decreasing poverty, empowers the terrible (mainly ladies in growing international locations), will increase get admission to fitness and education and builds social capital among terrible and prone communities (Khandker, 2005; Westover, 2008).

The self-assist organization (SHG) technique is a brand new paradigm into the sphere of rural improvement which important targets are to growth the well being of the terrible human beings, offer get admission to assets and credit score, growth self-confidence, shallowness and growth their creditability in all factors of lives (Matiki, 2008). Self-assist organization is a voluntary and self-controlled organization of ladies, belonging to comparable socio-financial characteristics, who come collectively to sell financial savings among themselves (Das Gupta, 2001). The poverty relief intervention of the SHG is withinside the shape of task financial programs to offer employment, giving micro finance offerings to the terrible in order to get themselves familiar with capabilities and occupational diversification. This new initiative turned into taken up via way of means of

Swarnajayanti Gram Swarozgar Yojana, functional in 1999, to arrange the terrible into self-assist organization.

This chapter focuses on how the microfinance specifically SHGs can be an effective tool for eradicating the evil of poverty. The purpose of this paper is to explore microfinance in more depth, describing examples of how SHGs has worked successfully for specific individuals, and discuss both the benefits and limitations of the microfinance approach to reduce poverty. This paper is arranged as- in the next section the area of the study, data base, methodology and analytical tool of the study has been discussed, then the profile of the study area, followed by impact of assessment of SHGs in the above mentioned directions through the probit regression model and finally the conclusion.

Data Source and Methodology

The objective of this study is to empirically examine the influence of activities under SHGs on poverty based on mainly primary data survey. This study has logically established that poverty depends on household size, landholding, average level of education of a household, per capita income, social security and average age of the family member of the household. All the factors also influence in participation in SHG which determine the probability of get rid of poverty. The data has been collected in 2018–2019 keeping in mind the above factors on the basis of Stratified Random Sampling in the first step to select the district on the basis of the development index of districts in West Bengal (Das, 2011). Two districts of West Bengal are purposely chosen from the developed districts and two districts are chosen from less developed districts on the basis of development index. This study has taken into account in terms of Monthly Per Capita consumption Expenditure (MPCE).

The status of poverty of participating households in SHG is examined with the help of probit model. The model also identifies the determinant of SHG, i.e., the factors which induce to participate SHG. Besides, the model represents a sigmoid curve. It corresponds to the Cumulative Distribution Function (CDF) of a standard normal distribution. Here, P_i is considered as standard normal CDF, which is assessed as a linear function of independent variable(s). Hence, the Probit model is stated as-

$$P_i = P(Y_i = 1)$$
$$= F(a + bX_i)$$

Here, $F(a+bX_i)$ is the CDF of the standard normal distribution so that

$$P_i = F(a+bX_i) = \int_{-\infty}^{a+bX_i} f(Z)dz$$

Where

Z is the standard normal variable and $f(Z)$ is the density faction of $Z \sim N(0, 1)$.

In Probit model, the log-likelihood function is-

$$\ln L = \sum_{i=1}^{n_1} Y_i \ln P_i + \sum_{i=n_1+1}^{n} (1-Y_i)\ln(1-P_i)$$

$$= \sum_{i=1}^{n_1} Y_i \ln F(a+bX_i) + \sum_{i=n_1+1}^{n} (1-Y_i)\ln[1-F(a+bX_i)]$$

Maximizing $\ln L$ with respect to a and b and solving, we get the estimates of the two unknown parameters.

It has been made known that $LR \sim \chi^2$ with degrees of freedom $k = $ number of independent variables in the model. Thus, the decision rule is: If $LR^* \sim \chi^2 > \chi_k^2$, reject the null hypothesis which means all the coefficients of the estimated model are simultaneously equal to zero, and infer that there is overall significance of the regression.

Profile of the Blocks

A block has been selected randomly from each district. Hooghly and Howrah are selected as developed districts. On the other hand, Twenty Four Parganas (South) and Birbhum are selected as underdeveloped districts. The blocks named Goghat II and Amta-I are selected randomly from Hooghly and Howrah, respectively. The blocks Mandir Bazar and Labpur are selected randomly from Twenty Four Parganas (South) and Birbhum, respectively. So, this is a purposively stratified random sampling.

50 households have been selected from each of the blocks. Panel a of Table 16.1 describes the distribution of households according to principal activity. The table shows that more or less 50% households are engaged in agricultural activity as principal status except in Amta-I.

Table 16.1 Percentage distribution of sample households (HH) with principal status activity (Panel a) and percentage distribution of population by age group (Panel b)

Panel a

Main Occupation of HHs	Mandir Bazar HH	Labpur HH	Gogbat II HH	Amta-I HH
Agricultural Activity	49.15	52.08	60.29	32.2
Taloring	11.86	10.3	7.42	25.4
Jori Work	10.17	9.98	11.38	18.6
Animal Husbandry	0.85	2.6	1.49	1.7
Food Processing	1.27	1.5	1.49	3.4
Other Non-farm Activity	2.12	2	2.99	5.1
Regular Employed	1.69	1.8	4.48	5.2
Migrated Worker	22.88	19.74	10.46	8.4
Total	100 (50)	100 (50)	100 (50)	100 (50)

Panel b

Age Group	Mandir Bazar	Labpur	Gogbat II	Amta-I
0–5	4.6	5.8	6.7	5
6–14	9.2	8.5	11.7	11.8
15–29	27.6	23.9	35.1	24.1
30–45	29	37.8	26.3	31.8
46–60	18.6	18.7	11.7	20.8
Above 60	11	5.3	8.5	6.5
Total	100	100	100	100

Source Authors' Field Survey, 2018–2019

Among the SHGs tailoring and jori works get priority. 1 to 3% of the households are engaged in animal husbandry and food processing activity. The animal husbandry practices basically include dairy, piggery firming, goatery, poultry, duckery, veterinary, etc. The other non-farm activities ensure cobbler, mason, barber, carpenter, and respiring taking the loan from SHGs.

The majority of the population belongs to low castes in most of the blocks. But Labpur is exceptional. Only 37.54% of the population belongs to low castes in the village. The panel b of Table 16.1 shows the percentage distribution of population by age group among sample households across blocks. About 15% population is below 14 years while 75% population is between 15 and 60 years, and only 11% population is above 60 years in Mandir Bazar. The dependency ratio is lower in Labpur. The percentages of population below 14 years are 18 and 16 in Goghat II and Amta-I, respectively. The working population for in Goghat II and Amta-I are 74% and 76%.

Data revels from panel a of the Table 16.2 that majority of households belongs to Rs. 50,000 to Rs. 75,000 classes across villages. But in case of Goghat II block 18% of households belong to less than 50,000 income level which is highest among the villages. Amta-I is relatively better than other agriculturally developed block. The data supports the evidence that the earnings from non-agricultural sector are relatively better than agricultural. Only 5% of households are below 50,000 income level.

From the panel b of the Table 16.2, it can be shown that land is evenly distributed to Goghat II. Only 12% households are land less and 63% households are marginal land holder. The percentage households having no land are 39, 16, and 48 in Mandir Bazar, Labpur, and Amta-I, respectively. From the above table, it is clear that about 50% households come from marginal land holder. Labpur is gifted of cultivable land on the ground that 32% and 3% of household are belong to small and medium farmer. But in Mandir Bazar small land holders are 11% and only 2% households belong to medium farmer.

More or less 30% workers are engaged in non-farm agricultural activity and near about 50% are engaged in agricultural activity in most of the blocks. Both the workers associated with farm and non-farm activities are involved in SHGs to finance their activity and marketing their product. So, the enhancement in SHGs with better finance facilities may augment their income and improve their standard of living.

Table 16.2 Percentage distribution of households by income group (Panel a) and landholding (Panel b)

Panel a

Household income (Rs.)	Mandir Bazar	Labpur	Goghat II	Amta-I
<50,000	11	9.5	18	5
50,000–75,000	53	45	29	52
75,000–100,000	22	34	25	17
100,000–125,000	9	7	7	12
125,000–150,000	2.8	1	10	7
150,000–175,000	0.7	1.5	9	3
175,000–200,000	0.5	0.75	1	2
225,000+	1	1.25	2	2

Panel b

Landholding (acres)	Mandir Bazar	Labpur	Goghat II	Amta-I
No land	39	16	12	48
0–2.5	48	49	63	46
2.5–5.0	11	32	24	5
5–10	2	3	1	1
10+	0	0	0	0
Total	100	100	100	100

Source Authors' Field Survey, 2018–2019

Impact of SHGs on Status of Poverty

Discussion on poverty examined that malnutrition can lead to a vicious cycle of poverty. Low quality food intake leads to low level of nutrition and it turns to low productivity which causes to low wages and low level of income. This leads to low level nutrition again and completes the cycle. If somehow, they can break the critical level of income through capitalization, marketing, advertising, and giving advice via SHGs, they will get rid of vicious cycle of poverty. Now, we have analyzed the consumption pattern of sample households across study blocks.

The Table 16.3 on consumption expenditure of sample households from Mandir Bazar shows that households spend the highest percent of their expenditure on food items (21.3%) followed by Labpur (17.5%). On the other hand in Goghat II, households spend 10.7% of their expenditure on food items. The highest percentage is spent on non-food item by households 26.8%, 27.7%, 33.6%, and 37.76% in Mandir Bazar, Labpur, Goghat II, and Amta-I, respectively, followed by other labor households. The highest percentage of expenditure on health and education are incurred by households in Goghat II.

Table 16.3 Percentage distribution of consumption of commodities and services

Item of consumption	Mandir Bazar	Labpur	Goghat II	Amta-I
Food grains	21.3	17.5	10.7	15.34
Vegetable, milk/animal products, and Fruits	35.1	35.8	34.5	29.86
Grocery	13.6	21.4	18.6	16.55
Intoxicant	3.3	1.7	2.6	0.49
Subtotal food	73.2	76.3	66.4	62.24
Total fuel	0.3	0.7	2.8	0.92
Clothing and footwear	13.7	9.4	10.9	9.81
Consumer durables	2	0	1.6	5.95
Health and education	4.7	5.8	8.2	4.56
Electricity	1.9	2.3	2	2.79
Other exp	2.4	4.4	6.2	10.63
Transport	1.8	1.1	1.9	3.12
Grand total	100	100	100	100

Source Field Survey, 2018–2019 and authors' calculation

MPCE has been used as a proxy indicator to measure the impact of SHGs on poverty levels of a household. The impact is likely to be positive if the increase in income has transferred into an increase in expenditure, particularly on food and essential items, of the household. We have tried to establish this in the Table 16.4 in a first-hand approach with any econometric analysis, and then we have seen the result with the help of Probit model.

On the basis of our primary survey, we have calculated the MPCE of the sample households and distributed them as the percentile classes. For Mandir Bazar, the 5th percentile of the MPCE distribution was estimated as Rs. 912 and the 10th percentile as Rs. 962. The MPCE of corresponding class for Goghat II are Rs. 1388 and Rs. 1482, respectively. But the MPCE of Labpur and Amta-I are relatively higher for the first two classes. Using consumer price index for agriculture labor of 2011–2012 and 2018–2019, we have estimated rural BPL line for West Bengal Rs. 1238. We can see that 60% of the population belongs to BPL in Mandir Bazar. The percentages of BPL households for other studied

Table 16.4 Fractiles of the distributions of sample households participating in SHGs according to MPCE

Fractile class of MPCE	Mandir Bazar MPCE*	% of HH**	Labpur MPCE*	% of HH**	Goghat II MPCE*	% of HH**	Amta-I MPCE*	% of HH**
0–5%	912	1	1579	2	1388	0	1457	5
5–10%	962	14	1632	10	1482	8	1677	9
10–20%	1016	21	1657	24	1535	17	1736	38
20–30%	1077	31	1680	35	1619	28	1936	43
30–40%	1135	37	1710	41	1743	35	2113	37
40–50%	1169	43	1740	48	1877	50	2168	49
50–60%	1212	47	1949	50	1979	52	2219	55
60–70%	1281	52	2128	52	2139	46	2274	52
70–80%	1417	52	2272	48	2386	49	2400	46
80–90%	1534	30	2508	25	2675	34	2888	27
90–95%	1675	19	2979	27	3052	21	3519	19
95–100%	1885	8	3173	11	3446	17	4625	8
All classes	1265	34	1601	37	1564	41	1805	44

*Average MPCE of the Class, **Percentage of HH Participating SHGs within the group
Source Field Survey, 2018–2019 and authors' calculation

blocks are 10%, 30%, and 5% in Labpur, Goghat II, and Amta-I, respectively. From the Table 16.4, it is clear that MPCE increases with increase in participation of SHGs for all studied blocks.

Results and Discussion

Status of poverty of a family (SPH) is binomial and we've assigned the values 1 and zero for under poverty and others, respectively. Any boom in family size (HHS) is anticipated to lower the provision of sources in according to capita feel and could lessen the extent of consumption. Studies in addition to be had records have showed that the creation of social safety scheme gives greater profits for households. Therefore, it's far anticipated to have a fantastic effect on consumption. In view of this, the variable social safety scheme (SPS) is blanketed to narrate with popularity of poverty analysis. The family belongs to which caste (HHC) is likewise a vital issue in figuring out the extent of ownership of sources in a financial system and the same old of dwelling relies upon of the class of social strata like caste. Consumption is a feature of profits. So, we've taken into consideration according to capita profits (PCI) as a determinant of poverty. Education is the human capita which increase the manufacturing talent of someone and complements the same old of dwelling. So according to head degree of education (PLE) of a family is an impotent variable for analysis. Per capita land holding (PCL) can set off employment possibilities through agricultural manufacturing of a family. To seize the poverty, we've taken into consideration PCL of a family. The SHGs offer economic backup for manufacturing and potential constructing achieving marginal regions to marginal people. This facilitates them to reinforce their profits. So, participation in SHGs is taken in attention for our analysis. The notations and specifications of status of poverty and its determinants are presented in Table 16.5.

Now let us analyze the data by Probit regression model.

Estimation states that PCI, SPS, PCL, and PLE have negatively related with Poverty of the households and all are statistically significant. But households' size (HHS) is significantly and positively related to poverty (Table 16.6). The household's size is positively related with poverty and statistically significant means that the probability of poverty increases with increasing household's size. But the result is quite different for caste categories. HHC positively related with poverty implies that other households are better than SC/ST categories. But this is not statistically significant.

Table 16.5 Notation, Mean, and SD of the Variables used in Probit Regression Model to estimate the effect SHGs

Notation of variable	Specification of variable	Mean	Standard Deviation	Minimum	Maximum
Dependent variable					
SPH	Poverty (Poor = 1, Other = 0)	0.255	0.43	0.0	1.0
Independent variable					
HHS	Household size	3.93	1.23	1.0	9.0
HHC	Households belongs to the caste (SC/ST = 1, Other = 0)	0.69	0.46	0.0	1.0
PCI	Per capita income of households	2318.93	2191.52	960	18,476
SHP	SHGs participation (yes = 1, No = 0)	0.555	0.49	0.0	1.0
PLE	Per head level of education	6.27	3.73	0.0	28
PCL	Per capita landholding in decimal	19.61	22.15	0.0	124
SPS	Social protection scheme	1815.63	3897	0	20,592

Source Authors' calculation

Table 16.6 Probit estimation of SHGs over sample households on poverty

	Coefficient	Std. Err	z	P > z	
Constant	5.532816	1.916449	2.89***	0.004	Number of obs. = 200
HHS	0.5711934	0.2620083	2.18**	0.029	LR $\chi^2(6)$ = 194.95
HHC	0.6098128	0.7154359	0.85	0.394	Prob. > χ^2 = 0.0000
PCI	−0.0034472	0.0012879	−2.68***	0.007	Log likelihood = −16.07780
SPS	−0.0007031	0.0003585	−1.96*	0.050	Pseudo R^2 = 0.8584
PCL	−0.040286	0.0235341	−1.71*	0.087	
PLE	−0.3829342	0.1394478	−2.75***	0.006	
SHP	−2.592624	0.5766914	−4.50***	0.000	

Note *, ** and *** implies significant at 10%, 5%, and 1% level of significance, respectively
Source Authors' calculation

The empirical results relating to the effect of participation in SHGs (SHP) over poverty has been estimated by Probit regression model. The result indicates that in Poverty is significantly influenced by the participation in SHGs. Household's level of education and per capita land holding are also negatively related with poverty and statistically significant. This empirical result has established that education and resource will reduce the level of poverty.

Conclusion

Poverty is the situation in which low-income people cannot meet the basic needs of life. The SHGs may be trained to prepare several products that can be possible to produce within the village, so that they can earn higher incomes with value addition. This paper examined the impact of SHGs as measured by the changes in the livelihood and the level of poverty. This study shows that SHGs are successful in augmenting the welfare of rural households. The formation of SHGs smoothens the financial availability. It provides training to its member and creates marketing facilities to the members. Thus, an income earning environment is created through introduction of SHGs. Generally, poverty is a consequence of lack of income opportunity and means of earning. SHG motivates its member creating income earning resources and helps to make a structural transformation in occupation.

References

Bateman, M. (2010). *Why doesn't microfinance work? The destructive rise of local neoliberalism*. Zed Books.

Cull, R., Demirgüç-Kunt, A., & Morduch, J. (2007). Financial performance and outreach: A global analysis of leading microbanks. *The Economic Journal, 117*(517), F107–F133.

Das Gupta, K. (2001, July–September). An informal journey through self-help groups. *Indian Journal of Agricultural Economics, 50*(3), 370–386.

Das, P. (2011). *Rural non-farm employment in India: Pattern of growth and determinants*. Firma KLM Pvt. Ltd.

Epstein, M., & Yuthas, K. (2011). The critical role of trust in microfinance success: Identifying problems and solutions. *Journal of Developmental Entrepreneurship, 16*(4), 477–497.

Fouillet, C., Hudon, M., Harriss-White, B., & Copestake, J. (2013). Microfinance studies: Introduction and overview. *Oxford Development Studies, 42*, 1–16.

Hartarska, V., & Nadolnyak, D. (2007). Do regulated microfinance institutions achieve better sustainability and outreach? Cross-country evidence. *Applied Economics, 39*, 1207–1222.

Khandker, S. R. (2005). Microfinance and poverty: Data from Bangladesh. *World Bank Economic Review, 19*(2), 263–286.

Matiki, R. E. (2008, July–September). A New Rural Development Strategy for Rapid and Sustainable development in developing countries. *Journal of Rural Development, A Quarterly of NIRD, 27*(3), 449–667.

Westover, J. (2008). The record of microfinance: The effectiveness/ineffectiveness of microfinance programs as a means of alleviating poverty. *Electronic Journal of Sociology*.

CHAPTER 17

Microfinance and Women Empowerment: An Assessment of Disparity in Rural Women Access to Micro Credit in Nigeria

Richardson Kojo Edeme, Henry Thomas Asogwa, and Yakub Yusuf

INTRODUCTION

Micro-credit, sometimes refers to micro banking or microfinance, is a channel of extending credit to non-traditional borrowers like the very poor in rural areas. It is usually in the form of small loans with no

---

R. K. Edeme (✉) · Y. Yusuf
Department of Economics, University of Nigeria, Nsukka, Nigeria
e-mail: richard.edeme@unn.edu.ng

R. K. Edeme
Institute of Development Studies, University of Nigeria, Enugu Campus, Nigeria

H. T. Asogwa
Department of Economics, Kogi State University, Anyigba, Nigeria
e-mail: henry.asogwa@unn.edu.ng

© The Author(s), under exclusive license to Springer Nature Singapore Pte Ltd. 2022
R. C. Das (ed.), *Microfinance to Combat Global Recession and Social Exclusion*, https://doi.org/10.1007/978-981-16-4329-3_18

collateral. Such arrangement makes it possible to reinforce the sense of collective responsibility. The essence of setting up microcredit system is to organize and structure existing local savings which cannot be easily mobilized through other means (Akinyi, 2011). Microcredit is set up in developing and transition economics; microcredit is established to create wealth. Microcredit allows for the financing of individual or group projects. It enables the poorest to participate in projects by advancing a portion of the initial investment.

The issue of empowering rural women through microcredit has been of major concern to stakeholders and policy makers because of its role in opening up access to capital, mitigate credit-market failures, and enhance growth with grater equity. In recent times, micro credit has become a dependable tool to improve the economic power of the poor. The studies such as Gaiha and Kulkarni (2013); Herath et al. (2015) held the view that access to credit by women would increase the number of new businesses, expand existing ones and improve productivity. Kasali et al. (2016) contend that improving women access to credit has the potency to improve women investment potentials and bargaining power. Access to credit is an important mechanism for reducing women's rural poverty and empowers them. To achieve this, the delivery of microfinance is one of the assured means of empowering rural women. Such arrangement will enable them start and expand small businesses (UNECA, 2014; Yogendrarajah & Semasinghe, 2015).

Toward improving the financial constraints of women in rural areas, microfinance institution was established in the 1980s. Since the 1990s, there is evidence suggesting that the number of microfinances has been on the rise. Despite the increase, women's ability to own business is still minimal, and it is often linked to inability to access micro credit. Apart from the immediate benefit to the family, financial freedom is also imperative to poverty and inequality reduction, consumption smoothening and enhances women participation and capacity in decision making process (Selvaraj, 2016). Lack of credit poses serious constraint to the empowerment of women, especially those in rural areas who find little or no access to credit. Micro credit for women has been the means of empowering poor women and pulling them out of poverty. Although there has been increase in the number of women that own businesses in recent times, majority still do not have access to formal credit (Morsy, 2020; World Bank, 2014). In Kenya, 48% of business owners are women yet, only 7% have access to formal credit (IFC, 2014). National Bureau of Statistics

(NBS) (2019) indicates that of the 40% of women that owned business in Nigeria, only with 5% have access to formal credit.

As part of the quest to reduce poverty among women and reduce the gender disparity, the Nigerian government has imitated several programs including the Better Life for Rural Women Programme, Family Support Programme, the G WIN-Project, the Women Fund for Economic Empowerment (WOFEE), the Business Development Fund for Women (BUDFOW), the Government Enterprises Entrepreneurship Programme (GEEP) which was established as an intervention program to tackle paucity of funding to the Micro, Small, and Medium Enterprises (MSMEs). Beside these efforts, the Central Bank of Nigeria has also introduced several activities and products to ensure that women are financially included. Notable among them are the establishment of the Medium and Small Micro Enterprise Development Fund (MSMEDF) and the inauguration of the National Financial Inclusion Special Interventions Working Group (NFISIWG). These and many more programs were aimed at offering skills, inputs, and start-up capitals so as to link women to the formal sectors and promote sustainable economic growth.

Apart from the establishment of Microfinance Banks, several other initiatives have been put in place to empower women, yet the ability of women to own business is limited. Microfinance has been seen as a veritable institution to facilitate and improve financial ability of rural dwellers. Although the country has experienced growth in the number of microfinances, its impact in poverty-inequality reduction and empowering women is relatively minimal (Edeme & Nlalu, 2018). Nycander (2008) find that in Nigeria, rural women income would improve further if they have enough access to microcredit.

Women empowerment is an economic empowerment that creates income-earning opportunities for women either through direct interventions or through the operation of market forces. According to Cohen and Richards (1994), the essence of women empowerment is to achieve equality and equity between men and women in terms of decision making. Batliwala (1994), Fernando, (1997), Kabeer (2001), and Mayoux (2002) see empowerment is a channel through which the vulnerable are empowered to improve their capabilities in the society. As demonstrated above, empowerment is multilevel and multidimensional in nature. The levels comprise of the family, community and the state while dimensions of empowerment usually include some aspect of decision making autonomy, mobility, self-efficacy and confidence, legal awareness, political involvement and freedom from violence (Sen & Batliwala, 2000).

Although findings on empowerment and microcredit are contradictory, studies that find no association between access to credit and women's empowerment conclude that women bear the burden on loans they may not have full control and are creating feminization of debt. Yadav and Sharma, (2015) and Linh et al. (2019) assert that the constraints being faced by rural dwellers can only be disentangled through access to rural credits. Evidence abound that some women are at greater risk for violence because of these loans and access to extra cash did little to modify women's status (Herath et al., 2015). In Bangladesh, several studies including Schuler and Hashemi, (1994), Amin et al. (1996) Pitt and Khandker (1995, 1998) have also demonstrated that access to credit empower women, lower their risk for domestic violence, and willingness to control fertility or contraceptive use. These studies provide evidence that households with credit had higher incomes and consumption ability compared to non-credit households. In furtherance, Pitt et al. (2006) articulate that credit programs improved household ability in decision-making, financial autonomy, and connections of women. Household level studies such as Malhotra et al. (2002) have also conceptualized wider perspective explicit frameworks and in identifying indicators that can capture features related to empowerment. Following the framework, Noreen (2011) finding suggests that age, inherited assets, level of education of husband, marital status, and number of children greatly influences women ability to access loan. At the household level, the amount given a loan also contributes to women empowerment. Even though it was not significant, the outcome indicates that the females use loan which has more enhanced results than loan used by male counterpart. Yogendrarajah and Semasinghe (2015) find that micro credit explains about 11% of the variation in women empowerment while education, experience, income accounts for 89.1%. Even though micro credit has facilitated the creation of self-employment and the growth of businesses and generated wealth. When women are self-employed through micro enterprises, their welfare is improved. Beside, demographical factors, such as age, education, and experience, also have moderating effect on women empowerment (Dubreuil & Miranda, 2010). Mushtaq (2008) explained that through micro credits, education of women can be improved, poverty alleviated, income and savings, nutrition and adequate food accommodation, clean water, and hygienic environment. Further, it was concluded that micro credit program is effective in generating employment and to meet short term needs. This was further supported by Asim (2008) by affirming that micro credit empowers women at the household level through increase in independent income, control over credit and savings, and ability to generate valuable asset to the household. Tadesse and Yousuf (2013) show that insufficient amount set aside for loan, lack of education and follow up, non-availability of nearby market and high cost of inputs were the major constraints to women ability to micro credits, suggesting that loan size should be given priority in the running of microfinance institutions.

Singh (2004) contend that women are more empowered through self-help groups. Such arrangement assists women to embark on activities that generate income, opportunities for self-employment. Talekar and Biraadar (2011) further affirm that self-help groups are imperative to overcome exploitation and fight rural poverty among women and build confidence among them. In a comparative study of impact of self-help projects on livelihood of semi-urban and rural areas dwellers, Bhuvaneswari, et al. (2011) find that people in rural areas took micro credit for non-income generating and domestic activities. Unlike semi-urban dwellers, they are involved in loans to assist them start new business ventures. Latha and Kumar (2012) opined that self-help groups have accentuated rural women profits which have given them better livelihood and sense of worth in the society. The study by Zaei et al. (2018) was to ascertain if income earned by members of women's self-help groups has empowered them. From the findings, it is apparent that such arrangement has improved women's income, savings, and reduced rural poverty. Nader (2008) findings affirm that microcredit programs improve rural women access to income and education of their children. Similarly, Swapna (2017) evaluated access to microcredit by rural women entrepreneurs and found that entrepreneurial skill and supportive regulatory framework have direct influence on access to credit while lending conditions has negative relationship with access to credit. A study on the determinants of microcredit access by the poor in South-West Nigeria by Kasali et al. (2016) also affirm that age, household size, worth of business, experience, level of education, assets, health standard, living standard, and income greatly influence accessibility to micro credit loan. Awojobi (2014) found that women who participated in microfinance projects have been empowered economically and socially. Al-hassan (2014) averred that despite the challenges faced by Microfinance, it a viable strategy for women empowerment. In another study,

Ganle et al. (2015) conclude that microcredit is a double-edged sword that both empowers and disempowers women. Ugwumba and Omojola (2013) found positive relationship between institutional credit access and productivity growth. Abraham (2018) estimated the effects of financial access on the poor farmers in rural Northern Nigeria and conclude that access to financial services benefits vulnerable women farmers.

It has been suggested that full participation of women is essential in the growth process; there is insufficient research on factors inhibiting rural women access to micro-credit. Even if women have had access to funding resources in the 1990s due to the establishment of microfinance institution, this access is not equal to men's and in most cases, they do not have control of these resources. While previous studies concentrate on whether micro-credit is an engine for empowering women or its impact on women empowerment, the main aim of this chapter is to analyze disparity in women access to microcredit by rural women in Nigeria.

Materials and Methods

Cross-sectional data generated from the Nigeria General Household Survey (GHS) 2016 was utilized for the study. The GHS provides data at the national level as well as at the zonal (urban and rural) levels. It provides data for a wide range of monitoring and impact evaluation indicators relevant given its large sample representation. Several approaches, such as the Lorenz Curve, Gini ratio, have been adopted independently to study inequality. The Bonferroni Inequality Index was employed to determine the inequalities in rural women access to micro credit. Bonferroni Inequality Index combines Theil-index of inequality, Gini index, and Entropy index approaches. The technique adopts the positional transfer sensitivity axiom which involves the Gini index as its inequality component. The Bonferroni Inequality Index of the type $P = F(\beta)$ is stated as:

$$p_{\text{Rural women Access}}(x, z) P_H \left(1 - \frac{1}{q^z} \sum_{i=1}^{q} \frac{1}{i} \sum_{j=1}^{i} x_j \right) \quad (17.1)$$

where xj is the women inequality distribution. The p-value of less than 0.05 were used to accept the result. All statistical analysis was conducted using STATA (version 11).

RESULT AND DISCUSSIONS

Table 17.1 presents the descriptive summary statistics of the different group of women in rural area.

The descriptive statistics indicates that the group means are significantly different as the p-value in *the Pr(|T| > |t|)* row (under Ha: diff ! = 0) is less than 0.05. On the average, more women in the rural areas do not have access to credit due to collateral which is a condition to access the credit.

As visualized in Table 17.2, there exist huge disparities among rural women access to micro credit as evidenced by the coefficient of variations.

Table 17.1 Descriptive statistics showing differences among rural women group

Do women have access to these credit	Summary of collateral required for credit			
Group	Obs	Mean	Std. Err	Std. Dev
Yes	739	1.5657	0.0182	0.4961
No	47	1.7659	0.0624	0.4279
Combined	786	1.5776	0.01763	0.49425
Diff		−0.20034	0.07405	
			$t = -2.7052$	

Source Authors' estimation

Table 17.2 Disparity in rural women access to micro credit

Indicators/index	Credit disparity	Borrowing disparity	Collateral	Rural women access to credit	Loan repayment1	Loan repayment2
Relative mean deviation	0.2	0.1513	0.1547	0.0530	0.2658	0.8884
Coefficient of variation	0.4473	0.3082	0.3133	0.2239	0.6378	24.9385
Gini coefficient	0.25	0.1513	0.1546	0.0530	0.3566	0.9152
Kakwani measure	0.0639	0.0309	0.0316	0.0105	0.1219	0.8219
Theil entropy measure	0.1064	0.0504	0.0517	0.0201	0.2132	5.5969

Source Authors' estimation

The result shows that Theil entropy coefficient of 0.0201 indicates that a minimal percentage of rural women have access to microcredit. The extent of disparity is reasonably high given the severity of variation index of 64%. The huge disparity incidence is an indication that more rural women are deprived from access to credit in rural areas. The result further indicates levels of credit disparities among rural women by 0.1064 under 45% coefficient of variation, alongside borrowing and credit collateral at 31 and 32% variation, respectively.

Conclusion

This chapter has evaluated disparity among rural women access to micro credit in Nigeria. Cross-sectional data generated from the Nigeria General Household Survey (GHS) 2016 was utilized for the study. In this study, it was established that poverty is still very predominant in rural areas. The depth of poverty suggests that despite the efforts of the government which has been aimed at and channeled at reducing poverty in the country, there is still a very high gap between the poor and the rich manifested in level disparity among women in rural areas that could not access credit in Nigeria. It is therefore necessary that in future financial inclusion program equal consideration should be given to households in rural areas so as to make their life better through access to finance. To guarantee future economic prosperity for rural women, financial inclusiveness must be taken seriously to reduce the level of disparity in rural areas.

References

Abraham, T. W. (2018). Estimating the effects of financial access on poor farmers in rural Northern Nigeria, *Financial Innovation*, 4(25), 2–20, ttps://doi.org/https://doi.org/10.1186/s40854-018-0112-2

Akinyi, J. (2011). Role of microfinance in empowering women in Africa. *The African Executive Magazine*.

Al-hassan, S. (2014). *Is microcredit a viable strategy for empowering women? A review of selected NGO programmes in Africa*. Accessed 16 October 2020.

Amin, R., Becker, S., & Byes, A. A. (1998). NGO-promoted Microcredit programs and women's empowerment in rural Bangladesh: Quantitative and qualitative evidence. *Journal of Developing Areas*, 32, 221–236.

Amin, R., Li, Y., & Ahmed, A. U. (1996). Women's credit programs and family planning in rural Bangladesh. *International Family Planning Perspectives*, 22, 158–162.

Asim, S. (2008). *Evaluating the impact of micro credit on women's empowerment in Pakistan*. Centre for Research in Economics and Business (CREB) Working Paper No. 2–9, The Lahore School of Economics.

Awojobi, O. N. (2014). Empowering women through micro-finance: Evidence from Nigeria. *Australian Journal of Business & Management Research, 4*(1), 17–26.

Batliwala, S. (1994). *Meaning of women's empowerment: New concepts from action*. Harvard University Press.

Bhuvaneswari, G. K., Patil, A., & Hunshal, C. S. (2011). Comparative study on micro credit management of self helpgroups in Peri-urban and rural areas. *Karnataka, Journal of Agricultural Science, 24*, 188–192.

Dollar, D., & Gatti, R. (1999). *Gender inequality, income and growth: Are good times good for women?* (Gender and Development Working Papers, No. 1).

Dubreuil, G. S., & Mirada, C. T. (2010). Micro credit and women empowerment: An empirical case-study based in Catalonia. *Proceedings from the 2010 International Society for Third Sector Research International Conference*, July 7–10, Kadir Has University.

Edeme, R. K., & Nkalu, C. N. (2018). Reducing inequality in developing countries through microfinance: Any correlation so far? In R. Das (Ed.), *Handbook of research on microfinancial impacts on women empowerment, poverty, and inequality* (pp. 281–301). IGI Global. https://doi.org/10.4018/978-1-5225-5240-6.ch014

Fernando, J. L. (1997). Nongovernmental organizations, micro-credit and empowerment of women: The role of NGOs: Charity and empowerment. *Annals of the American Academy of Political & Social Science, 554*, 150–177.

Gaiha, R., & Kulkarni, V. S. (2013, September 10–11). *Credit, Microfinance and empowerment, invited contribution to expert group meeting on policies and strategies to promote empowerment of people in achieving poverty eradication, social integration and full employment and decent work for all*. United Nations Secretariat Building.

Ganle, J. K., Afriyie, K., & Segbefia, A. Y. (2015). Microcredit: Empowerment and disempowerment of rural women in Ghana. *World Development, 66*, 335–345, available from https://doi.org/10.1016/j.worlddev.2014.08.027

Gita, G. A., & Chen, L. C. (Ed.). (2000). *Population policy reconsidered: Health, empowerment, and rights*. (pp. 127–138). Harvard Center for Population and Development Studies.

Guirkinger, C., & Boucher, S. R. (2008). Credit constraints and productivity in Peruvian agriculture. *Agricultural. Economics, 39*(3), 295–308.

Hanak.I. (2000). Working her way out of poverty: Micro-credit programs undelivered promises in poverty alleviation. *Journal of Finance, XVI/3*, 303–328

Herath, H. M., Guneratne, L. H., & Sanderatne, N. (2015). Impact of microfinance on women's empowerment: A case study on two microfinance institutions in Sri Lanka. *Sri Lanka Journal of Social Sciences, 38*(1), 51–61. https://doi.org/10.4038/sljss.v38i1.7385

Honohan, P., & Beck, T. (2007). *Making finance work for Africa*. World Bank.

International Finance Corporation (IFC). (2014). *Microfinance in Africa banking for the smallest businesses inclusion and their impact on GDP and inequality* (IMF Working Paper 15/22). International Monetary Fund, Washington.

Jalilian, H., & Kirkpatrick, C. (2002). Financial development and poverty reduction in developing countries. *International Journal of Finance & Economics, 7*(2), 97–108.

Kabeer, N. (2001). Conflicts over credit: Re-evaluating the empowerment potential of loans to women in rural Bangladesh. *World Development, 29*, 63–84.

Kasali, T., Ahmad, S. A., & Fan, L. M. (2016). Determinants of microcredit access: Empirical analysis from South-West Nigeria. *Journal of Economic Cooperation and Development, 37*(4), 125–148.

Kazi, M. H., Leonard, & J. E. (2012). Microfinance, poverty and youth unemployment of Nigeria: A Review. *Global Journal of Human Social Science, Sociology, Economics & Political. Science, 12*(13), 45–59.

Khanna, T. (2000). Business groups and social welfare in emerging markets: Existing evidence and unanswered questions. *European Economic Review, 444*(6), 748–761.

Koenig, M. A., Saifuddin, A., Hossain, M. B., Alam, K., & Mozumder.A. B. M. (2003). Women's status and domestic violence in rural Bangladesh: Individual and community-level effects. *Demography, 40*, 269–288.

Kongolo, M. (2009). Factors limiting women's involvement in development: Lesson from Ithuseng. *South Africa, African Research Review, 3*(4), 13–30.

Latha, M., & Kumar, G. C. (2012). A study on agricultural women self help groups (SHGs) members microcredit analysis in Trichy district, Tamil Nadu, International. *Journal of Exclusion Management. Research*, 2. Available from http://ijemr.in/wp-content/uploads/2018/01/A-study-on-Agricultural-women-Self-Help-Groups-SHGs-Members-Micro-credit-Analysis-in-Trichy-district.pdf. Accessed on 15 November 2020.

Leikem, K. (2012). *Microfinance: A tool for poverty reduction?*. A Project submitted to University of Rhode Island.

Linh, T. N., Long, H. T., Chi, L. V., Tam, L. T. & Lebailly, P. (2019). Access to rural credit markets in developing countries, the case of Vietnam: A literature review, *Sustainability, 11* (1468), 2–18. https://doi.org/10.3390/su11051468

Malhotra, A., Schuler, S. R., & Boender, C. (2002). *Measuring women's empowerment as a variable in international development*. The World Bank.

Mayoux, L. (2002). *Women's empowerment and participation in micro-Finance: evidence, issues, and ways forward*. Retrieved October 2018 from http://www.genfinance.info/Case%20Studies/India_genfinance.pdf

Montgomery, R., Bahattacharya, D., & Hulme, D. (1996). Credit for the poor in Bangladesh. In H. David & M. Paul (Eds.), *Finance against poverty*, 2 (pp. 86–158).

Morsy, H. (2020), Access to finance, why aren't women leaning in? *Finance &Development*, 5 (1). Accessed from https://www.imf.org/external/pubs/ft/fandd/2020/03/pdf/africa-gender-gap-access-to-finance-morsy.pdf

Nader, Y. F. (2008). Microcredit and the socio-economic wellbeing of women and their families in Cairo. *Journal of Socio Economics, 37*, 644–656.

National Bureau of Statistics. (2019). Poverty and Inequality in Nigeria. *National Bureau of Statistics*, Abuja.

Noreen, S. (2011). Role of microfinance in empowerment of female population of Bahawalpur district, proceedings from International Conference on Economics and Finance Research IPRED, IACAIT.

Norwood, C. (2014). Women's empowerment and microcredit: A case study from rural Ghana. *Journal of International Studies Development, 4*, 1–22.

Nycander, L. (2008). *Empowerment of women through micro credit: Micro credit and social protection mitigating social exclusion and empowering women*. Retrieved from http://64.233.169.104/search?q=cache:K-mpiz6-IOJ:www.pksfbd.org/speechs%2520%26%2520Papers/Ms.%2520LottaNycander/Empo

Ojoh, A. C. (2012). *Empowering Nigerian women in the 21st century: Measuring the gap*. GRIN Verlag.

Pitt, M., & Khandker, S. (1995). *Household and intra-household impacts of the Grameen Bank and similar targeted credit programs in Bangladesh*. Paper presented at workshop on Credit programs for the poor: Household and intra-household impacts and program sustainability, by the Education and Social Policy Department; Washington, DC and Bangladesh Institute of Development Studies; Dhaka

Pitt, M., & Khandker, S. (1998). The impact of group-based credit on poor households in Bangladesh: Does the gender of participants matter? *Journal of Political Economy., 106*, 958–996.

Pitt, M., Khandker, S. R., & Cartwright, J. (2006). Empowering women with micro finance: Evidence from Bangladesh. *Economic Development & Cultural Change, 54*, 791–831.

Purokayo, S., Babalola, J., & Aminu, U. (2013). Challenges and contributions of women to the Nigerian economy: A strategy for achieving the Millennium Development Goals (MDGs), *The Journal of Economics, 113*,

138–146. Available from https://sites.google.com/site/photonfoundationorganization/home/the-journal-of-economics

Rankin, K. N. (2006). Social capital, microfinance, and the politics of development. In J. L. Fernando (Ed.), *Microfinance perils and prospects* (pp. 77–96). Routledge.

Schuler, S. R., & Hashemi, S. M. (1994). Credit programs, women's empowerment and contraceptive use in rural Bangladesh. *Studies in Family Planning*, 25, 65–76.

Selvaraj, N. (2016). Impact of micro-credit on economic empowerment of women in Madurai, Tamilnadu: A study. *Journal of Global Economics*, 4(4), 227. https://doi.org/10.4172/2375-4389.1000227

Sen, G. (Ed.). (2000). *Women's empowerment & demographic processes* (pp. 15–36). Oxford University Press.

Sen, G., & Batliwala, S. (2000). Empowering Women for Reproductive Rights. In H. Presser & G. Sen (Eds.), *Women's Empowerment and Demographic Processes*, Oxford University Press, (pp. 15–16).

Singh, S. K. (2004). *Micro-Finance and empowerment of scheduled caste women: An impact study of SHGs in Uttar Pradesh and Uttaranchal*. Planning Commission, Government of India, New Delhi.

Swapna, K. (2017). Impact of microfinance on women empowerment. *International Journal of Business Administration and Management*, 7(2), 229–241.

Tadesse, Y., & Yousuf, J. (2013). Constraints of rural women to utilize Microfinance institutions: The case of members of Microfinance institutions in rural districts of Dire Dawa Administration. *Ethiopia DerejeKifle, Developing Countries Studies*, 3(7), 24–28.

Talekar, S. D., & Biraadar, M. B. (2011). *Micro credit management by women's self-help groups* (pp. 33–37). Discovery Publishing House.

Ugwumba, C., & Omojola, J. (2013). Credit access and productivity growth among subsistence food crop farmers in Ikole Local Government Area of Ekiti State, Nigeria, *ARPN Journal of Agriculture and Biological. Science*, 8, 351–356.

UNECA. (2014). *Improving access to finance for the empowerment of rural womenin North Africa*. Publication based on case studies of Tunisia, Morocco, Algeria and Egypt.

Vong, J. et al. (2013). Impact of microfinance on gender inequality in Indonesia. In P. Mandal (Ed.), *Proceeding of the International Conference on Managing the Asian Century* (pp. 201–206). New York. https://doi.org/10.1007/978-981-4560-61-0_23

World Bank. (2014). *Expanding Women's access to financial services*. Washington DC: World Bank. Accessed from https://www.worldbank.org/en/results/2013/04/01/banking-on-women-extending-womens-access-to-financial-services

Yadav, P., & Sharma, A. K. (2015). Agriculture credit in developing economies: A review of relevant literature. *International Journal of Economics and. Finance, 7*(12), 219–244.

Yogendrarajah, R., & Semasinghe, D. (2015). A study on empowerment of rural women through Microcredit facilities in Sri Lanka. *Management Studies, 3*(9), 10, 237–246. https://doi.org/10.17265/2328-2185/2015.0910.002

Zaei, M. E., Kapil, P., Pelekh, O., & Nasab, A. T. (2018). Does Micro-credit empower women through self-help groups? Evidence from Punjab, Northern India. *Societies, 8*(3), 48. https://doi.org/10.3390/soc8030048

CHAPTER 18

Predicting the Likelihood of Loan Default Among Marginalised Population: A Case Study on Rural Bengal

Amit Kumar Bhandari

INTRODUCTION

The last five years have been an unfavourable time in the Indian banking and non-banking systems. Indian banks are sitting with $150 billion in bad loan, and cleaning it up is a massive challenge for them. The non-performing assets in the bank have increased a lot. Any disruption in the banking sector has a profound and lasting impact on the economy. With the recent NPA crisis, investment growth and economic slowdown have emerged. According to the Reserve Bank of India data, the gross non-performing assets of local lenders have increased to 10% as a result of the economic slowdown. Public sector banks are the most affected by this

---

A. K. Bhandari (✉)
Department of Economics, Rishi Bankim Chandra Evening College, Naihati, India
e-mail: amit.kumar.bhandari@gmail.com

IZA Institute of Labour Studies, Bonn, Germany

crisis because they have the lion's share of these toxic loans. The NPA problem in India is the ticking time bomb that could lead to another crisis for the industry.

Indian households borrow mainly from two sources, the formal and informal sources. The formal sector is made up of all institutional credit agencies, viz. commercial banks, cooperative banks, regional rural banks, etc. Informal sectors, on the other hand, are formed with landlords, money lenders, traders, relatives and friends. The government has pressured its credit agencies to increase credit availability, with special emphasis being given to agricultural credit. Formal banks have unlimited funds but lack credit proper credit monitoring. Information lenders may affect the opportunistic behaviour of the borrowers, but they lack the needed capital. There is a huge difference in lending methodology between borrowing from formal and informal sources. Informal credit is quickly recovered because the process recovery techniques like the reputation of the creditors or third-party application make it more effective. This is why the growth of microfinance in India has been greatly expanded.

The recovery performance in the priority sector is meagre. The repayment performance of small loan takers is also execrable. Delinquency in Kisan Credit Card is rising, which increases the amount of NPA of the banks. The NPAs in small accounts are below Rs 10 lakh. As a result, banks are facing a dreadful crisis. NABARD supply finance for the progress of agricultural activities and overall rural development. The problem faced by NABARD is its large amount of bad debt. A study shows that farmers have not repaid about 40% of the total loan. The state-level evaluation shows that the unpaid cash dues of formal institutions are 68% in West Bengal, whereas at all India level, it is 57%. However, the unpaid cash due to non-formal institutions amounts to 32%, which is lower than the country level (43%) in 2002 (NSSO, 2005).

Most of the literature on repayment activities of MFIs dealt with group-based lending or group liability as group lending is a substitute for microfinance activities. These studies greatly emphasised the role of joint liability in group lending such as peer selection (Ghatak, 1999), peer monitoring (Varian, 1990) and peer enforcement (Besley & Coates, 1995). The study showed that group lending could alleviate moral hazard, adverse selection and information asymmetries handled by the MFIs. Due to micro-credit programmes, the high repayment rate is maintained (Silwal, 2003). The deep connection between repayment capability and availability of microfinance shows that with the increase in repayment capability, access to microfinance also improves. Therefore, MFIs must combine microloans and other services as well as products to increase the efficiency of loan use, which will further aid in building the confidence of the borrowers in repaying the loans (Xia et al., 2011).

D'espallier et al. (2011) described the female client's repayment performance in microfinance in 70 countries. The study shows that other things being an equal higher percentage of female borrowers have better repayment rates, fewer write-offs and lower perceived credit risk. This trend is enhanced when loans are offered by NGOs, individual-based lenders and regulated MFIs. As far as repayment in microfinance is concerned, women are found to have a higher repayment rate (Armendariz & Morduch, 2005). In Bangladesh, Grameen Bank's experience shows that as a result of repayment difficulties related to male borrowers, the female clientele has substituted them (Hossain, 1988). The unwillingness of borrowers or their inability to pay loans have contributed to high default rates (Coyle, 2000). Unavoidable circumstances such as natural disasters and personal emergencies also affect loan payment (Stern, 1995).

The present study highlights the strategies adopted by the MFIs to cope with the economic recession. Maintaining a steady loan repayment performance of the customers is one of the significant challenges faced by the MFIs. The study was conducted in five districts of rural West Bengal. This chapter estimates the default risk by using the factors affecting the repayment behaviour of the borrowers of MFIs. Among the determinants, the study applied different socio-economic and loan-related factors of the borrowers as a determinant of credit repayment performance. For this, we have used a multivariate static technique to understand key factors that contribute to the default risk of a loan.

The rest of this chapter is organised as follows. The next chapter explores the resilience of MFIs during the time of economic recession, followed by the issues of creditworthiness of the borrowers of MFIs. Section "Methodology" describes the methodology of the study. Section "Data and Variables" describes the data and sample used in the study. Section "Discussion of Results" presents the results and discussion. Finally, Sect. "Summary and Conclusions" concludes the study.

THE RESILIENCE OF MFIs DURING THE RECESSION

There is no way to ignore that microfinance has saved the poor in access to credit. MFIs are regarded as the most effective tool in the fight against global poverty. Still, it has to go a long way to financing those who are still unserved from the essential financial services. As per reports of SIDBI, India's microfinance customer has exceeded 42 million, and the number is still growing. As per Microfinance Institutions Network estimates, microfinance has reached 30% of the household. It will still have to go a long way in terms of growth and expansion. Demonetisation hit the microfinance sector hard with the delinquencies, which resulted in the jump in NPA as a percentage of advance at 15%. However, after one year after demonetisation, the default rate reduced quickly to the normal state, indicating the resilience of the MFI sector to the shock in the financial system. During this crisis, many MFIs started to diversify their business; they started offering housing loans, various consumer loans and small micro-enterprise loans.

Since microfinance is linked with the global financial market, any economic recession makes MFIs fragile. If we look at history, we found that MFIs around the globe survived the 2008 crisis caused by subprime mortgages in the USA. With the development of microfinance, some powerful institutions emerged that focussed on funding the poor people, which in turn attracted private investors in this sector. Commercial banks have now been playing an important role in financing MFIs and helping them provide traditional services. Backed by robust growth and a robust regulatory framework, banks are now more confident in giving loans to this sector. Banks lend generously to small and medium-sized small lenders after Bandhan becomes a bank. According to MFIN, 66% of the current microfinance portfolio goes to the rural sector, half of which goes to agriculture and 46% go to commercial and small manufacturing units. In contrast, the rest goes to family finance. After the merger of Bharat Financial Inclusion (BFIL) with Induslnd Bank in 2019–2020, banks hold the largest share of microfinance portfolio, followed by NBFC-MFIs and Small Finance Banks holds the second and third position, respectively.

During the economic recession, MFIs face difficulty in raising funds. The lack of funds delayed the distribution of loans to clients and forced them to revise the overall growth strategy. During the time of crisis, MFIs diversified their debt sources, reduce their dependency on a single source. MFIs started focussing on equity as a source of funding, which reduces dependence on external sources and increases the chances of survival. Increasing the term of loans helps the MFIs to avoid the crisis. It is essential to investigate the root cause of the market failure so that effective financial products can be designed and interfered with. For example, the lack of information about creditworthiness hinders the effectiveness of the loan programme. The following section highlights the underlying importance of the creditworthiness of the individual borrowers.

Issues of Credit Worthiness

In many developing countries, the functions of formal financial institutions have been restrained due to weak loan repayment record. Due to these large defaults and delinquencies, the long-term efforts to form feasible lending institutions in rural areas have been ruined. If the loan is not repaid to the lender, he will not be able to revolve funds due to which the borrowers will not be able to avail credit from the sources which acted as last resorts (Spio, 2006). It has been observed by Hunte (1993) that too many debts and high default rate of the financial institutions indicate the inefficiency, either, because they funded unproductive investments or has failed to procure the money lent. Due to poor understanding of financial instruments, assessment of the rural finance market project has often been deceptive (Von Pischke et al., 1983). As a result, most of the time, loans for particular purposes are side tracked towards non-productive uses, especially consumption (Adams & Vogel, 1986). When loans are used for productive purposes, it produces extra income, which increases the repayment capacity of the borrower. On the other hand, loans used for non-productive purposes do not generate income and lead to the debt burden.

Maintenance of creditworthiness individual borrowers is an essential indicator of obtaining credit in the future and for self-respect. The creditworthiness of any borrower depends mostly on trust. The basis being trust encompasses innumerable aspects like better credit history, reimbursement behaviour and borrower's status and reputation. Often, measurements of creditworthiness take into account the principles and values of the family and its ancestry instead of limiting itself to the individual level (Harriss-White & Colatei, 2004). A lender often takes two aspects into account while granting loans. The first is household-specific characteristics, that is, the family reputation and history, its financial background and ethics. The other aspect is the individual, which relates to the quality of the borrower.

Material aspects are also important, but their estimation becomes subjective. Land, building, jewellery and livestock—all comprise tangible assets. So far, the land is concerned; its quality plays the most significant role. The formal institutions favour families having higher possession over cultivable lands due to their excellent repayment capacity (Pal & Laha, 2013). In addition to that study also reveals that the capability to provide physical collateral is a strong indication of a household's creditworthiness.

As far as income is concerned, the number of earning in a family and the regularity of income play important roles. The guarantor is a crucial part of the loan transaction. Lenders try to make sure that the guarantors and borrowers have a definite connection. Here, kinship, neighbourhood and even SHG membership come into play. Juggling and manipulation are common practice where debt is contracted at someplace and repaid at some other place. The system of borrowing and repayment of money makes the poor suffer as there are widespread circulation and money laundering. Rotation of loans is either a result of certain constraints or planned arbitration.

In recent years, the effectiveness of micro-credit to fight global poverty has been in question, with several studies showing that micro-credit has little or no effect on the welfare of the family. Many micro-credit programmes require weekly loan repayments, which follows a strict weekly schedule leads to difficulty for borrowers to repay their loans. It takes time to get a return from productive investments. As a result, borrowers experience financial blows in the form of dissolution of their tangible and intangible assets. They are forced to sell their house, land, jewellery and livestock because a significant portion of their income goes into repayment. Their social connections get lost. Thus, they slowly become insolvent and socially degraded. The present study analysed the impact of the determinants related to borrower-specific and loan-related factors on the loan repayment performance of the borrowers among rural borrowers.

Methodology

In order to investigate the repayment performance of the borrowers, we estimate the impact of the determinants on the risk of loan default. The repayment of current loan status has been classified into two categories. One category paid their dues on time, and others become defaulters who did not pay instalment even after 12 months of the due date. In the study, we consider those independent variables which significantly influence the repayment performances. The functional form of the borrower's repayment performance can be represented as follows:

$R = f$ (Different borrower-specific and loan-related characteristics) where $R =$ If a borrower defaults on a loan.

The logistic regression model is used to analyse the relationship between the determinants of creditworthiness of rural borrowers and the probability of borrowers' likelihood of loan default. The probability of defaulting (Y) is estimated with the explanatory variables (X).

The dependent variable of the model is presented as

$Y = 1$ Default
$Y = 0$ Non default

We use logistic regression, where the cumulative logistic distribution function can be represented as:

$$P_i(Y_i = 1) = \frac{1}{1 + e^{-(\alpha + \beta X_i)}}$$

P_i is the probability of defaulting loan of the ith borrower, the vector X_i contains borrower's characteristics, and β is the unknown regression coefficients to be estimated. The probability P_i ranges between 0 and 1 and is nonlinearly related to the X_i attributes. The probability of not defaulting loan can be represented as:

$$1 - P_i = \frac{1}{1 + e^{(\alpha + \beta X_i)}}$$

The odds ratio is defined as:

$$\frac{P_i}{1 - P_i} = \frac{1 + e^{(\alpha + \beta X_i)}}{1 + e^{-(\alpha + \beta X_i)}} = e^{(\alpha + \beta X_i)}$$

The odds ratio is the ratio of default to no-defaulter. This likelihood of loan default depends on the values of the explanatory variables. Taking the natural log of the above equation, we get the final logistic regression equation.

$$L_i = \ln\left(\frac{P_i}{1 - P_i}\right) = \alpha + \beta_i X_i + \varepsilon_i$$

The coefficient of the regression represents a change of log odds of loan default due to the change in a unit of the parameters. The maximum likelihood method is adopted for estimating the parameters.

Data and Variables

Primary data were collected from the field survey conducted in the five districts of West Bengal. The research was conducted in five districts of the southern part of West Bengal, viz. Howrah, Hooghly, Bankura, North and South 24 Parganas. The data were collected from households that belong to gram panchayat areas. A structured questionnaire was used to elicit information of households relating to gender, age, education, income and family size, which used to identify key household-level factors that influence creditworthiness among rural populations. Several loan-related characteristics such as the purpose for credit has taken; default in payment, any credit was taken previously, asset holdings, business experience, etc. were collected. Table 18.1 presents a variable description along with the percentage distribution of the borrowers concerning various determinants.

Discussion of Results

It was observed from the sample dataset that the percentage of defaulter was higher for female than male borrowers. The age-wise distribution reveals that the majority of the borrowers belong to 31–50 years age group (Table 18.2). The loan defaulter was higher for borrowers above 50 years of age group (40%), while the lowest defaulter found from 31–50 years of age group (22.8%). The education level of the respondents reveals that the majority of the borrowers (46.6%) have above primary to higher secondary education level. The percentage of the defaulter is decreasing as the level of learning of the borrower increases. Loan defaults are the lowest among graduates and above borrowers. As far as the occupation of the borrowers is concerned, the majority of the borrowers are self-employed (28.8%), 22.6% were involved in business, 16.4% were involved in different services and 9% are wage labour. The default rate was the highest (34.8%) among the wage labourers. We have divided the borrowers into five categories. The percentage of loan defaulter decreases at the higher income levels. The percentage of loan defaulter among the borrowers were almost the same who have farmland and those who do not. If we look at the source of the borrower's loan, it is seen that 61.8% of borrowers took loans from non-formal sources. Of those who took loans from non-formal sources, 42.1% of them were defaulters, while only 4.7% of borrowers default who borrowed from formal sources. If we look

Table 18.1 Socio-economic characteristics of respondents

Variables	Description	Defaulters	Non-defaulters	Total sample
Gender	Male	22.6	77.4	59.2
	Female	35.3	64.7	40.8
Age (in year)	Upto 30	27.5	72.5	21.8
	31–50	22.8	77.2	55.2
	51 and above	40.0	60.0	23.0
Educational	Upto Primary	42.3	57.7	31.2
	Class V to XII	25.8	74.2	46.6
	Graduate and above	11.7	88.3	22.2
Occupation	Farming	26.0	74.0	19.2
	Wage labour	34.8	65.2	9.2
	Service	31.7	68.3	16.4
	Business	22.1	77.9	22.6
	Self-employed	27.1	72.9	32.6
Respondent's Income (in ₹/month)	≤ ₹3,000	30.4	69.6	22.4
	₹3,001–₹6,000	36.9	63.1	35.8
	Above ₹6,000	18.7	81.3	41.8
Households Income (in ₹/month)	≤ ₹5,000	39.7	60.3	28.2
	₹5,001–₹10,000	26.2	73.8	45.8
	Above ₹10,000	17.7	82.3	26.0
Dependents	≤3	26.1	73.9	76.0
	>3	33.3	66.7	24.0
Agricultural land holdings	Yes	28.1	71.9	57.0
	No	27.4	72.6	43.0

(continued)

Table 18.1 (continued)

Variables	Description	Defaulters	Non-defaulters	Total sample
Sources of credit	Formal	4.7	95.3	38.2
	Non-formal	42.1	57.9	61.8
Loan size (in ₹)	≤ 5,000	37.2	62.8	15.6
	5,001–10,000	44.4	55.6	19.8
	10,001–20,000	32.4	67.6	21.0
	20,001–50,000	19.5	80.5	24.6
	Above 50,000	8.4	91.6	19.0
Purpose of credit	Agriculture & allied activities	20.0	80.0	11.0
	Consumption & emergency	46.8	53.2	21.8
	Business	24.8	73.2	50.0
	Acquisition of personal assets	19.0	81.0	8.4
	Personal	15.9	84.1	8.8
Business experience	≤5 years	37.5	62.5	49.0
	>5 years	18.4	81.6	51.0

Source Author's calculations

Table 18.2 Results of logistic regression on the risk of loan default

Variables	Coefficient	Standard Error	Odds ratio
Gender (= 1, Male; = 0, Female)	−0.487[b]	0.283	0.614
Age	0.259[c]	0.446	1.296
Education (Ref: Upto Primary)			
Class V to XII	−0.439[c]	0.286	0.645
Graduate and above	−0.667[c]	0.432	0.513
Dependent	0.174[c]	0.122	1.190
Households income (Ref: ≤ ' 5,000)			
' 5,001–' 10,000	−0.711[a]	0.302	0.491
' 10,000	−0.579[c]	0.392	0.561
Distance	−0.007	0.049	0.993
Agricultural land (= 1, Agricultural land; = 0, No agricultural land)	0.443[c]	0.252	1.557
Other assets (=1, other assets; = 0, no other assets)	−0.347	0.321	0.707
Credit sources (=1, formal sources; = 0, non-formal sources)	−2.079[a]	0.346	0.125
Loan Sizes (Ref: ≤ Rs. 5,000)			
(Rs. 5,001–Rs. 10,000)	1.254[a]	0.383	3.503
(Rs. 10,001–Rs. 20,000)	1.239[a]	0.436	3.451
(Rs. 20,001–Rs. 50,000)	1.263[a]	0.505	3.538
(Above Rs. 50,000)	0.853[c]	0.632	2.346
Loan purpose (Ref: Consumption & emergency)			
Agriculture	−0.328	0.497	0.721
Business	0.451	0.356	1.570
Acquisition of personal assets	−0.520	0.555	0.594
Personal	−0.997[b]	0.523	0.369
Business Experiences (=1, > 5 years; = 0, <5 years)	−0.904[a]	0.256	0.405
Constant	−1.093	2.368	0.335

(continued)

Table 18.2 (continued)

Variables	Coefficient	Standard Error	Odds ratio
−2 Log Likelihood	467.875		

Dependent variable: Repayment performance of borrower's (1 = Defaulter and 0 = Non-defaulter)
Note First category is the reference category. Model Chi-square = 126.179, p <0.001
[a], [b] and [c] Show significance level of 1%, 5% and 10%, respectively
Source Computed by the author from the field survey data

at the loan the relationship between defaulting loans with the amount of loan, shows that the default rate is lower among those who have taken a bigger loan. Considering the purpose of borrowing, it is found that most borrowers have taken loans for business and emergency purposes. 18.4% of those with business experience over five years of age are loan defaulter.

This study was designed to investigate the loan repayment behaviour of microfinance borrowers from rural areas using various indicators. The odds ratio of borrowers signifies that the ratio of the probability that a borrower will not be repaying loans to the probability that he will, for a unit change in an explanatory variable. The intercept term of the model indicates the probability of defaulting a loan by the borrowers if all the predictor variables are zeroed. The result of the logistic regression shows that the majority of the determinants have expected signs and are statistically significant.

Against the general expectation, we found that female borrowers are more likely to default on loans than male borrowers. Many women borrowers have no control over the use of debt in rural areas, in fact, male members of the household control it. This can negatively affect women in the rate of repayment of loans. The probability of loan default increases with the age of the borrowers and the coefficient is statistically significant. Borrowers from younger age groups and those who belong to rural areas are the most productive in the life cycle in terms of earnings. They have ambitions to earn higher incomes, so they are expected to be more active in terms of saving and accumulating wealth. Over time, respondents of this age group acquire knowledge and experience in the business. This will help them settle and earn more capital than old. Hence, the loan repayment performance is favourable for them. At the same time, the aged borrower lacks motivation and energy to start up a new venture and increases the chances of default.

The coefficients of the education level of the borrowers have a positive impact on credit repayment performance. The level of education significantly reduces the chance of defaulting a loan. Higher educational qualification enriches borrowers' business information, systematise their business and make prudent business decisions. An educated borrower is likely to have more knowledge on several aspects of the loan and other formal contracts. A borrower with a decent education is quicker to respond to technological innovation and keener on using modern means of production to enhance the output and hence utilising his/her earnings to repay the debts. The odds ratio favouring loan repayment performance increases by a factor of 0.645 and 0.513 as compared to the reference category (primary education) for borrowers who have completed their study up to higher secondary (from class five onwards) and graduation and above, respectively (Table 18.2).

The number of dependent members puts pressure on the family budget, which increases the chances of debt not being repaid on time. Households with more than three dependents increase the risk of defaulting loan. The possible explanation is that a big household size needs more financial support for their livelihood. They used this loan for consumption and emergency purposes instead of productive investment, which resulted in an increased risk of loan default. The odds of loan defaulting on a loan is 1.190 times higher as compared to the number of dependents less than equal to three.

The relationship between a household's income and defaulting on a loan is expected to be positive. The results are consistent with previous expectations. The odds ratio of defaulting of a loan decreased by a factor of 0.491 and 0.561 as compared to the reference category (income less than equal to Rs 5,000) for households whose incomes are falling in the range of Rs 5,001–Rs 10,000 and above Rs 10,000, respectively. With the increase in income, households that require loans regularly are expected to have higher incentives to repay loans because defaulting on a loan reduces the chances of getting a loan in the future.

The effect of agricultural landholding on the probability of loan default is positive and significant. The use of credit is limited to productive purposes because small farmers are suffering from financial distress. The loans for agricultural work are used to pay for consumption purposes, so they could not pay off the loan on time. The result shows that another asset possesses by the borrower is having a negative impact on defaulting on a loan. These other assets may be used as collateral securities for accessing loans. Lack of collateral and guarantor for the rural poor is the impairment of the availability of credit from the formal credit institutions. Banks fail to assess the risk associated with a particular borrower because of the absence of the guarantor. The odds ratio on defaulting on a loan decreases by a factor of 0.707 as compared to the non-holding of other assets. The negative impact of the other assets possesses imply that respondents feel more confident in repaying loans if they borrow and lenders also have believed that other assets could be used as collateral in the event of lending money.

The sources of credit also influence the loan repayment capacity. It is seen that borrowers tend to default on loans if loans are taken from formal credit sources. Loans from non-formal sources are more likely to default than formal sources, which is contrary to the prior expectation. Formal lenders hesitate to lend poor rural households because of their inadequate monitoring mechanism and asymmetric information about the borrowers. So, in the event of the lending process, banks generally go through cumbersome documentation processes and take security deposits to ensure the creditworthiness of the prospective borrower. The odds of loan repayment performance were decreased by a factor of 2.079 times as compared to the borrowers who had borrowed from formal sources.

Looking at the results of the purpose of loans, it can be observed that the risk of default increases for loans given for consumption and emergency purposes than other categories, namely agriculture, purchase of assets and personal loans. It is assumed that individuals with extensive business experience will be able to manage the business successfully rather than inexperienced. So, it is expected that the experienced person will be able to repay the loan in time if he takes the loan. Higher business experiences reduce the loan default. The odds of loan repayment performance decline by a factor of 0.405 times as compared to the borrower who is having a business experience of less than five years.

Summary and Conclusions

It was microfinance that showed the potential from financial inclusion to the ability to endure the financial crisis. During the time of economic downturn, maintaining the loan repayment performance of micro borrowers is one of the biggest challenges for the MFIs. This chapter used a multivariate statistical technique to identify the key factors of microloans that contribute to the risk of default. We have used various socio-economic and loans-related factors to identify the key determinants of loan default from the rural borrowers. This study has brought some interesting facts about small rural borrowers.

The finding of this study revealed that the risk of loan default higher for female borrowers than their male counterparts. The aged borrowers increase the risk of loan default. Household financial commitments increase with the age of the borrowers, which affect their income negatively and the risk of not pay off their debts on time increases. The risk of default decreases with the education level of the borrowers. A borrower having higher education are more likely to repay debts on time than those who are in the below-average learning experience. Borrowers who have a large number of dependents in the family were more likely to be more defaulters than households with a lesser number of dependents. The higher financial burden due to the bigger family size leads to deviate the purpose of loans and utilise the loan for unproductive purposes. Hence, the probability of loan defaulter is higher among borrowers with lower income levels compared to households that belong to the higher income group. Paying the dues is a matter of dignity for the rural people, and the borrowers will not become wilful defaulter until the situation will force them. It is also observed from the result that borrowers tend to default loans if loans are taken from non-formal credit sources. A mixed response has been found in asset holdings; the probability of defaulting loan is more likely for borrowers who have farming land, while those with other assets holdings have more tendency to pay off their debts. The probability of loan repayment performance increases with the increase in business experiences. Business experiences give a reliable platform for the knowledge and ideas of the borrower. Their entrepreneurial skill enhances, which helps them to provide stability in the source of income, and they will be capable of repaying their loans on time. Furthermore, this study found that the source of credit is also an important determinant of loan repayment default. The results of this study have a significant impact on the credit assessment and the monitoring of loans by MFIs, particularly during the time of economic recession when the financial institutions are seeking ways to get out of the financial crisis. High-risk borrowers can be separated from low-risk borrowers. Thus, if the borrowers can be segmented in the multidimensional scale as per the default, MFIs can adopt a better pricing strategy, reduce the loss from such loan default and solve the problems of the borrowers.

References

Abraham, G. (2002). *Loan repayment and it is determinants in small-scale enterprises financing in Ethiopia: Case of private borrowers around Zeway area* (MSc, Thesis). AAU.

Adams, D. W., & Vogel, R. C. (1986). Rural financial markets in low income countries: Recent controversies and lessons. *World Development, 14*(2), 477–487.

Armendariz, B. A. D., & Morduch, J. (2005). *The economics of microfinance*. MIT Press.

Berhanu, A., & Fufa, B. (2008). Repayment rate of loans from semi-formal financial institutions among small-scale farmers in Ethiopia: Two-limit Tobit analysis. *J. Soc. Econ., 37*, 2221–2230.

Besley, T., & Coates, S. (1995). Group lending, repayment incentives and social collateral. *Journal of Development Economics, 46*, 1–18.

Coyle, B. (2000). *Framework for credit risk management*. Chartered Institute of Bankers.

D'espallier, B., Guerin, I., & Mersland, R. (2011). Women and repayment in microfinance: A global analysis. *World Development, 39*(5), 758–772.

Duy, V. Q. (2011). *Factors affecting on access to formal credit of households in the Mekong Delta, Vietnam*. Retrieved from http://papers.ssrn.com/sol3/papers.cfm?abstract_id=1972944

Gebeyehu, A. (2002). *Loan repayment and its determinants in small scale enterprises financing In Ethiopia: Case of private borrowers around Zeway area*. Retrieved from http://etd.aau.edu.et/dspace/bitstream/123456789/985/1/Abreham%20Gebeyehu.pdf

Ghatak, M. (1999). Group lending, local information and peer selection. *Journal of Development Economics, 60*, 27–50.

Harriss-White, B., & Colatei, D. (2004). Rural credit and collateral question. In B. Harriss-White & S. Janakarajan (Eds.), *Rural India facing the 21st century*. Anthem Press.

Hossain, M. (1988). *Credit for alleviation of rural poverty: The Grameen Bank of Bangladesh* (Institute Research Report 65). Washington, DC: International Food Policy Research.

Hulme, D. (1991). The Malawi Mudzi Fund: Daughter of Grameen. *Journal of International Development, 3*(3), 427–431.

Hunte, C. K. (1993). *Loan default and efficacy of the screening mechanism: The case of Ddvelopment Bank of Guyana* (Unpublished PhD Dissertation). Columbus, OH: The Ohio State University.

NSSO. (2005). *Household indebtedness in India*. All India Debt and Investment Survey, NSS 59th Round, Report No. 501 (59/18.2/2), January–December 2003.

Orebiyi, J. S. (2002). Agricultural loan repayment performance and its determinants in the rural credit markets of Imo State, Nigeria. *International Journal of Agriculture and Rural Development, 3*, 37–45.

Pal, D., & Laha, A. (2013). *Sectoral choice of credit in rural India*. Retrieved from http://www.business-standard.com/article/finance/credit-complementary-services-can-uplift-rural-lending-iim-a-study-113031200272_1.html

Roslan, A. H., & Karim, M. Z. A. (2009). Determinants of microcredit repayment in Malaysia: The case of Agrobank. *Pertanika Journal of Social Science and Humanities, 4*(1), 45–52.

Silwal, A. R. (2003). *Repayment performance of Nepali village banks* (Unpublished Master Dissertation). Swarthmore College, Swarthmore.

Spio, K. (2006). *The impact and accessibility of agricultural credit: A case study of small scale farmers in the Northern Province of South Africa* (Unpublished PhD Thesis). University of Pretoria, South Africa.

Sterns, K. (1995). *The hidden beast: Delinquency in micro enterprise credit programme* (ACCION Discussion Thesis Document No. 6).

Varian, H. R. (1990). Monitoring agents with other agents. *Journal of Institutional and Theoretical Economics, 146*, 153–174.

Vitor, D. A. (2012). Determinants of loan repayment default among farmers in Ghana. *Journal of Development and Agricultural Economics, 4*(13), 339–345.

Von Pischke, J. D., Gordon, D., & Dale, W. A. (1983). *Rural financial markets in developing countries: Their use & abuse.* Johns Hopkins Univ Press.

Xia, L., Christopher, G., & Baiding, H. (2011). Accessibility to microcredit by Chinese rural households. *Journal of Asian Economics, 22*(3), 235–238.

Zeller, M. (1998). Determinant of repayment performance in credit groups: The role of program design, intragroup risk pooling, and social cohesion. *Economic Development and Cultural Change, 46*(3), 599–621.

Index

A
Andhra crisis, 9, 211, 212, 216, 217, 220, 221, 223
Asset quality, 6, 15, 22
Audit, 82, 83, 92

B
Banco Solidario Group (BancoSol), 17, 18, 20–23
Bandhan microfinance, 19, 20
Benchmarking, 108

C
Capacity building, 5, 133
Capital to Asset Ratio (CAR), 16, 18, 20, 22, 23
Collateral, 5, 12, 13, 18, 25, 31, 72, 97, 132, 148, 162, 232, 264, 269, 270, 281, 290
Constant Returns to Scale (CRS), 105, 109
Credit, 4–7, 12–14, 18, 24, 25, 30, 31, 33–40, 42, 43, 45–47, 51, 55, 56, 65–67, 69, 72, 82, 84–86, 88, 89, 91, 92, 98, 108, 116–121, 133, 149–152, 161–163, 165, 167, 168, 178, 179, 181–185, 187, 195, 200, 210, 211, 229, 232, 234–236, 239–243, 245, 250, 263, 264, 266–270, 278, 279, 281, 284, 286, 289–292
Credit rationing, 6, 30, 35, 36, 38, 41, 42, 46
Credit unions, 7, 82–84, 89, 91, 92, 210
Creditworthiness, 31, 47, 279–281, 283, 284, 291
Crisis, 6, 9, 11–16, 18, 20, 24, 25, 30, 32, 53, 64, 68, 148–153, 184, 210, 212, 216–218, 220, 222, 223, 277, 278, 280, 291, 292

D
Data Envelopment Analysis (DEA), 7, 99, 100, 102, 107–109

Decision making trial and evaluation laboratory (DEMATEL), 7, 85, 89–92
Default risk, 6, 279
Development, 4, 5, 10, 14, 18, 30, 31, 39, 52, 53, 55, 56, 58–60, 67, 72, 77, 82, 87, 88, 92, 108, 109, 114, 116–120, 132, 134, 145, 148, 151, 157, 162, 164, 167, 169, 170, 179–184, 186–188, 209, 232, 236, 238, 242, 243, 245, 251, 280

E
Economic downturn, 6, 13, 30, 31, 44, 115, 291
Emerging economies, 3, 5
Employment, 8, 13, 15, 17, 30, 51, 87, 99, 103, 114, 115, 118, 121, 131, 132, 139–141, 144, 145, 150–153, 155, 157, 165, 166, 179–181, 186, 187, 250, 258, 267
Entrepreneur, 4, 64, 84, 86–89, 117, 132, 152, 163, 164, 178, 267
Estimated Generalized Least Squares (EGLS), 9, 202, 206
E-transaction, 123
Excess reserve (ER), 35

F
Finance, 5, 12, 14, 20, 23, 24, 33, 52, 53, 64, 67, 72, 82, 83, 98, 103, 106, 108, 114, 117, 120, 121, 131–133, 136, 138, 141, 144, 163, 165, 166, 178, 195, 198, 204, 231, 254, 270
Financial accelerator, 31
Financial autonomy, 266
Financial inclusion, 8, 14, 19, 89, 101, 103, 106, 108, 109, 113, 114, 116–119, 121, 122, 124, 162–171, 232, 233, 235, 245, 270, 291
Financial services, 12, 13, 17, 18, 20, 72, 82, 85, 103, 113, 114, 116–122, 162, 163, 167, 169, 171, 177, 178, 185, 233, 268, 280
Financial volatility, 21
Fixed effect (FE), 56–59, 216
Formal credit, 25, 30, 100, 236, 264, 265, 290, 291

G
Gender and politics, 9, 179, 187
Generalised Method of Moment (GMM), 56, 57, 59
Gini Index, 9, 199–206, 268
Global financial crisis, 11, 15, 16, 26, 32, 72, 149
Global Findex Index, 114, 122, 167
Global recession, 3, 5, 6, 13, 18, 20–22, 24, 25, 63, 68, 72, 76, 77, 131, 148
Grameen Bank, 18–23, 65, 71, 180, 181, 185, 230, 279
Granger Causality, 9, 197, 199, 202, 204–206
Gross domestic product (GDP), 7, 13, 30, 54–56, 58–60, 108, 131, 149, 180, 184, 185, 196, 199–201, 203, 207
Growth, 3–8, 11, 13, 15, 31, 51–56, 68–72, 76, 81, 82, 85, 108, 118–120, 131–136, 140, 141, 144, 145, 150, 157, 164, 166, 168, 170, 178, 179, 184, 185, 199–201, 210–212, 219, 230, 232, 237, 250, 264–266, 268, 277, 278, 280

I

Impact of global crisis on MFIs, 6, 13, 16
Income inequalities, 8, 168, 201
Inequality, 8, 9, 64, 67, 87, 117, 120, 132, 183, 195–207, 264, 265, 268

L

Loan defaulter, 284, 289, 292
Loan portfolio, 14, 18, 56, 152, 184, 212, 217–219
Logistic regression, 283, 287, 289
Logit model, 7, 135

M

Macroeconomic factors, 52–54
Make in India, 245
Manufacturing enterprises, 7, 132, 134, 138
Micro credit, 10, 64, 87, 107, 200, 233, 263, 264, 266–270, 282
Microfinance, 4–10, 12, 13, 15–22, 25, 29–33, 51–56, 60, 64–73, 76, 77, 82–92, 98–100, 108, 118, 132–136, 138, 140, 144, 145, 147, 148, 150–152, 157, 162–171, 178–188, 195–202, 204–207, 209–211, 222, 223, 230–235, 238, 245, 250, 251, 263–265, 267, 278–280, 289, 291
Microfinance institutions (MFIs), 4, 6, 7, 9, 10, 12–16, 18, 20–26, 31–33, 51–60, 65–72, 76, 77, 82–84, 86–89, 98–109, 114, 115, 120, 132, 148, 152, 162, 163, 165, 166, 168, 171, 178–181, 183–185, 188, 195, 196, 198, 200, 202, 206, 207, 209–217, 219–224, 229–241, 244, 245, 250, 264, 267, 268, 278–280, 291, 292
Microloan, 10, 19, 31, 67, 179, 279, 291
Micro, Small and Medium Enterprise (MSME), 6, 30, 31, 34, 39, 41, 45, 47, 98, 118, 121, 131, 133, 265
Mobile money, 7, 114, 119, 120, 122–125
Monetary transmission, 47
Multiple Criteria Decision-Making (MCDM), 213

N

National Bank for Agriculture and Development (NABARD), 19, 68, 70, 71, 74, 134, 155, 166, 209, 278
National Sample Survey Organisation (NSSO), 134, 135, 138, 139, 278
Non-performing assets (NPAs), 34, 38–41, 43–45, 211, 277, 278, 280

O

Overall technical efficiency (OTE), 101–103, 106, 108

P

Panel cointegration analysis, 8
Penetration, 99, 119–121, 161, 165
Performance of MFIs & conclusions, 54
Political economy, 9, 179, 185–188
Potentiality, 3, 148, 150
Poverty, 3–5, 7, 9, 12, 15, 17, 31, 33, 51, 64–66, 68, 71–77, 82, 83, 85–87, 89, 98–100, 103,

108, 109, 115–117, 133, 150, 162, 165–169, 177–183, 185–187, 195–200, 229, 230, 232, 245, 249–251, 256–258, 260, 264–267, 270, 279, 282
Poverty alleviation, 5, 7, 12, 31, 65, 72, 74–77, 116, 165, 167, 180
Poverty reduction, 7, 10, 14, 18, 76, 120, 123, 124, 150
Profit at Risk (PAR), 16, 20–23
Purchasing capacity, 150

R
Random effect (RE), 56–59, 216
Recession, 3, 4, 6–8, 10, 12, 15–17, 20–26, 29, 30, 32, 38, 39, 46, 63, 64, 76, 108, 151, 279, 280, 292
Regulations, 88, 100, 169, 170, 185, 204, 210, 236
Repayment behaviour, 279, 289
Required Reserve (RR), 35
Responsible microfinance, 170
Return on assets (ROA), 9, 16, 20, 22, 23, 212, 216–218, 222
Return on equity (ROE), 9, 216–219, 222
Risk diversification, 157
Rural development, 85, 278
Rural women, 10, 264, 265, 267–270

S
Security, 19, 86, 120, 138, 148, 164, 245, 251, 291
Self-help groups (SHGs), 9, 33, 148, 152, 154, 155, 166, 200, 210, 230, 231, 238, 239, 245, 250, 251, 254, 256–260, 282
Services, 4, 6–8, 10, 12, 17, 32, 33, 60, 72, 82, 84–86, 89, 108, 114, 116, 118–121, 124, 148, 155, 157, 161, 162, 164, 169, 171, 178, 203, 211, 220, 222, 231–233, 235, 236, 238, 241, 245, 256, 279, 280, 284
Sinking and slowdown, 26, 150, 152, 277
Social exclusion, 3, 5, 6, 8, 10
Social inclusion, 5, 6, 9, 10, 179, 183, 187, 229, 230, 232–236, 241, 245
Social performance management, 170
Social protection, 151, 241, 259
South Asia, 54, 132, 169, 196
South Asian Association of Regional Cooperation (SAARC), 9, 196, 197, 206, 207
Steady state equilibrium, 45
Strategy, 53, 72, 107, 108, 165, 177, 232, 267
Structural break, 212, 216, 217, 221, 223
Sustainability, 8, 9, 15, 24, 26, 32, 52, 56, 64, 67, 68, 84, 100, 101, 103, 152, 162, 171, 180, 181, 188, 211–213, 215–224, 231, 233

T
Technique for Order of Preference by Similarity to Ideal Solution (TOPSIS), 92, 213–215, 217, 222
Turkey, 7, 83–85, 89, 91, 92, 165, 180

U
Unbanked people, 17, 72
Unorganised sector, 131, 132, 134

V
Value added, 8, 203, 244

Vector Error Correction Mechanism (VECM), 8

W
West Bengal, 7, 10, 19, 33, 99, 101, 102, 108, 221, 222, 231, 238, 251, 257, 278, 279, 284

Women borrowers, 148, 165, 235, 289
Women empowerment, 19, 183, 230, 265–268

Y
Yield on gross portfolio (YGP), 9, 216–219, 222

CPSIA information can be obtained
at www.ICGtesting.com
Printed in the USA
LVHW010019230723
753203LV00014B/957